NEIGHBORHOOD TOKYO

D0373576

*Studies of the East Asian Institute,
Columbia University*

The East Asian Institute is Columbia University's center for research, publication, and teaching on modern East Asia. The Studies of the East Asian Institute were inaugurated in 1962 to bring to a wider public the results of significant new research on Japan, China, and Korea.

Neighborhood Tokyo

THEODORE C. BESTOR

Stanford University Press
Stanford, California

Stanford University Press
Stanford, California
©1989 by the Board of Trustees of the
Leland Stanford Junior University
Printed in the United States of America

Original printing 1989
Last figure below indicates year of this printing:

08

Published with the assistance of the Suntory Foundation
and a special grant from the Stanford University Faculty Publication
Fund to help support nonfaculty work originating at Stanford

CIP data appear at the end of the book

For Arthur and Dorothy

Acknowledgments

Anthropological fieldwork, perhaps more than research in other subjects, depends on the willing cooperation, support, and encouragement of a vast number of people. This work is no exception, and I owe major debts of gratitude to the many residents of Miyamoto-chō who graciously allowed my wife and me to intrude into their lives for two years, and who endured my persistent and at times bewilderingly naïve questions. We arrived as total strangers and left with what I hope will be lifelong friendships. Friendship and gratitude should be repaid with open thanks, yet promises of confidentiality throughout my research require anonymity. Moreover, it would be impossible to mention all the many residents of Miyamoto-chō who so graciously helped me. I can only hope that I have not violated any confidences, and that this book does justice to the people and to their community.

I gratefully acknowledge the following support that made fieldwork possible from May 1979 to May 1981: a Japan Foundation Dissertation Fellowship; a National Science Foundation Doctoral Dissertation Improvement Grant (BNS 7910179); a National Institute of Mental Health Predoctoral Training Fellowship (MH 08059); and an International Doctoral Research Fellowship awarded by the Joint Committee on Japanese Studies of the Social Science Research Council and the American Council of Learned Societies. Stanford University's Center for Research in International Studies provided additional support while I was completing my dissertation after returning from Japan.

A grant from Sigma Xi helped make possible a brief return trip to Tokyo in September 1983 to gather information on local politics. A grant from the Wenner-Gren Foundation for Anthropological Research and a short-term fellowship from the Japan Foundation permitted two months of field research on landholding patterns in Miyamoto-chō during the summer of 1984. Awards from Columbia University's East Asian Institute and its Council for Research in the Social Sciences, as well as from the Northeast Asia Council of the Association for Asian Studies, supported another trip to Tokyo in June and July of 1986, for a further examination of landholding and its relation to small business. During this most recent trip I also gathered more information on changes in the neighborhood and tried to assure old friends that I really did intend to publish a book after all these visits. Although I include only some of the materials collected during these later trips in the present volume, the chance to return to Miyamoto-chō was invaluable for checking data gathered earlier and tracing out recent developments.

A grant from the Suntory Foundation during the preparation of the final manuscript provided valuable assistance for mapmaking and indexing. I am grateful to Marilyn Oldham for her conscientious cartography and her care in checking references and details of the manuscript. Nick Fusco's cartographic advice was invaluable. Anne Muldowney and Catherine Casse Sutton were also extremely helpful in the final stages of preparing the manuscript. Kim Brandt and Claire Cesareo provided welcome extra eyes for proofreading.

During my original fieldwork I was a research student in the Department of Sociology of Tokyo Metropolitan University. I deeply appreciate the kindness and guidance I received from Professor Shogo Koyano, who arranged my affiliation before his retirement; from Professor Susumu Kurasawa, who acted as my sponsor and adviser during 1980–81; and from Professor Nozomu Kawamura, who gave me thoughtful advice during my fieldwork and in the years since. I am especially indebted to Toshiko Bunya, now completing her doctorate in the department, for her extremely able and enthusiastic assistance, as well as her friendship, throughout my research. Particular thanks go as well to Hiroyoshi Noto, then of the Inter-University Center for Japanese Language Studies, who was my tutor, confidant, and close friend while I did fieldwork. Terayasu Hirahata of the Tōkyō Shisei Chōsakai kindly allowed my use of its library on municipal government. Innumerable officials of the Shinagawa Ward Office and the Tokyo Metropolitan Government were unfailingly helpful in answering my questions, providing me reports, and guiding me to relevant sources of information.

Throughout my research and writing I received the careful advice and trenchant criticisms of my faculty advisers at Stanford University: Harumi Befu, Peter Duus, Bernard J. Siegel, and Sylvia J. Yanagisako. I am grateful to them all, but especially to Harumi Befu for his long and patient tenure as my principal adviser.

Much of the present manuscript was written while I served on the staff of the Social Science Research Council from March 1983 through December 1985. Kenneth Prewitt, then president of the SSRC, generously allowed me the time to work on this book and to return to Miyamoto-chō on several occasions; my colleagues made it possible through their willingness to take on additional tasks during my absence. Special thanks go to Sophie Sa.

Gary Allinson, Carol Gluck, Chalmers Johnson, Nozomu Kawamura, Blair Ruble, Robert J. Smith, Thomas C. Smith, and James W. White made incisive comments on drafts of the manuscript, in whole or in part. Their criticisms and suggestions helped me immensely to sharpen this study's focus. Family members patiently read and reread the manuscript, and gently protested when the forest disappeared among the trees. In particular, Dorothy Koch Bestor's extensive editorial suggestions vastly improved the book's style and organization. Arthur Bestor's support—both moral and computerized—was invaluable. Barbara Mnookin, who combined critical editing with patient good humor, was immeasurably helpful throughout the final production of the book.

No dedication can do justice to the patience of loved ones.

Anthropological research is a collective enterprise, and the contributions of one's spouse during fieldwork are beyond number. Without my wife, Victoria Lyon-Bestor, this book would not have been possible. Throughout our stay in Miyamoto-chō she was an enthusiastic researcher in her own right, contributing data, ideas, and contacts that I would otherwise have overlooked. During the writing and revising of the manuscript, she has been my patient sounding board, excellent editor, and gentle critic. Nothing I can say will adequately express or discharge my debts to her.

I remain, however, solely responsible for the findings, interpretations, and conclusions expressed in this book.

T.C.B.

Contents

Four pages of pictures follow page 124

Tables and Maps

Tables

Maps

Explanatory Note

All Japanese terms are romanized in the modified Hepburn system used in *Kenkyusha's New Japanese-English Dictionary* (4th ed., 1974). Japanese names are listed in the Western fashion, personal name first and family name second. I have created pseudonyms for Miyamoto-chō and the names of all organizations, institutions, and persons in the neighborhood past or present to protect the confidentiality and anonymity of neighborhood residents. The identities of residents are further disguised by the alteration of minor details of age, occupation, or family background. All translations from Japanese sources are my own.

I have adopted the convention of referring to residents of Miyamoto-chō as "Mr. Takahashi" or "Mrs. Horie." I do so to convey some flavor of the formality with which neighborhood residents address one another; personal names are almost never used except among relatives and the most intimate friends. In almost all contexts when referring to or addressing people other than one's relatives, the suffix *san* is obligatory. To have rendered residents' names with san, however, might confuse readers accustomed to the linguistic differentiation of gender. Other suffixes used in forms of address, such as *chan* (a diminutive form of *san*), *kun* (a masculine form that teachers and neighbors use in addressing boys, and that business executives use to refer to their close male subordinates), and *sama* (an exalted form of *san*, often used when referring to deities), do not have graceful English equivalents, and so appear unaltered in this book.

I have also retained the honorific *sensei* ("master" or "teacher"), a term of respect that replaces san after the family name. Like san, sensei is used only by others when they speak someone else's name (never one's own or a relative's). Sensei is applied to the names of schoolteachers, instructors of traditional dance and tea ceremony, university professors, television commentators, and politicians.

At several places I refer to the Japanese National Railway, the backbone of Tokyo's transportation system. In 1987 the railway was privatized; it is now universally known by the English initials "JR" for Japan Railway.

In discussions of money I have not given dollar equivalents for yen amounts, because changing exchange rates over the past several generations would distort relative values expressed in dollars. Before the Second World War, the exchange rate remained stable for several decades at roughly two yen to the dollar. During the American Occupation the exchange rate was arbitrarily set at 360 yen to the dollar, at which level it remained until the early 1970's. During my fieldwork the rate fluctuated between about 190 and 230, and, as I complete the manuscript, in early 1988, it stands at about 125.

Throughout the book I refer to the following conventional eras of Japanese history: Tokugawa period (1603–1868); Meiji period (1868–1912); Taishō period (1912–26); and Shōwa period (1926–1989).

NEIGHBORHOOD TOKYO

Form is possibility

—Cecil Taylor, jazz pianist

Introduction

OLDER SECTIONS of Japanese cities often are divided into well-defined neighborhoods. These are not merely administrative devices (such as postal zones or police precincts) that correspond only slightly to the social categories and groupings important in the daily lives of most residents. Nor do such neighborhoods exist primarily as eponymic emblems or symbols of larger social divisions of the city, such as New Yorkers might have in mind when referring to Wall Street, Williamsburg, and the West Village; or San Franciscans when talking of the Tenderloin, Nob Hill, and North Beach. Instead these Tokyo neighborhoods are geographically compact and spatially discrete, yet at times almost invisible to the casual observer. Socially they are well organized and cohesive, each containing a few hundred to a few thousand residents.

In the vastness of Tokyo these are tiny social units, and by the standards that most Americans would apply, they are perhaps far too small, geographically and demographically, to be considered "neighborhoods." Still, to residents of Tokyo and particularly to the residents of any given subsection of the city, they are socially significant and geographically distinguishable divisions of the urban landscape. In neighborhoods such as these, overlapping and intertwining associations and institutions provide an elaborate and enduring framework for local social life, within which residents are linked to one another not only through their participation in local organizations, but also through webs of informal social, economic, and political ties.

This book is an ethnographic analysis of the social fabric and internal dynamics of one such neighborhood: Miyamoto-chō, my pseudonym for a residential and commercial district in Tokyo where I carried out fieldwork from June 1979 to May 1981, and during several summers since. It is a study of the social construction and maintenance of a neighborhood in a society where such communities are said to be outmoded, even antithetical to the major trends of modernization and social change that have transformed Japan in the last hundred years. It is a study not of tradition as an aspect of historical continuity, but of traditionalism: the manipulation, invention, and recombination of cultural patterns, symbols, and motifs so as to legitimate contemporary social realities by imbuing them with a patina of venerable historicity. It is a study of often subtle and muted struggles between insiders and outsiders over those most ephemeral of the community's resources, its identity and sense of autonomy, enacted in the seemingly insubstantial idioms of cultural tradition.

The late 1950's saw the beginning of an enormous outpouring of foreign scholarly work on almost all aspects of Japanese society and culture. It is surprising, therefore, that although Japan ranks among the world's most highly urbanized societies, very little attention has been paid to urban communities, to the micro-texture of life in Tokyo or other large Japanese cities, since the publication of R. P. Dore's *City Life in Japan: A Study of a Tokyo Ward* (1958). Based on research carried out in 1951, when the American Occupation had not yet ended and the Japanese "economic miracle" could hardly be imagined, *City Life in Japan* has stood for a generation as the only comprehensive study of urban Japanese society in English. As the first major study of Japanese urban life and institutions, Dore's book ranged across a wide spectrum of social phenomena. Many of the topics he first touched on have since become the subjects of considerable research in their own right. Monographs on diverse aspects of Japanese culture and society—on the dynamics of domestic life in white-collar families, on the social organization of workplaces, on educational attainment and social mobility, on urban politics, on religious life and institutions in mass society, on migration and mobility in urban areas, on the dynamics of decision-making in Japanese organizations, and on dozens of other topics—have explored in great detail many of the social patterns and institutions first examined in Dore's seminal work. Of the many subjects Dore covered, only the structure of urban community institutions and social relations has not been the subject of more recent, comprehensive research by Westerners.

Many readers may note similarities between the patterns of community life that I found in Miyamoto-chō and those that Dore described for Shitayama-chō a generation ago. As I interviewed Miyamoto-chō's residents the whimsical thought occasionally struck me that they had read Dore's book just before speaking to me. I suspect Dore would not have predicted that the patterns of neighborhood social life he found would remain common throughout Tokyo 30 years later. From his vantage point in the early 1950's, the old order with which neighborhood social institutions usually are inseparably associated must have seemed so clearly on its last legs that these patterns could not have been expected to survive another generation without radical change. Although this seeming stability is one subject of my analysis, I should warn readers that I did not intend or attempt to replicate Dore's encyclopedic work, nor did I design my research to be a follow-up comparison of city life then and now; I draw few explicit parallels or contrasts between my findings and his.

Instead, I describe social life in Miyamoto-chō in the late 1970's and early 1980's, and analyze forces both internal and external to the neighborhood that create and maintain a framework within which local community life thrives. Dore used the community of Shitayama-chō as a glass through which to consider Japanese urban life generally; in many respects his analysis of various domains of urban life does not focus on their intersections within Shitayama-chō. My study focuses more closely on a particular neighborhood and how things work within it, but I also consider broad questions of how a neighborhood interacts with and is shaped by its larger urban environment. I relate the internal social life of Miyamoto-chō to the particular niche it occupies in contemporary Japanese society, and outline some of the social, cultural, and political forces that have formed Tokyo since the turn of the century, making Miyamoto-chō the kind of place it is today. By considering such questions as the relationship between Tokyo's early-twentieth-century growth and the creation of neighborhood institutions, or the social status of neighborhood leaders as an aspect of the class dynamics of Tokyo as a whole, I assess Miyamoto-chō not in isolation or as a community sustained solely by internal forces, but as a neighborhood that can be understood only within the context of Tokyo. By examining this wider setting I suggest that the seeming stability of urban community structure results from the interaction between neighborhood and city, not from the inner workings of an isolated community or class. Further, I argue that apparent continuities such as these are the results of processes of traditionalism—the interpretation, creation, or manipulation of contemporary ideas about the past to bestow an aura of venerability on contemporary social relations. These cultural processes not only shape social relations within Miyamoto-chō, but also play a significant though often ignored role in structuring contemporary patterns of social organization across a wide array of social domains.

Since this is an ethnographic study of a single community, I cannot claim that my findings apply to all urban Japanese neighborhoods. Still, I believe Miyamoto-chō is typical for a wide area of Tokyo at least. Though the specific local combination of elements that make up neighborhood life in Miyamoto-chō may be unique, the elements themselves can be found throughout Tokyo, and the processes that combine and link various institutions and social patterns to form this or any other neighborhood are of a general character.

In selecting the research site I chose a neighborhood with no obvious idiosyncrasies that would set it apart from others in Tokyo. Compared with the criteria used by White (1982: 267–71) to select three neighborhoods for a comparative study of migration and adaptation to Tokyo life, mine were impressionistic. I looked at neighborhoods a bit removed from major thoroughfares, large railway stations, or other facilities that would bring bustling crowds of commuters through the area, making them less arenas for local social interaction than passageways to somewhere else. I wanted an essentially residential but socially diverse neighborhood that had a full range of local amenities and institutions. I looked at neighborhoods whose shopping districts cater primarily to local trade, districts that do not attract customers from great distances because of any outstanding variety or quality of shops. I wanted a neighborhood with a smattering of small workshops and factories that were not linked to a single industry. I was not interested in neighborhoods that clearly specialized in electronic equipment, like Akihabara; used books, like Kanda's Jinbō-chō; lumber, like Kiba; Buddhist altars, like Inari-chō; or children's toys, like Asakusabashi. I was attracted to neighborhoods with shrines within their boundaries, but small community shrines, not shrines large or famous enough to be tourist attractions. I wanted a neighborhood with a heterogeneous mixture of homes and apartments, not a suburban area dominated by huge apartment blocks or housing developments for the employees of a single company. Finally, I looked at neighborhoods that were neither old enough to have been part of the old city of Edo (as Tokyo was known before 1868) nor so new that housing development (and the creation of community life) had occurred largely after the Second World War.

In my search for a neighborhood that met these general requirements, my several years of previous residence in Tokyo guided me. From firsthand experience living in half a dozen Tokyo neighborhoods, including upper-class suburbs and working-class industrial neighborhoods, from visits over the years to dozens of other neighborhoods throughout Tokyo, from stays in Kyoto and Nagoya, and from shorter visits to many other Japanese cities, I had a clear idea of the kind of neighborhood I wanted to examine.

I was not searching for anything out of the ordinary. A few minutes walk from most of Tokyo's 70 National Railway stations will lead one through a neighborhood that meets these criteria. But in many ways searching for the ordinary is more difficult than searching for the special. With my desiderata in mind, my wife and I spent several weeks walking through dozens of neighborhoods scattered across Tokyo. We even went

looking for Dore's Shitayama-chō, and to our surprise found our-
selves walking past the Sugiura family's shop, the subject of
John Nathan's documentary film on "downtown" Tokyo, *Full
Moon Lunch*.

It was a frustrating search; my criteria for an ordinary sort of
place were so precise (or perhaps so broad) that it was puzzling
to try to decide which one among possibly thousands of typical
Tokyo neighborhoods I should choose. The question was not
simply an academic one, however. Because I wanted to join in
local life as fully as possible, my wife and I planned to live in or
very near my research site. If a neighborhood did not work out,
we would have to move to another for my research. Given the
astronomical sums of cash required to negotiate an apartment
lease in Tokyo, relocating would be almost impossible. We had
to hit it right the first time.

Luck, so often the unsung heroine of anthropological fieldwork, brought our search to an end. A fellow student, Christena
Turner, sagely advised me to "choose a network, not a neighborhood": to figure out where my existing contacts were strong-
est and seemingly most reliable, and then see where they led me.
A day or so later, some friends (who had patiently put us up for
several weeks as we searched throughout Tokyo) suggested we
look at a neighborhood near their home, where the husband had
grown up and where his father was (and is) a well-known retired
local politician. We visited the neighborhood and found it to be
just the kind of place I was looking for. Miyamoto-chō, as I now
call it, turned out to be a mixed residential and commercial area,
with a bustling shopping street a block away from a small but
well-maintained Shintō shrine. Local bulletin boards and fliers
tacked to lampposts advertised local events; a weathered neighborhood hall stood among the stores of the shopping street; residents paused to chat with one another in shops or on the
streets. We spent an afternoon walking around Miyamoto-chō,
and the neighborhood grew on us. But the real test was whether
our contacts would actually give us entry into local life: would
anyone ever talk to me? Our friends led us to a local real estate
broker, whom they knew from PTA meetings for their daughter's nursery school. In turn the broker showed us a vacant apartment above a shop on the main shopping street. As I chatted

with Mr. Takahashi, the shopowner and landlord, he mentioned he was the vice-president of the neighborhood association, in which he had been active for decades; better still, as our conversation continued it became obvious he loved to talk. Quickly I signed the lease, and a day or so later we moved in.

By any standards Miyamoto-chō is an ordinary place, similar to hundreds of other Tokyo neighborhoods. As Robert E. Park put it, writing some 50 years ago about another neighborhood in another city on another continent, "The community with which this volume is concerned is nondescript; it is a place of unusual interest" (1976: xvii). Miyamoto-chō contains a mixture of homes, inexpensive apartments, small factories, and shops operated as family businesses; the small-scale entrepreneurs for whom it is both home and workplace dominate the neighborhood socially and politically. It is not old enough to be part of the true *shitamachi*, the old merchant quarter of central and eastern Tokyo that dates from the preindustrial era. But as an urban neighborhood that dates from well before the Second World War, it is old enough to have absorbed some of the customs and cultural values that characterize shitamachi, and that, in the thinking of many Japanese, make shitamachi not simply a place but a way of life. Miyamoto-chō's residents often explain the neighborhood's institutions and customs as a variant of shitamachi life, by which they mean they see their community as friendly, openhearted, unpretentious, generous, and neighborly. Residents are proud of Miyamoto-chō and take pleasure in pointing out aspects of its life that distinguish it from other neighborhoods. At the same time they consider it an ordinary place full of ordinary people, and they freely admit that Miyamoto-chō resembles hundreds if not thousands of other neighborhoods throughout Tokyo. I can offer no evidence that contradicts them.

This study examines the social life in Miyamoto-chō from the perspective of those for whom the neighborhood means most. I describe the texture and the patterns of the social life that shape the community, particularly the institutional framework for local life created by the neighborhood association, or *chōkai*, and the relationship of this formal structure to more informal patterns of interaction and association among residents.

I examine how the neighborhood exists as an important social arena for many of its residents. I also set out a historical account of how the neighborhood developed in the ways it did, and explain how the characteristics of the neighborhood and its self-definition as a community have been and continue to be shaped in response to broader forces of economic, social, and political change in Tokyo and throughout Japanese society.

The approaches I take to these topics do not arise solely from my goal of providing a descriptive ethnography of Miyamoto-chō. Some issues reflect perspectives on Japanese society that bear directly though not exclusively on urban neighborhoods. Others are more general themes that occur throughout the study of Japanese social organization.

Three interconnected views dominate discussion of urban Japanese neighborhoods. The first is the hoary cliché that Tokyo is little but a congeries of villages. This perspective argues that there is some form of direct historical continuity linking preindustrial village life and present-day urban neighborhoods. As evidence of this persistence, much is made of stable patterns of contemporary community organization that seemingly evoke the rhythms of life in a rural hamlet or in preindustrial Edo.

A second major interpretative thrust sees urban neighborhoods almost exclusively in administrative or political terms. One subargument runs that but for the imposition of administrative institutions by various levels of government onto the fabric of daily urban life, neighborhoods would not exist as identifiable divisions of the urban social landscape. Another version holds that neighborhoods exist only because of the calculations of territorially defined political machines.

A third view interprets the stability of traditional urban neighborhood life as an expression of the lifestyle of the so-called old middle class of small-scale self-employed merchants, factory owners, and craftspeople. This lifestyle is seen as existing in relative isolation from the major currents of social, cultural, economic, and political life in contemporary Japanese society. In this isolation, or so the argument goes, the members of the old middle class are able to preserve and sustain an old-fashioned, "feudal," and outmoded way of life, which includes as a crucial element the preservation of anachronistic forms of community organization that owe more to a rural village society than to an urban, industrial way of life.

I disagree with each of these characterizations. Urban neighborhoods are not rural villages, and they do not exist as lingering remnants of moribund social forms. Neighborhoods are not exclusively political and administrative entities. To conceive of them in these terms alone is to ignore the realities of social relationships and cultural values that give meaning to urban neighborhoods for their residents, who perceive them as communities. Without the social glue that local institutions, shared values of community, and a sense of communal identity impart to neighborhoods, neighborhoods could not effectively achieve the political and administrative ends that observers so often see as their sole reasons for existence. Finally, although members of the old middle class do indeed play a central role in sustaining and creating urban neighborhoods as social arenas, they do so not because they are isolated from or immune to the influences that shape the rest of society, but because they are responding to those larger influences. Their role in sustaining neighborhoods is a strategic response to the contemporary structure of Japanese society, not an index of their isolation from it.

In examining Miyamoto-chō and assessing these common interpretations of urban social organization, I have two ethnographic or descriptive goals. First, I aim to provide a detailed ethnography of the mundane, almost unnoticed but nonetheless significant institutions of urban neighborhood life—the texture and structure of social relationships—in an ordinary middle- or lower-middle-class Tokyo neighborhood. Second, by focusing on social relationships in such a neighborhood, in many respects this book becomes a study of the territorially structured social life of the old middle class. Despite common images of Japan as a corporate monolith, characterized by the neatly dressed and well-behaved white-collar employees of Japan Inc., members of the old middle class—self-employed small-scale entrepreneurs—constitute a surprisingly large segment of contemporary society. In 1982 self-employed entrepreneurs and family members employed in nonagricultural small-scale enterprises totaled more than ten million people, almost 20 percent of the private sector labor force (Patrick and Rohlen 1987: 336–39).

The people who run the small businesses of Japan form a large portion of the urban population. In Miyamoto-chō and elsewhere they contribute greatly to the texture and quality of neighborhood social life, and they figure prominently in determining the economic, political, and demographic character of Japanese cities. The old middle class forms a large, dynamic, and diverse population, yet the lives of small-scale business people and their place in urban society are rarely examined by foreign observers of Japan.

Ignoring the old middle class seriously distorts our understanding of contemporary Japanese society, and I hope this study may focus attention on this important segment of the urban population. I argue that the old middle class should not be understood as a stagnant force whose trajectory through the contemporary social firmament is solely inertial. Instead, by examining the role of these people in creating, maintaining, and defending community institutions, one can understand their lifestyle as a dynamic element in contemporary patterns of social stratification and conflict within Japanese society, not as something held over from the past.

On an analytic level as well, this study has two goals. The first, already outlined, is to evaluate the three interrelated views of the historical development and social character of urban neighborhoods, and to question their underlying assumptions about the social and cultural processes that shape urban life.

Related to this, my second analytic goal is to examine the role of "traditionalism" as an important process sustaining contemporary Japanese patterns of social organization. In my view traditionalism is a common Japanese cultural device for managing or responding to social change. The social and cultural processes that sustain urban neighborhoods as seemingly traditional forms of social organization reflect a tendency widespread in contemporary Japanese society.

Although my case study of Miyamoto-chō focuses on patterns of community life and the role of the old middle class in sustaining these, it also examines the relationship between the past and the present, which I suggest is not as simple as it seems. Put simply, in the minds of many Japanese and foreign observers alike, culture is history, culture is not something affected, changed, or generated by the lives of living people. That which is cultural is thought to be necessarily a product of the past. I examine ways in which residents invoke tradition to legitimate the present by reference to an idealized, ahistorical past, in ways that are as common to accounts of the dynamics of Japanese family life, the nature of industrial relations, or the relationship between individual and society as they are to interpretations of community structure. I argue that these reinterpretations and manipulations of a traditionalistic ethos—these presentations of the cultural present as the (a)historical past—often mask the dynamism and fluidity of Japanese social life. Throughout almost every realm of Japanese society, the seeming continuities this process stresses (and creates) all too often strike observers more forcefully than the changes and transformations that at once set the stage for the manipulation of tradition and are cloaked by its success.

CHAPTER ONE

Miyamoto-chō, a Portrait

FROM THE FINANCIAL DISTRICT of Marunouchi, from the fashionable shops of the Ginza, from the government ministries in Kasumigaseki, it is a quick twenty-minute ride on the Japanese National Railway's efficient commuter trains to Otani station, and from there it is a brief ten-minute stroll through crowded shopping streets and narrow, winding, densely packed residential streets to Miyamoto-chō. It is an easy journey to and from the center of Tokyo,[1] and this trip, or a similar one to and from other destinations throughout the Tokyo metropolitan area, is made twice a day by many residents of Miyamoto-chō: by white-collar *sarariiman* ("salarymen") in three-piece suits and college students in blue jeans, by young *O.L.* ("office ladies") in the latest fashions and high school students in sailor suits, by day laborers in pantaloons and factory workers in khaki uniforms.

Many other residents, however, make this trip infrequently. For them Miyamoto-chō is the world in which they conduct much of their social lives. Their work, their children's education, their friendships and rivalries, their political intrigues, their recreation, and in the end their funerals all take place within the neighborhood.

Miyamoto-chō is an ordinary place, resembling hundreds of other neighborhoods that surround central Tokyo in a wide swath to the northeast, east, and south. It is set off from the rest of Tokyo by no particular economic, occupational, or social coloration, by no racial, ethnic, or religious differences, and by no physical or geographical barriers. But for those who live there Miyamoto-chō is a special place, set apart from its surroundings by the crosscutting and overlapping social ties and local institutions that define it as a discrete social unit and breathe life into this definition through the activities and interactions they engender. Especially important in sustaining community life is Miyamoto-chō's neighborhood association, or *chōkai*.[2]

In possessing an institutional framework that fosters a sense of place and identity, Miyamoto-chō is typical of neighborhoods in Tokyo and other Japanese cities.[3] Throughout Tokyo neighborhood social life both thrives on and creates pride of place. In Miyamoto-chō as elsewhere the neighborhood naturally occupies a special niche in the hearts of local inhabitants who consider it home: uniquely superior and ineffably different from other places. But there is nothing extraordinary about Miyamoto-chō. Neither the kinds of social ties that bind the neighborhood together and provide a satisfying arena within which to lead one's life, nor the local opinion that Miyamoto-chō exists as a social arena set apart from its surroundings, is unique to the neighborhood. The specifics of Miyamoto-chō's patterns of community life are not precisely duplicated elsewhere, but nonetheless they reflect cultural, historical, political, economic, and social forces that interact in common and generally predictable ways throughout the urban environment.

The Place

Miyamoto-chō is a tiny plot of land in the midst of a metropolitan area that stretches for dozens of kilometers in an almost unbroken expanse of cityscape. The neighborhood is about six kilometers from the center of Tokyo and one kilometer beyond the Yamanote line of the National Railway, a commuter line that rings the central city. Tokyo Bay lies only a couple of kilometers to the east, but Miyamoto-chō and its surroundings are too far inland to be affected by or to take notice of the port.

The neighborhood extends in a rough rectangle from what

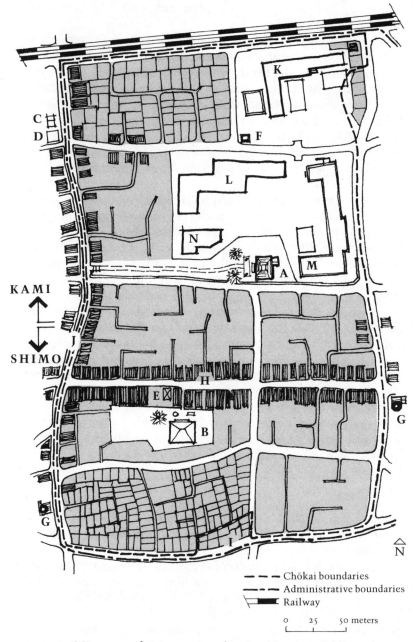

KAMI

SHIMO

C
D
F
K
L
N
A
M
J
H
E
B
G
G
I
N

- - - Chōkai boundaries
—·—· Administrative boundaries
▱▰ Railway

0   25   50 meters

MAP 1. Miyamoto-chō, 1979–81, showing density of housing and networks of alleys for representative portions of *kami* and *shimo*. Shaded areas are residential; shops are indicated with stripes. See the key opposite for individual landmarks.

was once a small river, across a level valley floor, and up a gentle hillside to the edge of a small plateau. The river was channeled underground in the early 1970's, and the one-lane, one-way street that was constructed over the riverbed has eased traffic congestion in the neighborhoods that line the river's former course. Along the flank of the plateau runs a railroad line over which commuter, freight, and high-speed express trains pass every few minutes, jarring nearby homes almost continuously. The railroad tracks mark one boundary of Miyamoto-chō; the former river five blocks—about 400 meters—away marks another. Two streets—two blocks and 250 meters apart—run roughly parallel to each other up the hillside from the river to the tracks to form the eastern and western boundaries of the neighborhood. (See Map 1.) These borders enclose an area of a little less than one-tenth of a square kilometer (0.071 sq. km), in which dwell 2,100 or so residents. There are roughly 750 households in Miyamoto-chō with approximately 1,920 members. In addition about 185 unmarried male workers live in two dormitories for employees of two large corporations that have factories a few minutes' walk from the neighborhood.

Miyamoto-chō lies far outside the limits of the sections of Tokyo that were urban at the time of the Meiji Restoration (1868). Until shortly after the turn of the twentieth century, it was part of an agricultural hamlet. The level valley floor was filled with rice paddies and bamboo groves, and the hillside and plateau were planted as dry fields, with a few tight clusters of houses scattered along the rim of the plateau. The area was engulfed by Tokyo's growth following the 1923 Kantō earthquake and by the

KEY TO MAP I

A	Shrine	H	Shopping street
B	Temple	I	Paved-over river
C	Jizō pavilion	J	Old road
D	Police box	K	Elementary school
E	Chōkai hall	L	Middle school
F	Volunteer fire	M	Company dormitory
	brigade hut	N	Ward branch
G	Public bath		office

early 1930's had become entirely urbanized. Today only a few remnants of the rural past remain, and these are hard to spot amid the network of streets and the densely packed houses, shops, and factories that occupy almost every available space.

Several stone figures of Jizō, the guardian deity of children and wayfarers, which were formerly scattered along paths running through the fields, now stand collected together in a tiny open pavilion next to the local police box, at what was once a minor crossroads. An old road that cut across the valley to link settlements on the plateau with others closer to Tokyo has become a narrow, heavily congested street running down the hill from the tracks to the covered-over river. This street—its twists and turns shaped long before the introduction of the automobile—forms Miyamoto-chō's western boundary. On the hillside the street passes the entrance to the local Shintō shrine; along the level valley floor it runs in front of a Buddhist temple. Both shrine and temple were founded centuries ago, and their ancient trees are now the major splashes of greenery in the otherwise totally built-up neighborhood.

The Shrine

Halfway up the gentle slope toward the railroad tracks, a large granite gateway marks the entrance to Tenso Jinja, the local Shintō shrine. Behind the torii (the characteristic Shintō portal topped by a gracefully curved lintel a few feet above a second crosspiece), a narrow tree-lined walk stretches off toward the shrine buildings, set back about 100 meters from the street. The walkway—a playground favored by local children—is bordered by a low fence of stone posts on which are carved the names of the several hundred people who donated money for the shrine's rebuilding a little over a decade ago.

The walkway ends at a few stone steps, dotted with moss, which lead to the inner shrine precincts and the shade of several massive old trees, almost the only large trees in the neighborhood. These bear metal plaques from the municipal government designating them historical and environmental monuments. The trees have their own aura of dignified antiquity, complementing the many monuments and plaques scattered around the shrine precincts that testify to the shrine's and the neighborhood's history. Tenso Jinja is the shrine of the local tutelary deity for seven adjacent neighborhoods, including Miyamoto-chō. The area that has now become these seven neighborhoods once constituted the pre-twentieth-century hamlet, and until the hamlet was amalgamated into a larger administrative unit, Tenso Jinja served as its official tutelary shrine.[4] Tenso Jinja's location in the neighborhood is a matter of some pride for local residents, and Miyamoto-chō's name is drawn from the shrine.[5]

The main shrine buildings themselves are not old. In the early 1970's the sanctuary was rebuilt in ferroconcrete in the style of traditional Shintō architecture. The handsome copper-roofed main building consists of an outer hall, in which semipublic religious ceremonies are held, and an elevated inner sanctuary, where the deity is enshrined. They are linked by an enclosed passageway in which the altar stands. No one except the priest approaches or enters the inner sanctuary, and a wooden railing and a large offering box bar the entry to the outer hall.

Alongside the main shrine stands a tiny old wooden shrine dedicated to O-Inari-sama, the deity of agriculture and commerce, who is always attended and symbolized by fox messengers. Two stone foxes guard the Inari shrine, planted at the head of a short avenue overarched by vermilion wooden torii and lined with several dozen red pennants donated by parishioners.

Behind the main shrine building is a cluster of corrugated steel storage buildings, which house festival paraphernalia for five of the seven neighborhood associations that support the shrine. Drums, carts for musicians, *mikoshi* (portable shrines carried through the streets of each neighborhood), strings of lanterns, and various odds and ends of decorations are kept locked away until the sheds are opened in August and September, when preparations for the autumn festival get under way.

The rest of the shrine's buildings consist of the priest's house on one corner of the precincts, a large meeting hall attached to it, a water font for ritually purifying the mouth and hands before praying, and an open-air (but usually shuttered) stage for Nō dramas and traditional dance.

The shrine precincts, though not especially large, provide the only open public space in the neighborhood. Local residents use the precincts constantly for relaxation, but infrequently as a place of worship. Most days only a handful of elderly parishioners visit the shrine to offer prayers and only rarely does the shrine transform itself into a site for public religious festivity. For a few days in mid-September, the precincts bustle with dozens of peddlers, who gather for the shrine's annual festival. On New Year's Eve hundreds of residents congregate to offer prayers at the stroke of midnight. On a few popular holidays throughout the year, a handful of parishioners stop at the shrine to offer prayers, purchase amulets, and receive the blessings of the tutelary deity, or *uji-gami*, familiarly referred to as the Kami-sama.

Otherwise the precincts are quiet: a promenade, a playground, a parking lot. The shrine earns income by renting two dozen parking spaces on the grounds for 10,000 yen a month; meanwhile, small eddies of life flow around the cars and the shuttered buildings. The shrine offers an ideal setting for small children to play hide-and-seek, and to practice writing their Chinese characters by tracing the many stone inscriptions. Middle-aged housewives walk their dogs and stop to chat with friends. Teenagers, too, like the seclusion the shrine offers, and occasionally one discovers a young couple furtively standing behind the Inari shrine, deep in private conversation and mild romance.

The Temple

Farther down the hill, along what was the old road, is the Buddhist temple. It stands in the center of a large block edged with shops and houses. The temple compound contains a ramshackle collection of buildings, including several religious halls, living quarters for the priest and his family, a hall for housing visiting parishioners and for funeral banquets, and a tiny bath house with what must have been, until its replacement in 1980, one of Tokyo's last *goemonburo* (a wood-fired iron bathtub resembling a cauldron, named after a famous medieval bandit—Goemon—who was put to death by boiling). On one corner of the block, just barely connected to the temple precincts, stands a three-story metal building, a former factory that the temple recently acquired in a complicated real estate swap. The building has been remodeled and now serves as a *kaikan* (a meeting hall), which the priest occasionally rents to local organizations.

The entryway to the temple grounds is bordered by high concrete walls covered with gaudy murals illustrating the major tenets of the temple's particular school of Buddhist teaching. Except for these didactic displays, the trees that can be seen through the gateway, and the incense that wafts over the walls of the compact graveyard, the temple is physically—and socially—almost invisible. The temple grounds are not generally open to the public because the priest discourages all but parishioners from entering the compound. In contrast to a Shintō shrine, which draws its parishioners from a given geographical area, affiliation with a Buddhist temple is a matter of family belief and tradition. Centuries ago most of the temple's parishioners may have lived in the immediate vicinity, but since they are now scattered throughout Tokyo and beyond, the temple has few ties to the local community. Only when funerals occur does the temple show signs of life. Even so, because most funerals are held at the home of the deceased, the temple is used infrequently. More common is the sight of the priest, dressed in his robes and carrying the necessary implements, hailing a taxi on his way to preside over a parishioner's funeral elsewhere in Tokyo.

The River and Old Boundaries

Half a block beyond the entrance to the temple, where the old road used to cross a tiny bridge over the river, the street makes a sudden jog before it passes over the boundary into another neighborhood. Even when the river flowed above ground, it was no more than three or four meters wide; since bridges crossed it at every block, it did not pose much of a physical barrier. It did, and does, however, serve as a boundary of some social significance. Long before there was a neighborhood known as Miyamoto-chō, the river was the boundary between two hamlets. The boundary has persisted and has been used time and time again. As administrative subunits have been shuffled and

readjusted in response to urban growth and to government efforts at administrative rationalization, the river has continued
to mark divisions.

In the late nineteenth century the hamlets on either side of
the river were amalgamated into larger administrative villages.
Then, in the early twentieth century, these became towns, still
separated by the river. In the 1930's the towns were absorbed by
the City of Tokyo and incorporated into larger wards, still separated by the river. When the local government system was re-
organized after the Second World War, the ward of which
Miyamoto-chō was then a part and the ward across the river were
combined. In the internal organization—both governmental
and nongovernmental—of the larger new ward, the river and the
street that now covers it remained a boundary: for neighborhoods, for school districts, for shrine parishes, for police precincts, for fire departments, for post offices, for voting districts,
for telephone exchanges, and for countless other organizational
purposes, both public and private.

Although these boundaries exist on maps and in the thinking
of local residents, there is no entrance—no gateway—to
Miyamoto-chō, and nothing to set it off physically from adjacent
neighborhoods. Most passersby would not notice that they were
crossing from one neighborhood to the next, unless they were
paying careful attention to the address plates on gateposts or to
the different styles of street decorations and light fixtures
erected by the merchants' associations.

The Contemporary Cityscape

Miyamoto-chō today is a totally urbanized cityscape. Little
of the past is preserved beyond a few barely visible traces. Concrete and a constant flow of traffic all but obliterate the twists
and turns of the old road and the gentle curve of the now-
subterranean river. The buildings, grounds, and monuments of
Tenso Jinja, the temple, and the roadside Jizō pavilion stand almost totally ignored in the daily comings-and-goings of Miyamoto-chō's residents.

Apart from a few well-preserved centers of historical and artistic tradition such as Kyoto or Kanazawa, Japanese cities are

generally gray and dingy. Both Tokyo and Miyamoto-chō con-
form to this norm. The neighborhood has long since lost whatever suburban air it had in the early twentieth century, and is
today a jumble of tightly packed houses and small apartment
buildings, interspersed with tiny workshops and factories, offices, and shops. The surrounding area was heavily bombed and
largely destroyed during the Second World War, but Miyamoto-
chō escaped serious damage (as did the nearby armaments factories, the nominal targets of the air raids).

Clusters of wooden shops and houses from the earliest phases
of urban growth in the 1920's therefore remain, but they have
survived long past their normal life expectancy and are generally
dilapidated, destined for replacement in the near future. By and
large Miyamoto-chō's buildings are the extremely plain, utilitarian structures of gray stucco characteristic of early postwar
construction. In the 1970's and 1980's new, more spacious
homes were built that, like the now-aging homes of the 1920's,
have small touches of traditional grace: more elaborate thresh-
olds and gateways, attractively tiled and gently curved roofs, or
space for a postage-stamp garden by a gate. But on the whole
Miyamoto-chō's buildings suggest a no-nonsense, unpretentious, and comfortable but not luxurious community.

Miyamoto-chō is densely populated, and almost no privately
owned space stands idle. The neighborhood has almost 30,000
residents per square kilometer, twice the density of Tokyo as a
whole (Sōrifu Tōkei-kyoku 1975: 3). These population figures
are all the more striking because hardly half a dozen buildings
exceed two stories, and much of the neighborhood is taken up
not by residences, but by a variety of public or semipublic institutions: the shrine, the temple, a government office building,
and three public schools—a nursery school, an elementary
school, and a junior high school, each with a playground or athletic field. Houses are built with walls almost touching. Few
have any semblance of a yard or garden, except for a few potted
plants on the doorsill or on a veranda used to hang the wash.
Often any open space around a home has been converted into a
parking spot or is occupied by a tiny steel shed storing possessions that cannot be accommodated in the house itself. On
many rooftops fenced platforms have been added for storage, for

airing clothes, for children's play areas, or for prized collections of potted plants. Despite the density, or perhaps because of it, every effort is made to preserve the privacy of the home from strangers and neighbors alike. Many houses fronting the streets are screened by high walls and gates that stand only inches away from the buildings' walls; windows have solid wooden or steel sliding shutters, which are closed every evening for protection, for privacy, or for warmth. Shopkeepers, too, roll down heavy steel shutters after business hours to cover their storefronts completely. As Bayley has noted (1976: 45), Japanese concepts of residential privacy are geared to sight, not sound. Japanese houses are anything but soundproof, and it is often impossible *not* to hear much of what goes on next door; yet at least visually and symbolically homes are carefully demarcated from the public sphere.

The streets running through Miyamoto-chō are narrow; though many of them have two-way traffic, most are wide enough for only one lane of traffic at a time. Even on the busiest thoroughfare—the one-lane, one-way shopping street that bisects the neighborhood—traffic often slows to a crawl as drivers maneuver around parked delivery vans, buses, cyclists, and pedestrians. For speed and convenience in getting through traffic, most local shopkeepers make their deliveries by bicycle or motorcycle. Only along this street are there sidewalks, and these are so narrow that two adults cannot walk abreast. In front of the elementary school a section along the edge of the road has been turned into a walkway with the addition of a steel guardrail. On other streets used by children going to and from school, pedestrian lanes are painted on the asphalt.

The public streets are all paved, but many homes in Miyamoto-chō are accessible only by dirt paths that wind through the interiors of each block, paved only with a few flagstones laid down the middle. These twisting alleys are at many points so narrow that one can touch the walls of houses on either side of the passageway with outstretched arms. Here and there along these back alleys, the neighborhood association has erected streetlamps, whose feeble light intensifies rather than dispels the gloom of nightfall.

On main streets and back alleys the principles of demarcation between the home and the public sphere are the same, but along the back alleys houses are much less likely to be walled; though windows have shutters, these homes are generally more open to the gaze of neighbors and passersby. Along these lanes, somewhat more than on the larger streets, interaction among neighbors is frequent and at times intimate; children run from one household into the next; housewives chat from one window to another across the alley while cleaning house or hanging bedding out to air; neighbors accept deliveries for one another and keep an eye on the house next door when its occupants are away; and on the death of a household member, immediate neighbors prepare for the funeral, take care of mourners, and serve at the funeral banquet.

Along the larger streets the traffic and the constant presence of passersby prevent the more relaxed and informal interaction of the back lanes and quieter side streets. Nevertheless, for main-street residents as well as back-alley dwellers, the streets and lanes, not their homes, are the settings for neighborly interaction. Housewives carrying shopping baskets over one arm—sometimes containing a well-groomed Pomeranian, Maltese, or some other tiny pet dog, usually of a Western breed—cluster for long conversations outside a gate or on a corner. During the day small children take over the side streets for games of hopscotch, jump-rope, or catch, pausing only when the ring of a bicycle's bell or the shifting of a car's gears urges them out of the way. In the evening two or three men linger to share cigarettes and local gossip outside Mrs. Maki's snack bar or on the corner outside Yokokawa-ya, the liquor dealer by the old river.[6] Shopkeepers pause as they close their shutters, chatting and watching their children scramble around the display cases in impromptu games of tag. During the summer months families stand in the street or alleyway in front of their homes at dusk, watching their children set off a few fireworks—sparklers, fountains, or pinwheels—which celebrate no particular holiday but are simply a part of the normal round of summertime pastimes enjoyed by small children and their indulgent elders. Without the institutionalized public gathering places found in other cultures—plazas, marketplaces, taverns, or open-air cafes—residents of Miyamoto-chō rely on streets and alleys for their informal interactions, the place to break through the formal privacy that otherwise surrounds and separates each family's home.

But social life and patterns of interaction are not uniform throughout Miyamoto-chō, nor is the neighborhood entirely homogeneous. Miyamoto-chō can be roughly divided into several areas, distinguishable by density, by the style of the houses, by the types of activities carried out in each area, and to some extent by residents' economic status.

The major distinction is between two areas—referred to by residents as *kami* ("the upper region" or "uphill") and *shimo* ("the lower region" or "downhill")—roughly demarcated by the main shopping street. Kami and shimo are not precise geographic subdivisions, although the areas generally correspond to local topographical contours, nor are the terms exclusively geographical in their implications. Rather, they reflect the subtle distinctions residents draw between the two regions—only incidentally derived from topography—based on perceived differences of social class and style.

Kami, the Upper Half

Kami extends from just behind the shopping street to the railway tracks. A few businesses are scattered throughout kami, primarily along the old road that runs down the hill in front of the shrine. These include a newspaper dealer, a barber, a beauty shop, and an undertaker, as well as the offices of several tax accountants and other professionals. Around the police box there is a small cluster of shops: a laundromat, a photographer's, a baker of old-fashioned Japanese sweets, a milk distributor, a pottery shop, a realtor, an electrical appliance dealer, and a *dagashiya*, a seller of small toys and candies, who caters to the children from the nearby elementary school. The houses of a couple of successful contractors—substantial, lavishly built homes advertising their skills—stand surrounded by storage sheds of wooden scaffolding, sawhorses, and other tools of the trade that poke out threatening to block the narrow paths and alleyways. But despite these businesses and a few other tiny workshops in kami, "uphill" is largely residential.

Kami's homes are generally prosperous looking; they tend to

be larger, newer, and fancier than shimo's, and are more likely to have a tiny garden, perhaps as much as three or four square meters. In particular the area bordering the shrine's gate is purely residential. With the borrowed greenery of the shrine's trees in the background, many of the nearby lanes are unexpectedly peaceful, disturbed only by the comings and goings of schoolchildren.

The streets of "uphill" are filled with schoolchildren, for kami contains all three of Miyamoto-chō's public schools. With their attached playgrounds and athletic fields, these schools occupy a sizable portion of the land between the shopping street and the railway tracks. They contribute heavily to the contrast with the industrial and commercial face of shimo.

The nursery school has the least-defined and most-extensive district; demand for preschool day care is so high that children are chosen by public lottery, and many of them come from well beyond Miyamoto-chō's boundaries. The junior high school draws students from three public elementary schools that encompass a dozen or more distinct neighborhoods. The elementary school's district is the most circumscribed, with pupils drawn only from Miyamoto-chō and parts of five adjacent neighborhoods.

Established in 1928, the elementary school is one of the oldest and most important institutions in local life. School activities attract the participation and interest of students, parents, and local residents who otherwise have no direct, day-to-day connection with the school. Social ties established through the school are important not only for children and parents themselves, but also for the many alumni and relatives of alumni who live in the area. Once established, ties between classmates often last a lifetime. Many lifelong residents of Miyamoto-chō and surrounding areas rely on school ties to classify other local residents, comparing the years they or their relatives graduated and using this to calculate the potential closeness of a relationship. Direct ties with classmates and the ability to create indirect connections through these calculations constitute an important framework of social reference. Such ties are useful for solidifying political contacts, for seeking the innumerable favors and introductions that daily life requires, and even for determining which of several possible coffee shops one may choose to patronize.

Kami contains several other institutions of local importance. Next to the elementary school a small cinderblock building houses the handcart fire engine of the volunteer fire brigade, which dates from the days of the old hamlet and now acts as an auxiliary to the professional fire department and as an honor guard at shrine festivals.

Across the street is the branch office (*shutchōjo*) of the ward government. Here local residents can file paperwork, get information, and make inquiries on a whole range of bureaucratic matters, including household registration, government pensions, school registration, passports, the registration of personal seals (*inkan*, used on legal documents in place of signatures), pet licenses, and public health inoculations. Branch offices, of which there are 12 in the ward as a whole, also are the conduits for most communications between the ward government and neighborhood associations.

Near the branch office are two company-owned dormitories for young unmarried men. The larger one houses about 175 employees of a large optical equipment factory located a few blocks from Miyamoto-chō. The smaller dormitory houses about a dozen employees of an electrical engineering research facility in an adjacent neighborhood. Although these dormitories and their residents are in no way disruptive, and the companies try to be good neighbors, the dormitory dwellers are seen as transient strangers who do not participate (and who are not expected to involve themselves) in any local events or organizations. They make few acknowledged contributions to the neighborhood as a community, though their patronage is probably important in sustaining some local shops and businesses.

Just across the neighborhood boundary, beyond the elementary school and the larger of the two dormitories, is the Kamiura station of a private railway line. This commuter line runs from the National Railway station at Otani, just a couple of stops away, out toward the west and southwest through increasingly exclusive residential areas of Tokyo. To the west of Miyamoto-chō the line intersects with several commuter lines that extend out into Tokyo's suburbs and the bedroom communities of the adjacent prefecture; it also intersects with the extensions of several subway lines leading into the heart of Tokyo. On an average day roughly 12,500 passengers use Kamiura station (SKNT 1979: 51), but compared with other stations on the same line, this is a very minor stop indeed. A tiny shopping district surrounds the entrance to the station and stretches down a sharp hillside away from Miyamoto-chō. Few residents of Miyamoto-chō shop there, in part because its geographical location orients the cluster of a dozen shops toward neighborhoods at the bottom of the slope. More important, few residents of Miyamoto-chō pass through the station for commuting, because the nearby Otani station of the National Railway is only a few minutes' walk away and for most destinations is more convenient, unless a person works or attends school in the western suburbs. Most of those who use Kamiura station are employees of several large manufacturing plants in the area, officials at a nearby government office complex, or students at several private high schools in the surrounding neighborhoods. The station's major effect on neighborhood life—like the dormitories'—may lie in the purchases commuters make as they pass through Miyamoto-chō on their ways to and from the station.

Despite the dormitories and the nearby station, despite the schools and the government branch office, and despite the handful of shops and offices located in kami, it is thought of as a quiet, prosperous, comfortable residential area. To residents of Miyamoto-chō this sharply distinguishes it from shimo, the commercial and social heart of the neighborhood.

Shimo, the Lower Half

Shimo stretches from the traffic bypass covering the river to the shopping street or a little bit beyond. In the loose classification scheme of local residents, the shopping street is "downhill," and shimo's major defining characteristic is the prevalence of industrial and commercial activities intermingled among the homes and apartment buildings.

Shimo contains several dozen tiny machine shops and assembly plants, small warehouses, shipping and construction firms, a factory that produces film cartridges, and a kimono-dyeing workshop. Most of the factories and workshops are hardly more than household operations, and many are subcontractors who process materials or produce parts for larger enterprises elsewhere, which may in turn be subcontractors for still-larger companies.[7] A few local factories produce parts for the nearby optical equipment factory. Other, smaller home workshops produce or assemble light bulb parts for an industry that was once centered in this section of Tokyo, but has declined in recent years because of competition from Southeast Asia. Although some areas of Tokyo have become famous for their locally specialized trade, Miyamoto-chō's businesses are not concentrated in particular specializations, nor are they integrated with one another through common sets of clients, suppliers, patrons, or brokers.

Originally, industrial activities came to be located in this area of Miyamoto-chō—and all along the river valley in the neighborhoods on either side of it—to take advantage of easily tapped water. Now that homes and businesses alike have access to a municipal water supply, water availability is no longer a factor. But industries are gradually moving out of Miyamoto-chō because of recent zoning laws prohibiting the building of new factories and the replacement or expansion of existing ones. Existing factories are protected by grandfather clauses, but government policy generally seeks to remove industry from the heavily congested, densely populated sections of inner Tokyo.

Scattered here and there along the back streets of shimo are many small shops: a laundromat with half a dozen small washers and dryers whose customers are mainly young men who live in tiny back-alley apartments; a late-night bar featuring home-style cooking, where many of these young men regularly eat, and where many older, married men will stop for a nightcap before returning home; a minuscule cigarette and candy shop— really no more than a window in the front of the Munekatas' home, where Grandmother knits, watches television, and every hour or so sells something to a passerby; a dry cleaner's shop run in the converted entryway of a housewife's home; and a busy liquor store, surrounded by mountains of bright yellow plastic beer cases and weathered wooden crates for *sake* bottles. Tucked beside a machine shop and a commercial laundry is a little flower shop that advertises a service to provide fresh flowers daily for home *butsudan* (Buddhist altars). Here too is the local pawnbroker, whose high walls and heavy *noren* (the curtains hung in a shop's entry that display the shop's name or crest) protect the privacy of those with whom he does business. Down alongside the old river, the Mutos, one of the very few local families that can trace their residence in the area back to the nineteenth century and before,[8] run a small lumberyard—with all the boards, beams, posts, and poles stored vertically to save space—which supplies most of the local contractors and carpenters. Along the old road beside the temple's entrance, and across from one of the three public baths that serve Miyamoto-chō, stands a row of small shops and businesses: a tailor, a tofu maker, a vegetable stall, a beauty parlor, a realtor, a barber, a yarn shop, a Chinese restaurant, a veterinarian, and a workshop that builds and refurbishes pianos.

Houses and apartment buildings are packed in among shimo's shops and workshops; "downhill" is home to roughly half of Miyamoto-chō's population. In general shimo's houses tend to be smaller, older, more tightly crowded together with fewer and smaller yards or gardens, and shabbier looking than those in kami. Apartment buildings are common and include some of the largest and most modern as well as some of the smallest and oldest. These latter, located on back alleys, are dark, two-story buildings of one-room apartments, generally occupied by transient young couples or single people who have little to do with their neighbors or the neighborhood. The mixture of shops, factories, and homes in shimo, producing an odd juxtaposition of old wooden homes with small factories of corrugated sheet metal, adds to the well-worn outward face of this part of Miyamoto-chō.

Given the grimy and unrelentingly urban cast of the landscape, one might think that shimo's residents would regret the paving over of the river and its transformation in the early 1970's into a one-way street carrying a heavy load of through traffic. Residents do not hold this romantic view; many recall the river as little more than an open sewer, which occasionally flooded low-lying homes and factories with its refuse-laden waters. My landlord, Mr. Takahashi, once spoke to me a bit wistfully about the river. He recounted how, following custom, he used to take decorations—ornamented bamboo fronds—from the Tanabata festival in July to cast them into the water. As he recounted this, he regretted the river's disappearance and wished his children could enjoy the same childhood pleasure, but it was a momentary regret, and few in Miyamoto-chō now feel much nostalgia for the river.

The crowded living conditions and the commercial/industrial character of shimo suggest to the casual observer that "downhill" residents are poorer than those of "uphill." Local opinion disagrees. When pressed, Miyamoto-chō residents argue that there are no great disparities in average wealth between dwellers in kami and shimo, and that if anything shimo may hold the edge in the number of *kanemochi*, or "moneybags." Certainly there are differences: the prosperous household head in kami is more likely to be a professional or white-collar worker, the one in shimo to own a business with which the family shares its living space. More frequently in "downhill" than in "uphill," residents lucky enough to have land and the capital to exploit it have become landlords, renting a few apartments tucked away down a narrow lane. To the white-collar resident of kami goes the public recognition of social standing by the standards of Japanese society as a whole; to the self-employed entrepreneur of shimo, through the complicated provisions of Japanese tax policy, goes a whole range of ways to shelter income and to enjoy the comforts of life behind a façade of grubby hard work.

Contrasting commercial shimo's cramped drabness with the relative spaciousness and neatness of domesticated kami, local residents often link the differences in outward appearance and stereotyped occupations to an implied social distinction between the two areas. For example, the main back street of shimo, which runs between and parallel to the shopping street and the old river, is sometimes called *gakkai-dōri* (gakkai street), a slightly derisive comment on the number of adherents of the Sōka Gakkai Buddhist organization who live in shimo. The Sōka Gakkai, like many other so-called New Religions, characteristically draws many of its members from the ranks of the lower-middle class; and the prosperous white-collar and self-employed residents of Miyamoto-chō who use the term gakkai street are implicitly stating a common, though not entirely accurate, appraisal of the social character of shimo.[9]

Only partly in jest residents compare shimo and kami with *shitamachi* and *yamanote*, the major divisions in the subcultural geography of Tokyo. Shitamachi (lit., "downtown"), the old merchant quarter, is a crowded, old-fashioned place, noted for the role self-employed entrepreneurs play in open and informal community life. Yamanote (lit., "the foothills") comprises the largely residential areas of western Tokyo, characterized by middle-class, white-collar sarariiman households and their more "modern," "rational," outwardly affluent, and less community-oriented lifestyles. The distinction between shitamachi and yamanote remains among the most fundamental social, subcultural, and geographic demarcations in contemporary Tokyo (R. J. Smith 1960; Dore 1958: 11–14; Bestor 1991). In suggesting that these distinctions are applicable within Miyamoto-chō, residents imply that the sarariiman households of kami are less concerned with neighborly ties and are less involved in neighborhood organizations, while the entrepreneurs of shimo interact more intimately with their neighbors and are more likely to be active participants in sustaining neighborhood life.

These contrasts are overdrawn, for most differences between kami and shimo are largely matters of outward appearance. All the same, there is an element of truth to these characterizations, and certainly the commercial shimo—whose merchants play leading roles in most neighborhood organizations and activities—is both the geographic and the social center of Miyamoto-chō.

The Shopping Street

Miyamoto-chō's shopping street is a two-block segment of a street that runs east-west—roughly parallel to the now-buried river—through a series of neighborhoods. Locally it is known as *basu-dōri* (bus street) or *sangen-dōri* (three-*ken* street), since it is 5.5 meters (roughly three ken) wide from storefront to storefront.[10] Narrow as the street is, the traffic load is heavy. It is a major cross-town route for this part of the ward, and forms one strand in a network that links the business district around Otani station with two major north-south highways running between Tokyo and Yokohama.

During one week in September 1980 the traffic safety committee of the neighborhood association patiently counted the passing vehicles. After 41 hours of observation on weekdays between 9:00 A.M. and 6:00 P.M., they calculated an average volume of 388 vehicles an hour, one every nine seconds.[11] The figures not only document the shopping street's heavy traffic, but are significant as well because their collection suggests something of the care and attention the chōkai is willing to devote to gathering information about local conditions.

Lined with small shops for its entire length, the street is the major local shopping area for the half dozen neighborhoods through which it passes. The two-block stretch through Miyamoto-chō, only 250 meters long, contains about 60 shops and other businesses. Almost all are owned and operated by members of local households and employ no other labor; all depend largely on local patronage. The shops in Miyamoto-chō are a cross section of businesses offering both goods and services (see Table 1), and though they do not offer a complete range of daily necessities, in combination with shops on back streets or in adjoining neighborhoods—a butcher, a small supermarket, a hardware store, a tea store, a baker of traditional Japanese pastries, and a *kanbutsuya* (a dealer in dried, salted, or pickled delicacies)—the shopping street can meet the ordinary needs of most households most of the time.

The density of small shops, all dependent on nearby customers, together with the presence of potential or actual rivals within a block or two up or down the street, creates competition among the *shōtenkai* (shopkeepers' associations) of the various neighborhoods to promote their own stretch of the street over adjacent stretches and nearby shopping areas. Among other things this has led to distinctively different styles of streetlights every two or three blocks, attempts at beautification that the merchants hope will distinguish their shopping area and invite greater patronage.

Such efforts by the Miyamoto-chō merchants' group to improve or beautify the shopping street take many forms. Each year it places seasonal decorations on the lampposts, wooden branches festooned with plastic foliage appropriate to the season: red and orange maple leaves in the fall; pink and white plum blossoms in the winter; pink cherry blossoms in the

TABLE I
Miyamoto-chō's Shopping Street, 1980

CROSS	STREET
Bakery	Cosmetics and sundries store
Women's Western clothing shop	Newspaper dealer
Jeweler	Motorcycle showroom [1]
Barber	Milk dealer
Printer	Mushroom dealer (wholesale)
Tofu maker	Futon store
Motorcycle repair shop [1]	Stationery store
Vegetable shop	Laundry and dry cleaner
Jewelry and toy store	Barber
Sporting goods store	Beauty parlor
Noodle maker	Rice dealer
Chinese restaurant	Snack food store
Fishmonger	Video game arcade
Sushi restaurant	*Soroban* (abacus) school
Beauty parlor	Vegetable shop
Used bookstore	Women's Western clothing shop
Sake dealer	

CROSS	STREET

CROSS	STREET
Pharmacy	Electrical appliance dealer [2]
Mahjong parlor[a]	Furniture store [2]
Coffee shop	Furniture store [2]
Ice, kerosene, and charcoal dealer	Vacant lot used for *chōkai* activities
Yarn shop	(lot owned by the Buddhist temple)
Electrical contractor [3]	Fire brigade storage shed[b]
Sewing-machine dealer	Clothing and dry goods store (Western
Liquor and grocery store	and Japanese style) [2]
Bicycle store	*Chōkai* hall
Fishmonger	*Chōkai* recycling hut
Women's Western clothing shop[c]	Judo school
Vegetable shop	Shoe store
Electrical appliance dealer [3]	Magazine and bookstore
Electrical contractor	Yarn store
Tailor	Jeweler and optometrist
Housewares store	Bakery
Chinese restaurant	
Used bookstore	
Chinese restaurant	

CROSS	STREET

NOTE: Residences and other buildings not used for businesses or other public purposes are omitted. A bracketed number after a business indicates that it is part of a single enterprise operating in more than one location. Thus the motorcycle repair shop and the motorcycle showroom labeled [1] are owned and operated by the same family.

[a] Formerly a coffee shop under the same management.

[b] The fire brigade subsequently moved its shed to a location near the elementary school.

[c] This shop opened and went out of business within the year.

spring; and green bamboo fronds around the midsummer Tana-bata festival. The loudspeaker system it erected, which can be heard the length of Miyamoto-chō's shopping street, broadcasts popular songs, light classics, and familiar folk tunes every after-noon during the peak shopping hours (from about four to six). Local shopkeepers feel that the music makes the area a more pleasant shopping district.

Other special events are designed to attract customers to the shopping area. Occasionally the merchants' group sponsors a one-day sale or offers some staple—milk or eggs or soy sauce—as a loss-leader to build traffic through the area. Twice a year posters go up to promote the shōtenkai's lottery; by accumulat-ing tickets from participating local merchants, shoppers can compete for prizes ranging from bottles of soy sauce to a new moped.

The merchants house their loudspeaker system in a long, low, aged wooden building in the middle of one block along the shop-ping street. This is the hall of the Miyamoto-chō chōkai, and a weathered sign identifies it as the meeting place of the old people's club (the *rōjinkai*) as well. The hall has a long row of large windows facing onto the shopping street, which are kept shuttered most of the time. When they are not shuttered—dur-ing the annual fall festival, for example—the interior of the hall is entirely open to the street. The hall is built on a plot of land leased from the Buddhist temple, and its rear windows look out over the temple's graveyard, which lends an unexpected and oddly idyllic bit of borrowed scenery to the interior.

Chōkai halls in surrounding neighborhoods are often rented out to businesses for temporary sales and are occasionally put to other commercial uses. But because the merchants' group jointly owns and maintains the Miyamoto-chō hall, local shop-keepers understandably object to the idea of its being used, even if for only a few days, for a business that might compete with them for sales; the use of the hall for any money-making venture is therefore prohibited.

The hall's main room is large and matted with tatami; at both the main entrance and the kitchen door, people remove their shoes before stepping up to the raised interior. The main room can seat about 60 people for a meeting or banquet. The chōkai and its women's auxiliary (the *fujinbu*), as well as the old people's club and the merchants' association, use the hall for regular membership meetings and for special events, such as New Year's banquets. From time to time it is rented for a nominal sum to other local groups and individuals, most frequently for bereaved neighborhood households to hold a banquet for mourners who have come to pay their final respects at a *tsuya*, or wake.

At one end of the main hall is a cramped kitchen and many cupboards of serving dishes and cooking utensils. Since banquets most often are catered with food delivered from nearby restaurants, the kitchen is used mainly to prepare soups and large kettles of tea, but the chōkai's pots, pans, dishes, teapots, and trays, as well as the hall's folding tables and seating cushions, can be rented by neighborhood residents at low cost for use at home during a wake or funeral banquet, or for a *tatemae* (roof-raising ceremony) celebrating the building of a new home.

At the other end of the hall is the main entrance, which doubles as a general storage room. In the entry and in the small loft overhead are stored odd bits of equipment: the chōkai banner, carried on outings by local children's groups; the flag of the old people's club, draped with a black ribbon and displayed in front of a deceased member's home during the funeral; bullhorns and helmets for Miyamoto-chō's disaster relief team; and the paper lanterns chōkai leaders carry on official occasions. From under the floorboards of the entryway, the scaffolding for the drum tower used in the annual Bon Odori folk-dance festival pokes out into the area where people remove their shoes.

Next to the chōkai hall a separate shed houses flattened cardboard boxes, bundled-up newspapers and magazines, crushed aluminum cans, and other recyclable materials deposited by local merchants and residents. Once a month a scrap dealer empties out the hut and picks up the residents' deposits at collection points scattered around the neighborhood; his payments for the material are a significant source of the chōkai's income.

Daily Cycles of Activity

Around the chōkai hall life along the shopping street ebbs and flows throughout the day. A very few enterprises begin their days early in the morning, as early as 4:00 A.M.: Mr. Matsue, the baker, preparing the buns and sandwiches he and his wife sell to commuters; Mrs. Naganuma distributing milk and yogurt to neighborhood households before she goes off to her job selling milk and snacks in downtown office buildings; the employees in Mr. Ide's factory starting work on the noodles they deliver to local restaurants, where they will be lunch for hundreds of workers from nearby factories and offices; young Mr. Goto, the apprentice in the Sumidas' fish store, going off to the wholesale fish market at Tsukiji in central Tokyo to buy the day's stock for his shop and for the Watanabes' sushi restaurant next door.

By 7:00 A.M. the morning rush hour is on in earnest, and hundreds of commuters scurry past the mostly still-shuttered shops on their way to or from the two railroad stations. A few shops are open to catch the morning trade, mainly those that sell prepared lunches, cigarettes, or magazines.

A little later clusters of schoolchildren emerge from back lanes and gateways on their way to the elementary school. Unlike their older brothers and sisters in junior or senior high school or their peers who go to a nearby private school, they do not wear uniforms. Each wears the leather knapsack standard for all Japanese elementary schoolchildren and a plastic badge listing his or her school, homeroom class, and name and address. For children who attend a school other than the local public elementary school, the badge also indicates whether they walk or take a train or bus to school; this last is to aid conductors and bus drivers in making sure small children do not mistakenly get on the wrong form of transportation. Pupils at the local school walk the two or three blocks together in residential groups, along streets the school approves; these are marked with special pedestrian lanes and signs to warn motorists that the street is a designated route for schoolchildren.

Shortly after these children have left their homes, mothers on bicycles take younger ones—each clad in a light blue smock and a navy blue sailor's hat—to the nursery school by the shrine. Since the school's regulations require that adults accompany children to and from the school, the streets near the shrine are crowded with bicycles and by the throngs of young mothers who stop to chat after dropping their children off or while waiting to pick them up.

Traffic gradually clogs the shopping street, and by midmorning it is packed bumper to bumper with cars, buses, taxis, and trucks inching along, while motorcycles and bicycles weave in and out among them, trying to beat the slow-moving stream of traffic. Shopkeepers raise the shutters that separate the shop interiors from the sidewalks, and roll display racks of merchandise out onto the sidewalks, further crowding the already narrow walkways.

By nine-thirty or ten most shops are open for business, but there are only a few shoppers in the morning. Shopkeepers spend their time arranging stock, or dusting it with long-handled whisks, before settling down to read the daily paper or to watch television (a standard piece of equipment in almost every shop). Around noon there is a small flurry of shopping; housewives rush out to get some forgotten item for lunch, and workers in local offices or factories take their lunch breaks and pause to browse in the bookshops or to make small purchases elsewhere.

The early afternoon is quiet as well, and shopkeepers often use these hours to make deliveries. Rice merchants, liquor dealers, and booksellers load merchandise into cases mounted on motorscooters, and set off to visit customers throughout the neighborhood and surrounding areas. Others, such as the stationer who supplies many business offices, use small vans or station wagons and cover wider territories. From time to time the old ice merchant lashes carefully sawn blocks of ice wrapped in heavy canvas onto the back of an aging bicycle to deliver them to local bars and restaurants.

Since most shops and businesses are owned and operated as household enterprises, there is considerable flexibility about staffing stores; merchants are free to make deliveries or keep other appointments because some other member of the household can keep an eye on things when they are away. In some shops any member of the family from an elementary school pupil to a grandparent of eighty may be left in charge awhile. Often (especially around meal times) no one will be in the shop itself, so customers have to call a member of the household out from the combination living room/dining room, usually one step up, just behind the shop.

Peddlers also make their rounds throughout the day. Most are semiregulars, appearing in the neighborhood once or twice a week: a purveyor of freshly made tofu and *nattō* (a delicacy made from fermented soybeans); a seller of bamboo laundry poles and plastic household items; occasional vegetable or fish merchants, who drive slowly through in trucks heavily laden with produce; a few elderly farm women from nearby prefectures, who go door to door selling fresh vegetables from heavy wicker baskets they carry on their doubled-over backs; wintertime sellers of *yakiimo* (roasted sweet potatoes), freshly cooked in charcoal furnaces mounted on handcarts or tiny pickup trucks; and the ubiquitous *chirigamikōkan* ("toilet paper exchange") trucks driven by scrap dealers who collect old newspapers, magazines, books, and cardboard from housewives in exchange for toilet paper or cash, the amount determined by the weight of the paper collected.

Many of the sounds and cries the peddlers make on their rounds are distinctive and even beautiful, such as the horn of the nattō peddler and the chants of the yakiimo sellers. Others are merely raucous and annoying, such as the amplified tape-recorded messages played by the chirigamikōkan trucks. They mingle with the other daytime noises of Miyamoto-chō: the honking of horns and the screeching of brakes; the blare of stereos and televisions on display in local shops; the many loudspeaker trucks making political, commercial, or public service announcements; the recorded music from the shopping street; the junior high school's outdoor public address system; the rumble of passing trains. Every once in a while the normal roar of the modern city is enlivened by the arrival of a troupe of wandering *chindonya*, a special type of street musician. The chindonya, who usually appear in groups of three wearing samurai costumes and heavy make-up, play traditional and popular songs on an odd assortment of instruments as they stroll along, carrying banners advertising a sale at a supermarket near Otani station or the grand opening of a new *pachinko* (pinball) parlor in the nearby entertainment district. It is a decidedly déclassé means of advertising, and if any Miyamoto-chō residents pay attention to the chindonya, they disguise it well.

In midafternoon the pace along the shopping street starts to pick up. Elementary and junior high school students begin to come home between two and three. Many local children study after school at Narita-sensei's private *soroban* (abacus) academy on the shopping street, and the street is animated by children running off to their classes or stopping later at the candy store and the video game arcade that flank the abacus academy. Otherwise one rarely sees any but the youngest children playing or meeting with their friends. The time of older children is consumed by the pressures to study long and hard for entrance examinations for schools more elite than the local public ones, and these pressures affect children as early as the third or fourth year of elementary school. After the first or second year of junior high school, children almost disappear from the neighborhood's streets after school, spending their time studying at home or in special examination preparation schools (*juku*) elsewhere in Tokyo.

As the last of the younger children are returning from school, about four in the afternoon, the public baths are opening, their boilers well stoked with beams and timbers the proprietors purchase whenever a local home is demolished. There are three large public baths (*sentō*) immediately adjacent to Miyamoto-chō—one on the old road across from the Buddhist temple, another just across the railway tracks beyond the police box, and the third on the shopping street on the way to Otani station. Three or four other public baths are within easy walking distance, and some Miyamoto-chō residents frequent these as well. In Miyamoto-chō, as throughout Tokyo, patronage of public baths is declining, but all the local sentō are still well patronized, serving as social centers for local residents, including many who could bathe at home but prefer the congenial atmosphere of public bathing. Many of Miyamoto-chō's elderly line up outside the doors early to get into the baths when the water is hottest and freshest. From four until eleven o'clock people carrying towels and small plastic wash basins—some in jogging suits, others in T-shirts and jeans, still others in *yukata* (a lightweight cotton robe) or *jinbei* (a cotton tunic and pair of shorts)—saunter down the street to one or another of the baths, often with a child in tow or carried piggyback, stopping on their way back to do a bit of shopping, to chat with friends, or to have a bowl of noodles in a restaurant.

From about four to six is the busiest shopping time, particularly for shops dealing in foodstuffs. Housewives in Miyamoto-chō, like Japanese housewives generally, shop for food at least once a day, buying fresh fish, meat, and vegetables for the evening meal a few minutes before starting to cook, and often determining the menu after scanning the day's best bargains. The late-afternoon shopping expedition is, moreover, a social event. Clusters of chatting housewives, shopping baskets on their arms, crowd the sidewalks in front of food shops. Younger ones are dressed in stylish skirts and blouses underneath aprons emblazoned with catchy slogans or designers' names, older ones in quiet kimono underneath white *kappogi* (a puffy-sleeved apron designed to be worn over Japanese-style dress). Lines waiting to be served at the butcher's or at shops that sell freshly prepared fried foods provide a chance to catch up on the latest gossip, to swap recipes, and to trade general information. Shopkeepers intersperse quick jokes, comments, and bits of gossip in among their urgings to try a new seasonal vegetable or to stock up on some staple at the current low, low price. Proprietors of food stores, especially the women proprietors, develop followings and often spend considerable amounts of time talking with regular customers. Local men jokingly compare the groups of housewives clustered around the hibachi in the back of the Okitas' vegetable stall or in front of the Sumidas' fish shop with *idobatakaigi*: the "well-side conferences" where women stereotypically gathered to gossip in the past.

There is no late-afternoon rush hour of returning commuters equivalent to the morning's, since so many workers stay at their jobs until late in the evening. Although the predinner shopping rush tapers off sharply after six, the shopping street stays moderately busy until eight or nine as workers and a few students return home, residents take strolls and walk their dogs, or people go to and from the public baths, stopping to chat with shopkeepers or make a few small purchases.

One shop in particular—Mr. Takahashi's grocery store—is a center of activity throughout the day, but especially in the eve-

nings. Mr. Takahashi, one of the chōkai's vice-presidents, keeps
the keys for the chōkai hall, and his shop is an informal gathering spot for local leaders. Because most chōkai activities and
other local events of any importance are discussed here, the shop
is also a central place for residents to hear the latest information
and gossip about any number of local issues, events, and organizations; people are constantly coming and going with bits and
pieces of information. Being at the center of this information
exchange, Mr. Takahashi is acknowledged as one of Miyamoto-
chō's experts on local affairs; sitting in his shop many evenings
during 1979–81 was an especially attentive listener, a foreign
anthropologist who by sheer luck (and possibly the unobtrusive
steering of understanding personal contacts) had rented an
apartment above his store.

Around nine, as patronage slackens, most shopkeepers begin
to move merchandise back inside, to close their shutters, and, if
they have them, to take down their noren. Few shops have a
fixed closing time, and no shopkeeper would turn away a customer who appeared just as the shutters were being drawn down.
A shop's closing time depends on the weather, the number of
people still on the streets, and the inclination of the person tend-
ing the shop. To discourage casual browsing yet indicate that
late customers are still welcome, shopkeepers often leave their
shutters open a few feet until the last family member finishes
straightening up the store.

By ten almost everything is closed, except for the public baths
and some *sunakku* (snack bars), *kissaten* (coffee shops), and
bars, which stay open well beyond midnight to catch the last
stragglers. One of Miyamoto-chō's few late-night bars and restaurants is located on a side street rather than on the shopping
street. This is the popular *akachōchin* (lit., "red lantern," a type
of bar so called for the large paper lantern that characteristically
hangs outside) run by the middle-aged Maekawa sisters, who
serve up home cooking as well as drinks. Patrons often drop in
for a nightcap on their way home from an evening of bar-
hopping, to catch a quick bite and to try to sober up, but few
leave more sober than when they entered. On the main street
Mrs. Maki runs a sunakku that serves as a hangout for local leaders, both men and women, after evening meetings or other

events. But generally when local men go out for an evening together, they leave the neighborhood and head for favorite bars or
restaurants a short distance away.

The nearby Otani station is surrounded by a moderately large
entertainment district similar to those common around most
Tokyo stations of the National Railway. It includes many mid-
dling quality bars, nightclubs, cabarets, sushi bars, stalls selling
skewers of *yakitori* (grilled chicken), and Korean barbecue restaurants, as well as Turkish baths,[12] room-by-the-hour "love hotels," and other types of establishments that enjoyed momentary notoriety during my research, such as *no-pan kissa* ("no
panty" coffee shops, where the waitresses wore see-through pan-
ties, or nothing at all, underneath their miniskirts). Even by the
low standards of Tokyo entertainment districts, the area around
Otani station is a dismal place,[13] and Miyamoto-chō's residents
tend to avoid it. This is partly because of the hoodlums who allegedly control many of the businesses. But more important, Miyamoto-chō men prefer places that are smaller and more intimate, where they know and are known by the owners, and where
the fuss made over them is more genuine than the synthetic, ef-
fusive greetings indiscriminately offered everyone in the Otani
nightspots.

The area near the private railway's Kamiura station contains
many more of the sorts of bars favored by Miyamoto-chō men
for a quiet night on the town with neighborhood friends and associates. Between Kamiura station and the line's terminus at
Otani station, the railway tracks are elevated at rooftop level.
Shops, restaurants, and bars fill the space underneath the via-
duct; a street too narrow for automobile traffic runs alongside
this row of shops for a couple of blocks before ending at a major
thoroughfare. The lack of automobile traffic permits this stretch
of alleyway to be a bustling shopping area during the daytime,
and the proximity of large businesses and government offices allows the bars here to do a thriving business until late into the
night. The street is far enough from Otani station, however, that
these bars and restaurants are small, intimate places where most
of the patrons are locals, well known to each other and to the
proprietors.

In bars near Otani station every patron who walks through

the doors is addressed as a *shachō* or a *sensei*—a company president or a university professor. In the bars the men of Miyamoto-chō prefer, regular customers are known by name and are greeted warmly by the staff with bantering bits of local gossip. A patron's favorite drink or snack is remembered and may appear on the counter before he has had a chance to order.

There is an amazing variety of bars and restaurants tucked away down alleys around Kamiura station and elsewhere within easy walking distance of Miyamoto-chō, each with a different ambience, a different type of clientele, a different culinary specialty: sushi counters, yakitori bars, noodle stalls, restaurants that specialize in regional cuisines, bars featuring *karaoke* sing-alongs,[14] and homey hole-in-the-wall akachōchin. Men often frequent a set of favorite spots—one in each of the above and other categories—which they patronize almost exclusively; as their loyalties solidify, they confirm their standing as regulars by leaving a bottle of whiskey marked with their name at each of several favorites. Cliques of friends go to the same bars, and friends usually know where to find one another late in the evening. If you want to find Mr. Maebashi the barber, look in Yoneda's eel shop. Looking for Ku-chan the carpenter?[15] Check the bar run by the Maekawa sisters. When Mrs. Tsunoda and her friends from the PTA go out for a bite to eat in the evening, they will probably be found at the pizza coffee shop run by the brother of Mrs. Tsunoda's childhood friend.

By about two in the morning, all but the hardiest souls are back home, and the shopping street is quiet except for the infrequent passage of taxis and the distant, eerie sounds of the *charumeru* flute of noodle vendors, who wheel pushcarts equipped with small propane stoves up and down the nearly deserted streets until almost sunrise, stopping occasionally in front of a mahjong parlor or on a street corner to prepare a bowl of noodles for a die-hard reveler. Once in a while on a summer weekend night, the quiet is shattered by the roaring passage of *bōsōzoku*, gangs of young male motorcyclists and sports car enthusiasts (see Loftus 1977; Littleton 1985). In the winter the quiet of cold, clear nights is more frequently interrupted by the howling sirens of fire engines rushing to extinguish a blaze caused by leaking gas, an overturned kerosene heater, or a forgotten cigarette.

If close enough, a fire will rouse many residents from their futon. Some are members of the volunteer fire brigade, but many are *yajiuma*, fire buffs, who come merely to watch, their curiosity mingled with a very real concern that the fire could quickly spread in the direction of their homes through the densely packed maze of Miyamoto-chō's wooden structures. But the fire department is efficient, and once a fire is extinguished Miyamoto-chō returns to sleep.

Miyamoto-chō is not just a random set of geographical boundaries encompassing a collection of unrelated individuals. To the outside observer and to the resident alike, Miyamoto-chō appears as a close-knit place where many people know and are known by their neighbors, where membership or participation in overlapping organizations and institutions provides many residents with a common set of social ties and experiences, where for many home and workplace are not so separate as to constitute distinct worlds.

These qualities—which are common to many Tokyo neighborhoods, though they may differ from one another in minor details—often lead observers to perpetuate the notion that Tokyo is nothing but a collection of villages bound together by very little. It is an appealing metaphor, but an appalling explanatory device. To confuse the closeness of social ties in a small corner of an enormous city with some residue of rural social values, or to try to account for the neighborliness of neighborhood life by constructing historical continuities with either rural or preindustrial urban life, seriously distorts our understanding of how Tokyo developed and of what urban life in contemporary Japanese society is all about.

The village metaphor distorts our understanding in several ways. First, it misrepresents the historical processes of Tokyo's development and the ways in which the creation of neighborhoods directly results from metropolitan growth. Second, in contemporary perspective, it distracts attention away from the connections between patterns of microcosmic social life and the social forces that shape the metropolis as a whole. It presumes that isolation is a major explanatory variable; that close social ties require closed social worlds. Finally, the village metaphor implies that one possible explanation for a highly urbanized society that maintains the integrity of community life, in which citizens play active and willing parts in upholding the social fabric of urban life, may be that the society is somehow not truly urban. It suggests that the patterns of Japanese social life differ from our Western-oriented expectations not because Japanese society could have developed alternative patterns of life in an urban, industrial society, but because they are incompletely "modern," that somehow social institutions and the behavior of individual Japanese are stuck in a premodern world.

CHAPTER TWO

The Development of a Neighborhood

MIYAMOTO-CHŌ IS A PLACE with a past, yet not the past its homey closeness immediately suggests. In its seemingly stable, traditional patterns of community life, the neighborhood appears to resemble the rural hamlet or the preindustrial city. But its history is far more dynamic and rather more self-conscious than one would expect from the common accounts of Japanese community organization, which dwell on an enduring resistance to change that supposedly sustains feudal social structure into the present.

Many analyses of urban neighborhoods—particularly those describing the older shitamachi districts of Toyko—link contemporary social patterns to the social structure of preindustrial cities. As Bellah (1957: 43) argues, during the Tokugawa period (1603–1868) the city "only to a limited extent represented a new form of social organization. . . . For many purposes it was merely a congeries of 'villages' in close geographic contiguity." Others, like Morioka (1966), see remnants of rural social patterns in the community life of newly urbanized neighborhoods on the fringes of older Tokyo. Whether the analysis starts with the premodern city or the agricultural hamlet, the findings seem strikingly the same, in part because many studies assume that the hamlet and the preindustrial city fundamentally resembled each other. In both cases, these approaches interpret contemporary patterns of urban community life as exemplifying a single set of social patterns linked to the present through direct (but often unspecified) processes of historical continuity.

Indeed, such views color interpretations of much more than just contemporary neighborhoods. Many scholars examine present-day Japanese social institutions with an eye to uncovering what they assume to be antecedents or continuities with traditions of the past. Observers often assert that the key to grasping the fundamental social patterns of contemporary Japan—whether corporate organization, government decision-making, or the structure of urban neighborhoods—is understanding the Japanese past. This past is viewed as fundamentally unchanging and homogeneous; historically it is usually located in preindustrial and preferably rural Japan.

Relying on the village as the source of Japanese social organization, Nakane (1970: 59–60), for example, draws structural parallels between the social patterns of the village and those found in many aspects of urban life, and Kamishima (1961: 71–89) sees the structure of village social relationships as at the heart of the human relations found throughout contemporary Japanese society. Fukutake (1962: 79–80) argues that the process of modernization involves the dissolution of traditional communities—the rural hamlet or *buraku*—and the liberation of the individual from traditional communal relationships. He believes this modernization has not yet occurred, in either rural or urban Japan, and argues that the "*buraku* as a social phenomenon exists not only in the countryside but also in the cities. . . . The social character of the *buraku* [is] the prototype of Japanese society" (p. 100).

These theorists are, of course, speaking of a broader range of urban social phenomena than just residential communities. Nakane in particular distinguishes the general social principles she discusses from their specific manifestations in neighborhoods or other communities. Yet urban neighborhoods are often explicitly equated with the rural hamlet and are cited as examples of the enduring gemeinschaftlich nature of contemporary urban Japan (Isomura and Okuda 1966: 141). Falconeri (1976: 34) views neighborhood associations as "a product of Japanese village orientations carried over into the urban setting," and Dore (1958: 286) refers to neighborhood social structure as "already anachronistic: . . . institutions which properly belong to the self-contained village." Elsewhere (1968: 186) Dore describes Edo as

a city to which the common description of preindustrial towns as a congeries of villages might well apply. Small territorial segments of 200–300 households called *chō* or *chōnai* were in some respects analogous to the nucleated hamlet settlements of rural Japan in that they had a distinctive name, a distinctive sense of identity, and a distinctive organization for the exercise of limited powers of self-government. . . . The *chōnai* was in some real sense a community containing within it most of the important social relations in which [its residents] were involved.

These *chōnai* have retained their identity two hundred years later.

Many analyses of the "urban village" focus on the role of particular segments of contemporary society in perpetuating these purportedly rural or feudal social patterns. Often that role is ascribed to the petty entrepreneurs of the old middle class, the stalwarts of local social life in many neighborhoods. As Ishida (1971: 57–58) puts it, only in the older merchant quarter, the shitamachi districts, where members of "the old middle class, such as shopkeepers, . . . have lived and worked in the same place for generations, has there been a solidarity . . . like that of the rural community." Compared with members of other social classes, the old middle class is seen as somehow less fully involved in and less fully affected by the processes of social change that have transformed Japanese society as a whole.

As folk models—or emic glosses—of change and continuity, these images of the city-as-village, the past-in-the-present, and the old middle class as heirs of the Tokugawa townspeople provide interesting and important insights on how Japanese themselves view the nature of their society. In this sense, at least, such beliefs constitute what Geertz (1973: 448) would call "a story [the Japanese] tell themselves about themselves." But these rural and historical metaphors often take on lives of their own, overpowering analysis both of the present-day social character of urban neighborhoods and the historical context of their development.

Those who argue for underlying structural and cultural continuities between past and present, between rural and urban, often distort the past, the present, and the processes of social and cultural change and continuity that link them. They assume that culture is an ahistorical constant, not an ever-changing construct created in historical moments and altered by historical change at the same time it changes participants' views of history. Assumptions of static continuity—in urban neighborhoods or in a wide variety of other Japanese domains—illustrate what Yanagisako (1985: 11) has called a "static concept of culture . . . inclined to discover sameness in surface similarity." As R. J. Smith (1973: 164) argues, scholars who contrast "traditional" and "modern" institutions frequently rely on "invented history" or "explanations of any contemporary phenomenon [that] often are made in terms of an imagined past condition from which change is believed to have occurred. . . . This procedure often falsifies the past in an effort to render the present more readily comprehensible." Analyses of Japanese social organization routinely do just this in presuming that contemporary institutions of urban community life originate in the rural, preindustrial past.

An examination of Miyamoto-chō's historical development leads overwhelmingly to different conclusions. On the one hand, the present-day community bears only the most tangential relationship to any physical settlement or social group existing in the area before the urbanization of the 1920's. On the other hand, even though residents may refer to the neighborhood's contemporary institutional patterns in ways that suggest stability and continuity with both rural and urban preindustrial institutions, present-day patterns are in fact products of Miyamoto-chō's development since urbanization began in the 1920's. The neighborhood's social framework continues to evolve and change in response to contemporary conditions; it is neither an ancient nor a static inheritance from the past.

In this chapter I address two major, interrelated aspects of Miyamoto-chō's historical development: Tokyo's early-twentieth-century expansion, which resulted in the urbanization of what is now Miyamoto-chō; and the simultaneous development throughout Tokyo of new institutional frameworks for urban neighborhood life. Later chapters will examine the on-going development and elaboration of what appear to be "tra-ditional" patterns of community life and their implications for understanding the nature of the contemporary neighborhood.

The Hamlet of Kumodani

Until the 1920's Miyamoto-chō simply did not exist. Before the Meiji period (1868–1912) the area that now corresponds to the shrine parish comprising Miyamoto-chō and six other neighborhoods was an agricultural hamlet named Kumodani.[1] The hamlet lay three kilometers beyond the outermost fringes of Edo, beyond the suburban villas of daimyo, beyond the post towns and barriers guarding the approaches to the city. The ham-let was one and a half kilometers from the nearest stretch of the great Tōkaidō highway that linked Kyoto and Edo.[2]

These are short walking distances, and even in the seven-teenth century the inhabitants of this insignificant hamlet did not live in a remote rural area. Kumodani had regular contacts with the post towns along the Tōkaidō highway. Like the ham-lets around it, Kumodani was obligated to provide labor for the upkeep of the highway's facilities (SKS, 1: 575–79). Beginning in 1639, for example, the hamlet was required to send six men each month for the nightly watch around Tōkai-ji, a major temple at the crossing of the Meguro River near the Shinagawa barrier. If a fire broke out near the temple, Kumodani was one of 22 ham-lets required to send men to fight the blaze; Kumodani had to provide 16 firefighters (SKKI 1979: 128–29).

Kumodani's inhabitants were "truck farmers," closely linked economically to the great metropolis. They produced onions, melons, eggplants, daikon, and carrots for the Edo market; in turn Edo provided the nightsoil that was their major fertilizer. In addition to these cash crops, the Kumodani farmers grew rice, barley, wheat, and several varieties of beans for their own con-sumption. Indeed, compared with other hamlets in the area, Ku-modani depended far more on strictly agricultural pursuits than on commerce or cottage industry. Wet paddy for rice cultivation constituted about 20 percent of the hamlet's fields; the remain-ing agricultural land was dry, upland fields (*hatake*). In the mid-dle of the Tempō era (1830–43), the hamlet's annual rice yield

TABLE 2
The Population of Kumodani, 1658–1889

Year	Households	Inhabitants
1658	15	72
1676	22	119
1799	46	241[a]
1872	55	305
1875	57	311[b]
1889	60	331

SOURCES: Ebara-ku 1943: 179–80; SKS, 1: 434; SKS, 2: 187.
[a] 121 males, 120 females.
[b] 168 males, 143 females.

was assessed for tax purposes at 273.1 *koku*, in principle enough to support a hamlet of about 270 adults (SKS, 1: 391, 433, 435).[3]

This assessed yield corresponds roughly to the hamlet's population during the Tokugawa and early Meiji periods. In the early Tokugawa Kumodani had between 80 and 120 residents in fewer than two dozen households. The population rose substantially after the completion of the Shinagawa canal in 1661, an irrigation project that opened more land for cultivation (SKS, 1: 435). Between 1676 and the end of the eighteenth century, the population doubled; by 1875 it had increased still further, to 311 inhabitants in 57 households (see Table 2).

After the Tokugawa Shogunate was overthrown in the Meiji Restoration of 1868, the Imperial capital was officially transferred from Kyoto to Edo, and Edo became Tokyo.[4] The many social, political, and economic changes of the era did not have any immediate major effects on life in Kumodani and other hamlets in the area. But the post towns along the Tōkaidō suffered major dislocations because of the end of the *sankin kōtai* system of daimyo's alternating attendance in Edo.[5] In 1872 Japan's first railway began to run between Yokohama and Shinagawa, roughly two kilometers from Kumodani. The official post station along the Tōkaidō at Shinagawa was abolished, and nearby hamlets, including Kumodani, were freed from their obligations to provide horses, labor, and grain to support the station; in the neighboring countryside there was reportedly "great happiness" (SKKI 1979: 174, 184).

Of course, the lives of Japanese peasants everywhere were affected by many of the changes instituted in the early Meiji pe-

riod—the legalization of land sales and transfers, the imposition of a new land-tax system, the introduction of the Western
calendar, the abolition of the feudal class system, and the creation of a conscript army. But these changes did little to alter Kumodani's status, and nothing to transform it from an agricultural settlement to something more urban (SKKI 1979: 184).

During the 1870's and 1880's the new Meiji leadership struggled to create a unified nation with governmental institutions
comparable to those of the European powers, and capable of winning the West's respect. The system of local administration
underwent a series of almost bewildering changes; units of local
government—from the prefecture to the lowliest hamlet—were
shuffled and reshuffled as the national government experi-
mented with various theories and systems of centralized control. The greatest changes affecting hamlets arose from the suc-
cessive government-mandated amalgamations of traditional agricultural settlements into larger administrative villages.
Between 1874 and 1886 this process went on at a modest pace,
with mergers reducing the number of towns and villages by only
about 10 percent. But in 1888 and 1889, after the government
enacted new regulations allowing it to force amalgamation even
in the face of local opposition, the total number of towns and
villages dropped dramatically, from 55,494 to 15,820 (Steiner
1965: 19–40, 46).

In 1889 Kumodani was amalgamated with four other hamlets
to create a new administrative village named Hiratsuka-mura
(SKS, 2: 187). Even within this new and larger administrative
framework, the hamlets continued to exist as village subdivisions called ō-aza; no evidence suggests that any profound social, political, or economic changes immediately altered life
within these subdivisions.

During the Tokugawa period the hamlet had been divided
into smaller clusters of households within which formal and informal relationships were maintained both by legal sanction
and by customary patterns of cooperation. These clusters,
known in Kumodani as *kumi* (SKS, 2: 510), were the local version of *goningumi*, the most basic units of administration and
social control in feudal Japan.[6] As administrative units, goningumi regulated the behavior of their constituent households

through elaborate, legally enforced systems of collective responsibility. As institutions of social life, they promoted mutual aid, labor exchange, joint rituals, and other nonadministrative forms of cooperation and interaction within the group. The
Meiji government abolished goningumi as compulsory organizations, but presumably they continued to exist in Kumodani's
ō-aza for some time as customary, though not legally obligatory,
institutions. Unfortunately, no records have survived to tell us
anything about the composition and precise activities of the
subhamlet groupings in what became Miyamoto-chō.[7]

A government ordnance map of 1886 shows that Kumodani
was a compact nucleated settlement (Rikuchi Sokuryōbu 1886).
Most of the houses were on the plateau (in contemporary terms,
across the railway tracks that border Miyamoto-chō). The
shrine, now at the center of Miyamoto-chō, stood at the farthest
fringe of the settlement, overlooking the valley; the Buddhist
temple stood in isolation on the valley floor, surrounded by
paddy fields. The settlement still lay well beyond the built-up
portions of Tokyo. When the western sections of the loop railway now known as the Yamanote line were completed in 1885,
the rail line skirted the edges of Tokyo's urbanized core, in many
places running through rural countryside (Tōkyō-shi 1928: 54;
Ishizuka 1977: 139). Kumodani was two kilometers outside the
loop.

Hiratsuka-mura remained an agricultural community until the end of the Meiji period (1912),[8] and the population increased only gradually, from 2,609 people in 473 households
in 1872 to 3,382 people in 618 households in 1909 (Kagami
1935: 8; SKS, 2: 187). The village continued to be both agricultural and slow-growing for a decade or so, until a combination
of external forces, including the outward expansion of Tokyo,
abruptly transformed village life near the end of the Taishō period (1912–26).

Tokyo's Growth and the
Urbanization of the Periphery

Hiratsuka-mura underwent massive urban development after
the Kantō earthquake of 1923. Several interrelated trends in the

population growth and physical expansion of the Tokyo metropolitan area, as well as local changes in land-use patterns, population density, and systems of municipal administration, set the stage for this change.

Population Growth

The early decades of this century saw phenomenal urban growth throughout Japan. In 1879 only 11 percent of Japan's population lived in cities with populations greater than 10,000; by 1920 the figure was 32 percent. Almost three-quarters of this growth came from rural-urban migration rather than from natural increase (Yazaki 1968: 390–91).

Growth was particularly rapid in the Tokyo metropolitan area. Between 1897 and 1920 the population of the City of Tokyo (Tōkyō-shi) and all outlying communities within Tokyo Prefecture (Tōkyō-fu) grew from 1.3 to 3.3 million.[9] In the inner portions of the metropolis—the City of Tokyo, which then roughly corresponded to the area inside what is now the Yamanote rail line—the population increased 94 percent; in the surrounding suburban and semirural areas it rose by 183 percent (Yazaki 1968: 391, 444). Hiratsuka-mura grew almost as fast. Between 1900 and 1921 its population rose from 3,386 to 8,522—an increase of 152 percent. But as can be seen in Table 3, that rate of growth pales next to the explosive growth of the following decade. By 1930 Hiratsuka-mura (renamed Ebara-machi in 1927) had a population of 132,108, an increase of 1,450 percent since 1921. In the same period the population of only the area that had been Kumodani rose from 763 to 17,510, an almost 23-fold increase (SKS, 2: 471, 476).

In 1932 Ebara-machi became one of 20 new wards in the City of Tokyo, and by 1940 its population reached 188,100, an increase of 42 percent since 1930 and an astounding 5,455 percent since 1900. On the eve of the Second World War, it was thickly populated, with 32,400 people per square kilometer: the seventh-highest density among Tokyo's 35 wards, and the second-highest among the 20 new ones created in 1932.[10]

According to the 1935 national census, a large proportion of Ebara's residents were of urban origin.[11] Almost half were born

TABLE 3
The Population of Hiratsuka/Ebara, 1900–1940

Year	Population	Households	Population per square kilometer	Cumulative percentage increase in population 1900	1921
1900	3,386	498	584	—	
1906	2,949	503	508	-13%	
1911	4,218	760	727	25	
1916	5,397	1,095	931	59	
1921	8,522	1,783	1,469	152	—
1926	72,256	17,903	12,458	2,034	748%
1930	132,108	30,433	22,777	3,802	1,450
1935	161,863	34,719	27,907	4,680	1,799
1940	188,100	40,865	32,431	5,455	2,107

SOURCE: Tōkyō-fu vols. for the years shown.

in Tōkyō-shi (both the old and the new wards). One in seven had been born in the old City of Tokyo (within the pre-1932 boundaries), 70 percent of them in shitamachi wards. Although 20 percent were natives of Hiratsuka/Ebara, only 2 percent of the total population had been born in Hiratsuka/Ebara before 1923 and the beginning of urbanization. Among those born outside Tōkyō-shi, one-third came from the surrounding prefectures (Tōkyō-shi 1935: 8–11).

Although rural-urban migration fueled Tokyo's population growth during the 1920's and 1930's, Ebara's growth came about not so much from direct in-migration from rural areas as from outward migration from central Tokyo. White (1978: 113, 114) suggests that migrants to Tokyo before the Second World War were less "rural" than we generally assume. His data show a steady increase between 1890 and 1940 in the proportion of migrants coming from the more urban areas of their prefectures, so that "the oft-stated general, undifferentiated descriptions of migrants as ex-peasants or 'urban villagers' are unrealistic and misleading." Data on Ebara's population during the 1930's, and my interviews with residents about their families' histories, confirm White's observations. Most new arrivals in Hiratsuka/Ebara, although not natives of the City of Tokyo, were not newcomers to urban life.

Land in the Early Twentieth Century

Population changes in Hiratsuka/Ebara accompanied dramatic alterations in land use and radical shifts in land values. Government ordnance maps reproduced in a local atlas (Shinagawa-ku 1972: 6–17) show few changes in Kumodani's settlement patterns between the early 1880's and 1916; it remained a tightly nucleated settlement surrounded by fields. But the 1929 revision of the maps shows the hamlet's entire area built up. The changes occurred not only because of population shifts away from central Tokyo, but also because of the related movement of industry into the area, the rapid expansion of suburban rail lines, and the willingness of landowners to convert their holdings to nonagricultural uses. All these trends, under way before 1923, accelerated rapidly after the Kantō earthquake that devastated central Toyko that year.

There were three major categories of privately held land: paddy land (*den-chi*), dry fields (*hata-chi*), and "residential land" (*taku-chi*), land registered for building sites, whether for residential, commercial, or industrial purposes. The proportions of land registered in these three categories were completely transformed between 1900 and 1940. From 1900 through the early 1920's about 10 percent of the land was paddy, roughly 80 percent was dry fields, and slightly under 9 percent was residential. After the mid-1920's agricultural land was swiftly converted to residential purposes. By 1940 less than 4 percent of the total was still in agricultural use (see Table 4).

The transformation of land use not surprisingly paralleled changes in land values. In 1900 the value of paddy land was 38 yen per *tan* (993 sq. meters), dry fields 15 yen per *tan*, and residential land 27 yen per *tan*. Agricultural land values remained almost unchanged through the mid-1920's, but by 1916 the value of residential land had risen 517.4 percent. Dry fields continued to be valuable for truck gardening. As the metropolitan area's population grew, so too did the demand for fresh produce; areas like Hiratsuka/Ebara were ideally situated to provide it (Ishizuka 1977: 142–45). But rising land values made clear the fate of local agriculture, including truck gardening; the price commanded by residential land continued to rise until there

TABLE 4

Changing Land Use in Hiratsuka/Ebara, 1900–1940

(Privately owned land)

Year	Total land in chō[a]	Percentage of total		
		Paddy	Dry fields	Residential[b]
1900	420.13	10.4%	80.8%	8.8%
1906	424.09	10.3	80.5	9.2
1911	427.27	10.2	80.3	9.5
1916	435.41	9.9	79.6	10.5
1921	455.49	9.3	76.7	14.0
1926	457.01	8.9	73.2	17.9
1930	465.88	7.2	51.9	40.9
1935	459.90	1.7	12.2	86.1
1940	446.17	0.4	3.2	96.4

SOURCE: Same as Table 3.

[a] One *chō* equals 10 *tan* or 0.922 hectare.

[b] Land registered for building sites, including commercial and industrial uses.

TABLE 5

Changing Land Values in Hiratsuka/Ebara, 1900–1940

(Privately owned land)

Year	Paddy		Dry fields		Residential	
	Yen per tan	Percent of 1900 value	Yen per tan	Percent of 1900 value	Yen per tan	Percent of 1900 value
1900	38.0	—	15.0	—	27.0	—
1906	38.5	101.3%	14.6	97.3%	26.3	97.4%
1911	38.5	101.3	14.5	96.6	134.6	498.5
1916	38.5	101.3	14.4	96.0	139.7	517.4
1921	38.6	101.6	14.0	93.3	146.2	541.4
1926	38.5	101.3	13.9	92.6	147.9	547.7
1930	37.2	97.9	13.7	91.3	144.9	536.6
1935	29.5	77.6	17.0	113.3	332.3	1,197.4
1940	28.5	75.0	22.1	147.3	721.8	2,673.3

SOURCE: Same as Table 3.

NOTE: One *tan* equals 993 sq. meters.

was no vestige of parity in the value of agricultural and non-agricultural land. In 1940 a tan of paddy was worth only 28.5 yen, about a twenty-fifth of the value of a *tan* of residential land (see Table 5).

Regardless of inflationary changes in the value of the yen and the cost of living during this period,[12] the value of residential land increased out of all proportion to other land values. Without adjusting for inflation, the 1940 value of paddy land was 75 percent of the 1900 level, dry fields 147 percent, and residential land an astounding 2,673 percent.

Unaided market forces alone did not impel land conversion. On the contrary, the government actively promoted and guided the process and appointed local landowners to the official bodies charged with supervising conversion in each village. Until the early Taishō period (1912–26) Hiratsuka-mura remained "a quiet agricultural village of spacious *hatake*" (dry fields; SKKI 1979: 191). But by then the government was promoting a movement throughout Japan to consolidate fragmented agricultural plots and rationalize field boundaries. The government commissioned Kōchi Seiri Kumiai (Cultivable Land Reorganization Committees) under the provisions of the national Kōchi Seirihō (Cultivable Land Reorganization Law) of 1909. Local landlords and other influential people sat on these kumiai, which planned the replatting and negotiated equitable exchanges of land, based on the size and quality of each owner's holdings. Nationally, field rationalization required about 20 years, but Hiratsuka-mura's kumiai finished their tasks rapidly. By 1918 almost all the paddy land had been replatted into uniform rectangular plots. The dry-field reorganization took longer to complete, until the early 1930's (SKS, 2: 478; SKKI 1979: 209–10).

This land reorganization paved the way not for a burst of increased agricultural productivity, but for urbanization and industrialization. As one local source puts it:

Ironically, within ten years the paddy land that had been consolidated and rationalized to increase the production of rice had been filled in one after another for factories and homes. The carefully laid out rectangular paddy fields were ideally suited for building sites. . . . The so-called consolidation and rationalization of plots served the purpose of setting the stage for the creation of industrial land. The rationalization of dry fields followed the same course. But in this case it was clear from the outset that the aim was to prepare for roads and to plan the conversion of land to residential use, and that the restructuring of agricultural land was nothing more than a nominal goal (SKKI 1979: 210).

In 1912, at the start of the Taishō period, only a few factories stood along the Meguro River north of Kumodani and along the coast of Tokyo Bay to the east. With the outbreak of the First World War and the disruption of European manufacturing and commerce, Japan experienced an unprecedented industrial boom, and industry rapidly developed in the areas surrounding Kumodani. Most factories were tiny plants that depended on subcontracting from larger firms elsewhere. The concurrent restructuring of landholdings into convenient parcels of land by the local Kōchi Seiri Kumiai, of course, aided industrial expansion.

Among the industries that developed in the area, several played major roles in shaping the future of Miyamoto-chō. A light bulb manufacturer who opened a factory in the town just across the river from Kumodani became an important world supplier of small bulbs for Christmas tree lights during the First World War, when production was disrupted in the West (SKKI 1979: 194–95). At its height the production of Christmas tree bulbs became a major industry in southern Tokyo, employing many tiny subcontracting firms. Some of these firms have survived in and around Miyamoto-chō—and a trade association still maintains an office building in the neighborhood—but in recent years the industry has declined because of competition from Southeast Asian manufacturers. Other industries that came to the area during and after the war were a precision optical equipment plant and a heavy machinery factory, both built a few blocks from Miyamoto-chō. Both became major suppliers of war materiel, the one producing bomb sights, periscopes, and binoculars, and the other tanks. During the Second World War both were early and frequent targets of the American bombing raids that leveled much of the area.

The overwhelming bulk of Miyamoto-chō's land—officially reclassified as residential land in the 1920's—continued to be the property of a small number of landowners until well after the Second World War.[13] In the early stages of Miyamoto-chō's urbanization, landlords leased plots of land as building sites for homes, shops, and factories. In some cases they became builder-developers themselves, leasing or selling the structures, while retaining the land. In other cases they leased land to commercial speculative developers, who then sold or leased the structures. And in still other cases landlords dealt directly with new arrivals, who arranged for the construction of homes, stores, or workshops on their own. But in almost all cases the land upon which Miyamoto-chō stood remained the property of village-era landlords.

Thus, in the early period of urban growth landlords played a decisive role in transforming Hiratsuka/Ebara from an agricultural village to a residential suburb, not simply through their collective activities in the Kōchi Seiri Kumiai, but also through their successful individual (or familial) decisions to convert their holdings from agricultural land to taku-chi, "residential land." The conversion of land from agricultural to other uses did not reflect the liquidation of family holdings by small-scale owner-cultivators to raise capital for entering new occupations. Rather, landowners could realize a greater return on their property by entering a new and more lucrative land market, renting not selling their land.

The dramatic local changes in population, land use, and land values of course reflected changes occurring throughout the Tokyo metropolitan area. Although the decisions of local governments and of landlords over the disposition of land shaped the course of Miyamoto-chō's development, the outward expansion of Tokyo was inevitable, given the sheer size and density of the city's population. On the eve of the Kantō earthquake, 14 of the City of Tokyo's 15 wards had population densities of 28,000 people per square kilometer or higher (Yazaki 1968: 448).[14] The destruction of much of inner Tokyo in 1923 launched an era of suburban development, a development that landowners and government agencies in the surrounding countryside already eagerly anticipated, even if they were not fully prepared for the rapidity with which it would occur.

The Earthquake and Its Aftermath

At 11:58 on the morning of September 1, 1923, an earthquake of an estimated 7.8 magnitude on the Japanese Meteorological Agency's scale struck the area surrounding Tokyo, the Kantō plain.[15] The damage from the quake itself and from fires raging out of control for several days afterward was catastrophic. Over half the area in Tōkyō-shi's 15 wards was engulfed in flames, and close to 60 percent of the population was left homeless. Almost 100,000 people died; 128,000 houses collapsed and 447,000 burned to the ground, and a further 126,000 buildings were partially destroyed (SKKI 1979: 198–99, 205). The toll of casualties was so staggering as to radically alter Tokyo's demography, politics, economy, culture, and social structure.[16] Miyamoto-chō was merely one among hundreds of neighborhoods subsequently created by the chaotic chains of events launched by the earthquake.

Because Hiratsuka-mura suffered little damage from the quake (SKKI 1979: 200), it became a temporary refuge for tens of thousands of people fleeing the stricken city. Yet they were not entirely welcome, either in Hiratsuka-mura or elsewhere. In the turmoil rumors swept the Kantō region that Japan's resident Korean minority was somehow responsible for the quake. Word spread of a Korean uprising, of Koreans poisoning wells, of roving bands of Koreans bent on murder and pillage. On September 2 the national government placed Tokyo Prefecture under martial law, but in many parts of the Kantō region, local residents formed vigilante groups (*keibidan* or *jikeidan*) to preserve order. Keibidan armed themselves; frequently they became mobs, attacking innocent Koreans (or strangers thought to be Koreans). In gruesome massacres that continued for days, vigilante mobs murdered several thousand Koreans throughout the Kantō plain.[17]

What is now Miyamoto-chō did not escape the hysteria. One old woman, now well into her eighties, told me how the bamboo groves that dotted the valley floor around the temple disappeared overnight as residents armed themselves with staves and spears. In at least one recorded case near Miyamoto-chō, spear-wielding vigilantes attacked and seriously wounded a Korean (SKKI 1979: 203). No other record of vigilante groups around Miyamoto-chō survives. Although some writers assume that keibidan were the direct precursors of the chōkai that became established throughout Tokyo in the decade following the earthquake (e.g. Steiner 1965: 219), there is nothing to suggest that in Hiratsuka-mura the keibidan survived the immediate crisis.

Local keibidan may have been short-lived, but the earthquake had other, more lasting effects on Hiratsuka-mura. In the re-

building of the Kantō region, many of Tokyo's homeless reset-
tled in the suburban towns and villages that ringed its 15 wards.
Among the 82 towns and villages in the five surrounding counties (*gun*), Hiratsuka-mura's population grew the most dramatically (SKKI 1979: 206), increasing from 8,522 in 1921 to 72,256
in 1926 (Table 3). Several factors made this phenomenal growth
possible. Compared with other towns and villages bordering Tokyo, Hiratsuka-mura's roads and other transportation facilities
were poorly developed, and so it had remained a "pristine agricultural village" with a small population and, most significantly, inexpensive land (SKKI 1979: 191, 206). Furthermore, because its population was small, it had remained administratively a village. As such it was exempt from the strict provisions
of the Urban Area Building Law (Shigaichi Kenchikubutsu-hō)
enacted in 1919 to regulate construction and promote urban
planning (Tōkyō-to 1979, 5: 546). For these reasons, after the
quake many barracks-style homes and temporary factories were
built in Hiratsuka-mura, and "large numbers of poor people
moved in" (SKKI 1979: 206).

As a result, Hiratsuka-mura soon far surpassed the minimum
population standards required of a town; indeed it had the highest population density of any village in Japan. Accordingly, in
1926 the central government upgraded the village to a town,
Hiratsuka-machi. In 1927 the town assembly renamed it Ebara-
machi, in part because the name Ebara had an ancient and distinguished history as a local place-name, and in part to distinguish the town from the many others throughout Japan also
name Hiratsuka-machi.[18]

Sudden, unexpected urban growth strained the new town's resources as its administration sought to provide new roads, new
schools, and other municipal services for the swollen population. Generally, the earthquake took its heaviest toll in
working-class and lower-middle-class districts of central Tokyo.
The refugees who flooded into Hiratsuka/Ebara were largely
poorly paid workers, left destitute by the quake. The town therefore faced the twin problem of a rapidly expanding demand for
municipal services and a totally inadequate tax base. Like many
of the suburban towns and villages surrounding Tōkyō-shi,

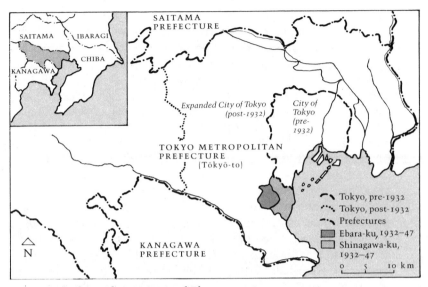

MAP 2. Tokyo, Shinagawa, and Ebara

Ebara-machi faced financial crisis, saved only by subsidies from higher levels of government. The outward expansion of Tokyo's population and the spread of truly urban areas far beyond the boundaries of Tōkyō-shi combined with the acute fiscal problems of the suburban municipalities to create support for the amalgamation of the suburbs into an expanded Tōkyō-shi.

This was accomplished after several years of study and negotiation by municipal, prefectural, and national agencies in the late 1920's and early 1930's. In 1932, 20 new wards—formed out of 82 towns and villages—were added to the original 15 wards of Tōkyō-shi. Ebara-machi became Ebara-ku, one of the new wards (see Map 2). Ebara was one of only two suburban towns or villages that survived the annexation intact.[19]

The Creation of Neighborhood Institutions

As the status of Hiratsuka/Ebara changed from village, to town, and then to ward in response to changes in the metropolitan region, other submunicipal institutions developed that contributed to the creation of neighborhoods as distinct administrative and social communities. These newly created neighborhoods did not grow out of previously existing local units.

During the Meiji period groups and organizations within the hamlets, or ō-aza, that made up Hiratsuka/Ebara apparently had not been exclusively or even primarily administrative in character. They were organized around agricultural cooperation and religious activity (Inoue 1932: 153–54). By the 1920's the kumi (or goningumi) of the pre-Meiji hamlet of Kumodani had long since withered away (Inoue 1932: 92). If local groups that reflected the organization of agrarian life in Kumodani survived into the Taishō period, they too must have disappeared as the original inhabitants were reduced to a tiny fraction of the area's population and abandoned farming for their new careers as landlords (SKS, 2: 510). By the early years of the current (Shōwa) period, no remnants of groups that originated in agrarian Kumodani were significant enough to be included in the comprehensive lists of town and lower-level associations, institutions, and organizations compiled in preparation for the amalgamation of Ebara-machi into Tōkyō-shi (e.g. Tōkyō-shi 1931).

Only a very few institutions from the hamlet era unquestionably survived into the 1930's. One was a school, now a public elementary school, near Miyamoto-chō, which traces its origins to a private academy founded by a village headman in the 1870's to educate the children of Kumodani. Others were the local shrine and the volunteer fire brigade, both of which had been strengthened immeasurably during the Meiji and Taishō periods. The shrine's position in local society was heightened by the incorporation of Shintō into nationally subsidized systems of ideological control. The fire brigade was continually upgraded by local and prefectural officials anxious to improve the infrastructure of public safety. In short neither institution survived into the Shōwa period simply on its own organizational merits, internal resources, or ability to command the affection and participation of residents.

The area's massive population growth caught the village/town without any effective administrative apparatus at a level lower than the municipality as a whole. In 1925, as a direct response to the pressures of growth, the government of Hiratsuka-mura instituted a new system of ku (wards), dividing the village into 47 wards (Ebara-ku 1943: 237–38). Eight of the ku covered old Kumodani, and one of the eight roughly corresponded to Miyamoto-chō. So far as can be determined from the scanty records of early neighborhood life, this was the first recognition accorded the neighborhood as a spatially, administratively, or socially separate unit.

No records remain to outline the activities or structure of the ku in Miyamoto-chō, but one account from the early 1930's states that all ku had essentially similar structures and functions; it presents a ward near Miyamoto-chō as an example (Inoue 1932: 83–85). Ward chiefs, who served four-year terms, and other local officers were "popularly elected," subject to confirmation by the town's mayor. Other officers included a representative and seven assistants selected by the ward chief, as well as a salaried ward clerk. The 1,300 households of this ward were divided into 13 units called *bu*, each with a section chief (*buchō*), an assistant section chief, and five counselors, all of whom served for two years. Each bu also had an official in charge of streetlights and one in charge of sanitation. The account lists five of the ward's major aims:

1. To help volunteer social workers (*hōmeniin*) in their efforts to aid the poor[20]

2. To complete and file governmental and police forms (at no charge) for those who were illiterate or too busy to attend to these matters themselves

3. To collect residents' monthly fees for night soil and garbage collection[21]

4. To send appropriate aid to other areas when a natural disaster occurred

5. To provide an official send-off for army inductees; all ward officials were to accompany the inductee to the local shrine and to the railway station

How faithfully these obligations were observed in Miyamoto-chō is unclear. One clue comes from an old photograph (one of only a handful of prewar photographs of Miyamoto-chō) that belongs to the Ide family. Mr. Ide, a young man whose family has owned a small factory in Miyamoto-chō since the 1930's, showed me a box of family photographs, one of which was of a neighborhood farewell for an army conscript, presumably a shop apprentice. The inductee and his relatives, several members of the Ide family, and some neighbors stand before the Ide's workshop, and at one edge of the group an elderly (and now unidentifiable) man wearing a military greatcoat carries a lantern that identifies him as a neighborhood official.

Some details about the administration of Hiratsuka/Ebara's wards can be gained from a list of duties appended to the proclamation that established the ku system in 1925 (Ebara-ku 1943: 240–43). Each ward was assigned 26 separate tasks in six general domains of responsibility: tax reporting, construction and public works, sanitation and public health, military affairs (i.e. dealing with inductees), household registration, and general administrative liaison. Wards were required to report to the town government all relevant local events and activities; to ensure that local residents properly filed required forms and adhered to all regulations; and to admonish (and report) residents who ignored or disobeyed government directives.

This ward system lasted only until 1932, when Ebara-machi became Ebara-ku, a ward within Tokyo's municipal government. Thereafter the legal status of units beneath the level of Ebara-ku becomes unclear, because a ward could not itself be divided into wards. Some areas had started neighborhood associations (chōkai) as early as 1923. Others established them during the era of the village/town's ward system, and within a year or two of the merger most neighborhoods in Ebara-ku had chōkai. When the forerunner of the present-day Miyamoto-chō organized its chōkai in 1933, it was among the last of the neighborhoods in Ebara-ku to do so (Ebara-ku 1943: 583–609). These associations continued to carry on some of the same functions as the old wards but did not have the same legal status as official units in Ebara-ku's administration.

As voluntarily organized bodies, moreover, these chōkai did not even necessarily correspond to the old administrative wards. There had been 47 administrative districts in Hiratsuka/Ebara, but by the early 1930's local residents had organized 78 separate neighborhood associations (Ebara-ku 1943: 557). These associations served a variety of locally defined needs beyond merely administrative functions, including promoting local business, administering shrine affairs, and stimulating sentiments of local identity and mutal aid. Taking as their boundaries those that local residents perceived as significant, chōkai provided a focus for community sentiment and identity. Consequently, they formed frameworks for neighborhood life within which (or parallel to which) formal and informal ties among residents could develop, local activities could be organized, and other groups and associations could be created within the geographical boundaries the chōkai established. The neighborhoods encompassed by these chōkai reflected the basic units within which could develop the full range of community life then becoming characteristic of Japanese urban society (and particularly the shitamachi version of city life).

The creation of Miyamoto-chō's shopkeepers' guild (shōten-kai) illustrates this process of parallel development of local groups separate from the chōkai but coterminous with it. The group's early history is documented by only a map and membership directory from the mid-1930's. The map, discovered by my landlord in 1980, illustrates how sheer luck can sometimes come into play in the often difficult task of trying to document the history of an urban neighborhood. As a schoolboy during the war, Mr. Takahashi had used the map to make a dust jacket for a dictionary his father had given him. He keeps the dictionary in his office and still uses it from time to time. One day he decided to replace the now-worn cover with something less shabby. When he removed the tattered paper and found the map and directory on the reverse, he was as surprised to discover the map as I was delighted to be shown it.[22]

Leadership in the new institutions of neighborhood life was mixed. On the one hand established residents of the area formed an elite. In the 1930's families with histories in the area dating back to the hamlet of Kumodani generally held economic and political power as local landlords. In addition to their economic power as landlords, they derived status from their families' former positions as village leaders and their long association with the shrine, the fire brigade, and the nearby school. All local organizations had members of the old elites as patrons, whether or not they played active leadership roles.

On the other hand the few surviving documents and photographs of organizational activities in prewar Miyamoto-chō suggest that the old elite did not actively lead or control local organizations. New arrivals rather than established residents had a much greater need for cooperative, communal action and much more to gain from organizing local activities to meet that need. Most local shops and factories were established by new arrivals, who formed the entrepreneurial core of the developing community. Gradually they shaped community organizations to foster their commercial interests. With the introduction of universal male suffrage in 1925, the control of local politics by the landed gentry lessened somewhat, although in and around Miyamoto-chō the landlord families continued to be central to political life. And, finally, new migrants clearly held the numerical balance of power in the area. The scanty records that survive suggest that by the 1930's, beneath the level of the patrons and honorary presidents of local organizations, the new arrivals provided much of the organizational impetus as well as the leadership for local organizations.[23]

Although the development of chōkai and other institutions of neighborhood life in Hiratsuka/Ebara coincided closely with urbanization and the rise of sentiments of community identity, it would be a mistake to interpret this institutional development as merely the transplantation of an established pattern of urban neighborhood life into a newly urbanizing setting. On the contrary, the urbanization of Hiratsuka/Ebara coincided with the development of neighborhood-level institutions throughout Tokyo.

Many observers assume that formally organized neighborhood associations formed a quintessentially traditional and enduring feature of urban life, particularly of life in the shitamachi districts of old Tokyo. In fact these organizations were late developments, creations of the 1920's and early 1930's that sprang up in the older and newer sections alike. A 1934 survey reveals that almost three-quarters of the chōkai in Tokyo (72.4%) were established after 1923, and only 2 percent antedated 1897.[24]

Neighborhood associations developed as urban Japan, particularly Tokyo, experienced unprecedented growth and upheaval. The economic, social, and political unrest that accompanied the era's industrial growth was compounded by the aftereffects of the Kantō earthquake. As H. D. Smith has noted (1978: 64), the 1920's saw the development in both official and unofficial circles of "a variety of urban improvement efforts along traditional moralistic lines." These efforts included the formation of urban neighborhood associations, among whose organizers there was "general agreement on the need to mobilize traditional values in an effort to stave off the debilitating effects of modern urban change."

During the 1920's and 1930's government ministries promoted various ideological campaigns to combat the evils thought to be inherent in the new urban industrial age. The Japanese government had long experience in attempting to control potential sources of social, political, or economic unrest through the conscious creation or manipulation of putatively traditional values and institutions. Moralistic edicts such as the Imperial Rescript on Education of 1890 and the government-mandated mergers of local shrines to bolster the legitimacy of new administrative villages (Fridell 1973) were earlier examples of this tendency. Not surprisingly, efforts to control urban society and organize urban neighborhoods in the 1920's were cloaked with similarly traditional ideological values evoking rural hamlet solidarity.

H. D. Smith (like Hastings 1980) argues that Tokyo's chōkai were not simply the products of government engineering, but reflected genuine grass-roots sentiments favoring communal organization to meet the needs of the urban environment. As he puts it (1978: 66), government efforts were overshadowed by "moralizing [that] came spontaneously from within the lower and particularly middle levels of Tokyo culture. . . . The most dramatic evidence of the internal potential of Tokyo culture for mobilizing traditional moral sentiment was the phenomenal growth of neighborhood organizations (chōnaikai). . . . Wholly spontaneous organizations, . . . the chōnaikai were essentially a means of sustaining local community solidarity in the face of rapid population turnover."

There is disagreement over the extent to which chōkai were wholly spontaneous organizations, but in any case they had no formal, legal recognition until the bylaws of Tōkyō-shi gave them official status in 1938 (Steiner 1965: 219). Thereafter they were rapidly incorporated into the authoritarian administrative system that developed in the late 1930's and was strengthened on the eve of the Second World War.

In September 1940 the Home Ministry issued Ordinance No. 17, requiring all neighborhoods throughout Japan to form neighborhood associations (called chōkai or chōnaikai in urban areas, and *burakukai* in rural areas); household membership in these and in lower-level bodies called *tonarigumi* was compulsory (Steiner 1965: 57). Shortly thereafter the Imperial Rule Assistance Association (Taisei Yokusankai)—created to forge political, social, and economic organizations into a single, tightly controlled arm of the government—incorporated all chōkai, burakukai, and tonarigumi into a national political front. This action standardized local organizations such as chōkai—which, having often arisen at local initiative, had taken diverse forms—consolidating them into a nationally centralized system.

By the following year, 1941, the ministry's edicts were having an impact on Tokyo's wards. Residents in Ebara-ku, for example, found that to strengthen supervision over their chōkai and to make them more uniform in size and operations, the ward government had redrawn the chōkai boundaries and reduced their number from 78 to 58 (Ebara-ku 1943: 556–60). This reshuffling created the present-day boundaries of Miyamoto-chō. A small neighborhood, comprising several blocks that straddled the rail line now forming one border of Miyamoto-chō, was divided among several adjoining neighborhoods, and one of the fragments was added to Miyamoto-chō. Although the records are spotty, this enlarged Miyamoto-chō probably had a population of slightly over 3,000 at this time. The part of the neighborhood that had been added was almost totally destroyed a few years later when the homes near the tracks were cleared away to create a firebreak to protect the rest of Miyamoto-chō from bombing aimed at the railroad.

The government closely controlled the activities of chōkai and tonarigumi during the war, and for many Japanese they became feared and hated institutions. One wartime apologist explained, "Every person . . . is required to become a member of his neighborhood unit, so that he can receive all the facilities given by the Government without undergoing any inconvenience" (Hozumi 1943: 990). But most Japanese probably agreed with the Occupation officer who later wrote, "With the *tonarigumi* the government reached into the lives of every citizen

through a medium more effective than the very effective police"
(Braibanti 1948: 139).[25]

Miyamoto-chō During and After the War

Miyamoto-chō was more fortunate than most of Tokyo. The
great bombing raids of 1944–45 that leveled much of the capital
missed the neighborhood. The surrounding areas were hit several times because the nearby optical equipment and heavy machinery factories and the adjacent rail line were strategic targets.[26] Though the bombing raids did not succeed in destroying
the factories, the neighborhoods bordering Miyamoto-chō were
incinerated. Luckily for the residents of Miyamoto-chō, the fires
were stopped roughly at its boundaries, in part because of several firebreaks that were constructed by pulling down homes
and businesses.

Of course, the residents of Miyamoto-chō did not come
through the war unscathed. Those who survived the war now
look back on their lives as combatants or as home-front civilians
in the neighborhood or elsewhere in Tokyo with a mixture of
pain and flashes of humor. Older men prefer to remember the
camaraderie of their days in the Imperial Guards, or the excitement of being sent off to China, or the absurd boredom of lob-
bing artillery shells through the thick jungle canopies of Bou-
gainville at unseen enemies. Most of those who told me of their
wartime experiences were children or adolescents at the time,
and so their memories are of incomprehension: Mr. Matsue and
his brother recalling numbly the firestorm that killed 100,000
people, including all the other members of their family; Mr.
Tsunoda's memories of sitting for hours in a drainage culvert
watching B-29's circle in the skies above; Mr. Takahashi's memories of his junior high school science class suddenly set to work
building flamethrowers. But for those who were young at the
time, often etched much more starkly in their minds are the
crushing poverty and gnawing hunger of the first years of the Occupation, when the bomb craters around Miyamoto-chō were
returned to agricultural production and every square meter of
wasteland was used to try to grow something, anything, edible.

TABLE 6
The Population of Ebara and Shinagawa, 1893–1984

Year	Ebara[a]	Shinagawa[b]	Year	Ebara[a]	Shinagawa[b]
1893	—	27,495	1944	—	395,770[c]
1897	3,275	—	1945	60,000[d]	143,490
1911	4,027	55,794	1950	—	288,545
1916	5,397	83,592	1955	—	374,184
1920	8,144	121,077	1962	189,394	414,520
1925	72,256	232,447	1964	191,300	415,728
1930	132,108	311,604	1971	182,177	388,122
1935	161,863	366,125	1976	162,577	354,950
1940	188,100	419,403	1984	144,577	343,074

SOURCES: SKNT 1961, 1984; Tōkyō-fu 1935, 1940; SKKI 1979: 243 (on evacuations).
    [a] Figures apply to the area encompassed by Ebara-ku (1932–47), now part of Shinagawa-ku.
    [b] Figures apply to the entire area now encompassed by Shinagawa-ku, including the former Ebara-ku.
    [c] Year in which bombing raids on Tokyo and mass evacuations began. Some 121,000 people were evacuated from Ebara and 237,000 from Shinagawa between February and May.
    [d] Estimated population.

Individuals survived and so too did Miyamoto-chō. But the neighborhood was irrevocably altered by the war and the immediate postwar years, which reshaped its demography, its institutions, and the relationship between land and local power.

Demographic Trends

The 35 wards of Tokyo had a population of 6.78 million in October 1940, and the figure fell only slightly in the midst of the war, to 6.56 million in early 1944. But by November 1945, two and a half months after the surrender, only 2.77 million people remained in the city; almost 60 percent of its prewar population had been bombed out or had fled (Tōkyō-to 1979, 6: 69). What was true for the city as a whole was repeated in Ebara and Shinagawa.[27] The population of what is now Shinagawa-ku, including what was Ebara-ku during the war and prewar years, was decimated by the war. The area reached its prewar peak population of some 419,000 in 1940; by 1945 the figure had fallen to about 143,500, only 34 percent of the 1940 population (see Table 6).

As American raids on Tokyo intensified in the spring of 1944, the government launched massive efforts to evacuate as many civilians as possible. The pupils and teachers of the local elementary school were removed en masse to a temple on the Japan Sea coast near Toyama, and many of Miyamoto-chō's leaders today recall the pain and bewilderment of being taken off to a strange and distant place. Formal evacuation programs, as well as individual and household decisions to flee the city, resulted in the departure of an estimated 121,000 people from Ebara alone between February and May of 1944. Roughly two-thirds of the ward's 1940 population left within four months. By the end of the war Ebara had an estimated population of only 60,000.

Some 15,000 dwellings in Ebara were destroyed by bombing, affecting at least 60,000 residents (SKS, 2: 754). Against a prewar total of 40,000 households, at least 40 percent of the housing stock was destroyed. The percentage was probably much higher, since many dwellings no doubt housed more than one household. As we have seen, Miyamoto-chō was fortunate in that firebreaks were built by government order both along the railroad and along one border. These firebreaks probably saved the rest of the neighborhood. In part because the neighborhood could still offer shelter, the population of Miyamoto-chō may have dropped less dramatically than that of Ebara generally, from a prewar high of roughly 3,000 to well below 1,500 by the end of the war.

In Ebara and Shinagawa, as elsewhere in the central metropolis, the postwar demographic recovery was gradual. It was not until 1964 that Shinagawa approached the prewar high of the combined old wards of Ebara and Shinagawa, with a population of 415,000. By then, new demographic trends were shaping the metropolis. The early 1960's saw the beginning of the shift of people from the central wards to the new cities of the Western suburbs. After reaching its postwar peak in 1964, Shinagawa's population steadily declined until the 1980's, when a plateau was reached. As of 1980 Shinagawa had lost almost 76,000 people, about 18 percent of the 1964 total (SKNT 1984: 13–14).

In general Miyamoto-chō has paralleled these population patterns. From an immediate postwar population estimated at somewhere between 1,000 and 1,500—at most only 50 percent of the neighborhood's prewar peak—the figure gradually rose to regain its prewar level by the late 1950's or early 1960's. In 1960 the neighborhood had 3,296 residents in 984 households (SKNT

1961). But the 1960's population decline was far more dramatic in Miyamoto-chō than in the ward as a whole. By 1980 Miyamoto-chō had only 2,115 residents in 899 households, a population loss of 35 percent in the 20 years since 1960 (Shinagawa-ku 1981).

Several factors account for the declining population. In part it reflects a shrinking household size (3.34 in 1960; 2.35 in 1980), which in turn reflects a declining fertility rate, as well as the aging of the population and the progress of domestic cycles in which older residents are now living without their children. A large part of the shift, however, reflects the outward movement of families and their replacement by young adults living in single-person households (see Appendix A). To a limited extent the population shift also reflects some loss of housing stock; expansions of the schools and government office buildings in the 1960's and 1970's displaced at least some residences in Miyamoto-chō. But even with so dramatic a decline, the neighborhood is hardly depopulated: in 1980 it still had a population density of better than 29,000 per square kilometer.

The wartime displacement of Miyamoto-chō's population, the gradual postwar recovery, suburbanization, and the changes in family size and composition all have had important effects on the neighborhood. Equally significant for understanding community social patterns is the extent to which the prewar and postwar populations of Miyamoto-chō contained different people. There is no direct data on returnees to Miyamoto-chō during the Occupation, but analysis of the earliest dates at which households were in the neighborhood shows a sharp break between the prewar and postwar periods and a bulge of new entrants during the immediate postwar years (see Appendix A). Old-timers in Miyamoto-chō report that the postwar years indeed saw a massive influx of new faces, and that many wartime evacuees simply never returned. Those families who stayed during the war or fled and returned were largely the families with some economic interest in the neighborhood. The landlord families, of course, remained part of the neighborhood no matter where they ended up after the war. Some residents had purchased the land on which to build a home or business before the war; those people, relatively few in number, had a stake in returning. And those who operated businesses in the area, whether or not they owned the land or the building, at least may have had livelihoods to which to return. The typical prewar resident, neither a property owner nor a local entrepreneur, had the least reason to come back. And many did not.

The Postwar Abolition of Chōkai

By the close of the Second World War, the Japanese government had reached its most centralized, most authoritarian stage. In defeat all levels of government—including its most localized institutions, the chōkai, tonarigumi, and burakukai— were thoroughly discredited because of their roles in the government's wartime campaigns to enforce ideological conformity, to mobilize the populace for military purposes, and to regulate the national economy.[28] To the policy makers of the American Occupation, chōkai were fundamentally undemocratic— John Embree compared them to the German Nazi's party organization (1945: 251)—and they were marked for abolition (Masland 1946; SCAP 1948, 1949).

But in the social, political, and economic turmoil immediately following the war's end, the authorities on the scene saw a continuing need for chōkai as a means of maintaining order. In some areas the police relied on them to control racketeering (Bennett and Ishino 1963: 283), and throughout Japan chōkai were entrusted with the vital rice-rationing program (SCAP 1947: 12–13). Nevertheless, the formal abolition of neighborhood institutions as quasi-governmental agencies remained a top priority, and when conditions had stabilized, the Supreme Commander for the Allied Powers (or SCAP, as both General Douglas MacArthur and his headquarters were known) directed the Japanese government to abolish tonarigumi, chōkai, and burakukai effective March 31, 1947 (SCAP 1949: 286–88). SCAP's order was followed by assurances that henceforth ration coupons would be issued directly to the consumer; neighborhood officials would no longer have anything to do with the process, not even determining a resident's eligibility. On May 3, 1947, the Japanese cabinet took additional steps to prevent the reestablishment of chōkai under new guises. All upper-level chōkai officials who had served in 1945–46 were barred for four years from holding any municipal office with responsibilities similar to their former chōkai duties. Former chōkai leaders were forbidden to issue any instructions or orders to the residents of their districts. Government officials were forbidden to issue instructions to neighborhood organizations. In addition, any group formed after the abolition of chōkai that performed similar functions was to disband. Other directives limited links between neighborhood organizations on the one hand, and Shintō shrines and local festivals on the other hand.[29]

Although chōkai were legally debarred, they did not disappear. Curtis (1971: 109) cites surveys indicating that neighborhood associations remained active in 86 percent of Japan's cities, towns, and villages during the official ban. After the ban lapsed in 1951, many new ones quicky surfaced; by 1956 they were functioning in 98 percent of Japan's municipalities. In Miyamoto-chō the chōkai survived the Occupation period in the guise of a "Crime Prevention Association," and it did not reclaim the title chōkai until the middle 1950's. The purges had little effect on local organizations in Miyamoto-chō. Apparently a few senior officers of the chōkai there and in surrounding neighborhoods were formally purged: generally these were the members of the old village-era elite who had held largely honorific positions as presidents and senior advisers in local organizations. The newly emerged active leadership—the young merchants and businessmen who had settled in the neighborhood in the 1920's and 1930's, and who had stayed in Miyamoto-chō during the war or returned to it afterward to try to resurrect their businesses—was barely touched by the purges.

Meanwhile, the government orders abolishing chōkai left room for the creation of new sets of local governmental institutions:

The certification of residence and other functions necessary under present conditions which were performed by the heads of *chōnaikai* and *burakukai* will be performed by the city, town, village, or ward offices. In order to effect this, as it may be necessary, it is conceived that subordinate members of the staff of city, town, or ward offices may be assigned to suitable districts (statement of the Minister of Home Affairs on Jan. 29, 1947, quoted in SCAP 1949: 287).

Local governments followed the letter of this directive. In April 1947 in the new Shinagawa-ku (formed a month earlier of the old Ebara-ku and Shinagawa-ku), the former Chōkai Renra-kujo (Chōkai Liaison Office) became the Kuyakusho Jimu Ren-rakujo (Ward Office Affairs Liaison Office). In June this office was subdivided into 12 branches, or *shutchōjo*, scattered throughout the new ward. Initially their duties centered on rationing rice and other staples, a responsibility formerly discharged by chōkai (Shinagawa-ku 1979: 3).[30] Gradually, the shut-chōjo assumed important liaison roles between the ward office and neighborhood organizations. In general this relationship has been a smooth one. But these formal links between government and neighborhood also create the potential for conflicts that from time to time pit the shutchōjo against Miyamoto-chō's neighborhood association.

Even in the 1980's memories of the wartime roles of chōkai and tonarigumi as organs of government regimentation color relations between the ward government and neighborhood groups. To a surprising extent—surprising at least to an American of my generation—the war and memories of wartime institutions loom large in the thinking of contemporary Japanese, both those old enough to remember it firsthand and those who grew up in its immediate aftermath. These memories play an important if implicit role in molding attitudes toward local institutions and influencing the nature of the interactions of local organizations with the government. And in turn these attitudes, plus the long-standing conflict within the Japanese political system between centralized control and local autonomy, contribute to the enduring tension between local and non-local that remains so important a theme even today in Miyamoto-chō. This tension between the chōkai in Miyamoto-chō and the ward government is central to understanding contemporary neighborhood life in Miyamoto-chō, as later chapters will discuss.

Land and Power in the Postwar Period

Although Miyamoto-chō and surrounding areas had long since ceased to be agricultural, the families of the village-era landlords continued to have some, though declining, economic power in the immediate postwar years. The Allied Occupation's land-reform policies, which applied only to land used for agricultural production, did not affect landholdings in Miyamoto-

chō or other already urbanized areas. Miyamoto-chō's residential and commercial land continued to be the property of the de-
scendants of the village-era landowners. By the late 1940's, however, this kind of landownership was no longer as important an
element of community power as before. Among other things,
massive postwar inflation eroded the landlords' return on long-
term fixed leases, and new land-tenure laws assured tenants of
the inalienable use of and first right to purchase leased land. As
shifting economic power combined with new democratic ideals,
landlord families lost any lingering positions of control over
community life. Other postwar changes have gradually fragmented the remaining large landholdings in and around Miyamoto-chō, including high inheritance taxes, the establishment
of partible inheritance as the legal ideal, and government programs to accept land in lieu of inheritance taxes and resell it to
tenants on reasonable terms. More and more local residents can
now, for the first time, hold title to the land upon which their
homes and businesses stand (Bestor 1984c).

In a neighborhood a few blocks from Miyamoto-chō stands a
massive house surrounded by a high wall, its heavily tiled and
gabled roof barely visible among a thicket of ancient trees. This
is the house of the Numata family, formerly the headmen of Kumodani and a leading landlord family in the area in the late nineteenth and early twentieth centuries. On the monuments dot-
ting the grounds of the local Shintō shrine, the names of generations of Numata men are carved: as leaders of the fire
brigade, as leaders of the shrine parishioners, as leaders of the
Land Reorganization Committee. A few families in Miyamoto-
chō and other neighborhoods are cadet branches of the main
family or are related to the Numatas by marriage. Some of these
collateral and affinal households play active roles in neighborhood organizations, but the main branch of the Numata family
has no hand at all in local affairs.

I once talked with Soeda-sensei, an elderly local leader from
a nearby neighborhood whose experience in local affairs
stretched back to well before the Second World War, about the
family's political role. During the 1920's and early 1930's, he
told me, the Numatas had been local stalwarts of the Seiyūkai,
one of the two leading parties of the day, and had effectively de-

livered local votes into the Seiyūkai camp. The importance of their political connections waned along with party politics in the 1930's, as the military played an ever-greater role in national politics and as local political autonomy (never very great in the first place) disappeared almost entirely. But their economic position as major local landowners remained secure, and they retained their social position: a Numata or a Numata relative stood at the head of almost every local organization, though increasingly as an honored elder statesman rather than as a mover and shaker of local life.

The Occupation brought the family's role in local life to an abrupt end. On the one hand the period's democratic ideals and disdain for "feudal" leaders (as well as the Occupation purges) destroyed any lingering political influence and removed the Numatas from leadership in local bodies. Inflation destroyed much of their economic position, and inheritance taxes took most of the rest of their wealth. In the decade following the war, the deaths of several elderly Numatas meant both that ruinous inheritance taxes were paid again and again, and that family leadership fell to members of younger generations less inclined to act as local gentry.

I ended my questioning by asking Soeda-sensei whether the current head of the Numata family could—if he wanted to— play a role in local politics. The elderly leader smiled at me: "Mr. Numata is a high school teacher. It's probably all he can do to keep that huge roof over his head."

In this chapter I have argued that the historical record of the establishment of Miyamoto-chō clearly shows that the neighborhood—both as a physical settlement and as a set of institutions—is the product of recent developments rather than of inherited patterns from the preindustrial past, whether rural or urban. There is little if any direct continuity with the village life that existed in the area before the beginning of this century. A few institutions—the shrine, the fire brigade, and a nearby elementary school—can lay some claim to bridging the centuries, but all underwent drastic modifications as they became incorporated into state institutions.

The community's class structure offers another possible

source of continuity. Yet though the leading families of the old hamlet became the landlords of the new neighborhood, little evidence suggests they were able to control the direction of its social development even during the first decades. Well before the Second World War, new arrivals to the area began to exercise leadership over the new institutions of neighborhood life, and the war and postwar reforms swept away both the landlords' political power and their economic base.

Demographically, the neighborhood has undergone two major transformations during the twentieth century, each creating breaks so sharp as to rule out any continuity linking the nineteenth-century hamlet, the prewar neighborhood, and postwar Miyamoto-chō. The first such upheaval came in the 1920's and 1930's, when floods of new residents dramatically shifted the area's demographic composition and set the neighborhood on a new course of institutional development. The Second World War, of course, created the second sharp break. Although the gradual but steady loss of population since the 1960's and the influx of transient households in the 1970's and 1980's have had a less marked impact, these trends too have eroded demographic continuities that might otherwise be thought to underlie Miyamoto-chō's social life.

There may be continuities between patterns of neighborhood life in Ebara-ku in the 1930's and the communal ethos of Tokyo's shitamachi—and certainly population movement from shitamachi to Ebara after the earthquake may have played a part in transmitting this ethos from one area to another. Yet here, too, whether neighborhood institutions "spontaneously" grew out of Tokyo culture or were carefully nurtured government devices, the fact remains that in prewar Ebara-ku, as elsewhere in Tokyo, these institutions were recent creations. Their establishment reflected both the government's insistence on social order and local residents' desire for calm and stability in the midst of population growth, urban expansion, and economic change.

The prewar creation of Miyamoto-chō, and of dozens if not hundreds of similar neighborhoods, was a response to these trends. The changes in metropolitan demography, politics, and economics that led to the populating of Miyamoto-chō gave rise equally to what were perceived as threats of social unrest throughout urban Japan, which the authorities sought to curb in part through the encouragement of urban neighborhood organizations that resembled those of the reified village. In sum, new institutions of neighborhood life that developed took on so strong a traditionalistic coloration, not because they were descended from rural hamlets, but because they reflected then-contemporary ideological currents in Japanese society that, as Havens (1978: 43) has so aptly put it, sought to "revive the past as a malleable ideal, not as an actuality."

CHAPTER THREE

Local Politics and Administration

LATE ONE HOT AUGUST NIGHT, after meeting to make arrangements for the upcoming festival, a handful of men retired to a local restaurant specializing in broiled eel, a delicacy noted for increasing one's stamina and virility. The group included several middle-aged men prominent in Miyamoto-chō's chōkai and in local politics, as well as a few younger men who play only occasional and peripheral roles in local affairs, like Mr. Ikeo, who with his wife and father-in-law runs a small cosmetics shop on Miyamoto-chō's shopping street. Sometime later, the politician Tsurumi-sensei showed up. The conversation turned to his recent trip to a political convention in Kyoto and his activities as a member of the ward assembly. During a lull in the conversation Mr. Ikeo called across the bar to Tsurumi-sensei. The merchant had been having difficulties filing some forms at the ward office. Tsurumi-sensei quickly made a few suggestions and told Mr. Ikeo to call him if he had any further problems. In less than five minutes of pleasant banter while drinking with the boys, Tsurumi-sensei had solved (or had promised to solve) a minor but annoying problem for a local resident. A few minutes later Tsurumi-sensei turned to Mr. Yamamura—a contractor who is one of his closest political allies—and said in a voice that carried throughout the tiny bar, "Mr. Ikeo is a great guy [*subarashii hito*]. It's too bad he's not given more chances to lead the neighborhood." Mr. Ikeo, who had moved to Miyamoto-chō as an adult and often confided to me his skepticism about neighborhood organizations and their leaders, beamed; Tsurumi-sensei had at once strengthened a friendship and solidified a future claim on support.

This trivial interchange illustrates the texture of politics in Miyamoto-chō and something of the way that politics interweaves through neighborhood life. These tangled interconnections between personal, local institutional, and governmental spheres lead many observers of Japanese communities to equate social relations with politics and to assume that neighborhoods exist almost exclusively for political ends. From this perspective politics subsumes all local social ties and institutions, and without political motivations to maintain local social life, urban community organizations and communal identity would cease to exist.

One variant of this argument holds that neighborhood organizations and the social ties that ramify from them are little more than devices through which local political bosses contrive to control conservative voting blocs. Thus, were it not for these political activities, neighborhoods would barely exist on the urban social landscape in any institutional form. Moreover, the argument runs, these political activities take the form they do because local politics remains the bailiwick of members of the old middle class—shopkeepers and other self-employed businessmen—people who are regarded as inherently conservative not only in their politics, but also in their social ideology. This social outlook, it is often held, is parochial and inclined to favor particularistic ties based on "feudal" values of hierarchy and old-fashioned community solidarity rather than "modern" forms of participatory democracy based on enlightened self-interest. McKean (1981: 194) quotes one activist in the environmental movement who expressed this common appraisal of neighborhood associations: "Our worst opponent was our local neighborhood association, which has power left over from the feudal age. [Association leaders] actually do no work for the benefit of the neighborhood at all; they just eat and drink and then do what the ward government tells them to do."

This reflects another but related point of view—namely, that neighborhoods are merely administrative mechanisms created by conservative local governments to do their bidding. Here, again, members of the old middle class are called to task for willingly subordinating themselves to government demands, both because of their assumed agreement with conservative government policies and because of their presumed subservience to hierarchical authority. Though the perspective is slightly different, the resulting analysis is much the same: neighborhoods have little social reality beyond the administrative roles that are thrust upon them. By extension, in either light, the informal social ties that bind residents to one another and the social institutions that interact *within* neighborhoods are ephemeral and insignificant.

Certainly there are elements of truth in these characterizations. Shopkeepers and factory owners do indeed dominate local politics. And both internal political relationships and external administrative guidance do indeed constitute important dimensions of neighborhood life. But to argue that without political and administrative roles, neighborhoods would cease to exist as social units reduces complex patterns of social relations to a single political-administrative dimension.

This reduction is common in studies of chōkai. Much of this research equates or confuses the existence of neighborhoods as meaningful social units with the existence of chōkai as political or administrative institutions. On the one hand most descriptive studies focus primarily on the formal institutions and thus simply fail to distinguish between formal and informal aspects of community structure. The implicit assumption appears to be that formal features of institutional structure create the informal and are the major index of the existence of a community. In Miyamoto-chō, as elsewhere, it is difficult to disentangle institutional structures from informal social relations and patterns of interaction among residents, but it is an analytic mistake to regard a community's social structure as simply the sum total of a community's formal institutions.

The priority given formal structures also reflects the common tendency to cast all social relationships and activities occurring under the aegis of the neighborhood in almost exclusively political terms, and to focus on political and administrative features of neighborhood structure to the exclusion of other, more broadly social aspects. Yet these other aspects are critical to the development of a sense of community and the feelings of social solidarity that enable urban neighborhoods and their formal institutions to play effective political and administrative roles. As Allinson remarks (1979: 201), "The mood created by these associations [is] in the end more important than any overt political actions they [may] have taken."

The generally one-dimensional view of neighborhood social organization as institutional and administrative (or political) rather than informal and social in character feeds on images of chōkai as little more than extensions of the government itself—largely created at government instigation, subservient to it, and manipulated by it to serve the government's ends. According to this line of argument, but for the government's imposition of these bodies upon neighborhoods and their residents, neither the institutions nor the neighborhoods-as-communities would exist. Implied here is a notion that neighborhoods totally share common interests with political parties or local administrative agencies, hence the relationship between the two sides is untroubled by questions of the legitimacy and the proper roles of actors at either level. Whether neighborhoods are seen as political machines influencing the municipality or as administrative devices carrying out the will of the bureaucracy, the relationship implied is assumed to be tranquil and mutually agreed upon.

Superficially this may appear to be the case, but I argue that neighborhoods (as self-defined communities) and municipal officials (as nonelected stewards of good government) often subtly disagree over what a community is, what its role in influencing government policy should be, and what attitude officials should assume in their dealings with citizens and local organizations. These opposing views rarely break out into open conflict, but the issues nevertheless remain important ones, at least in the minds and behind the actions of neighborhood leaders. Observers seldom note that seemingly close and stable ties between a generally conservative chōkai and the local government can paradoxically embody persisting tension and latent conflict. That such situations can and do exist surely demonstrates the strength of the internally created sense of community and the contemporary independence of this communal self-definition from direct government control. These strains demonstrate that definitions of community structure based solely on administrative and political criteria fail to represent the entirety of community life. Moreover, they symbolically signal the unwillingness of a community to be dominated by external agencies such as those of the government.

In this chapter I discuss several dimensions of the relationship between neighborhoods and the government. First, I examine the role of the local politician in mobilizing (as well as creating and strengthening) communal sentiment, and the ways in which Miyamoto-chō therefore exists as a base for electoral politics. Second, I discuss the administrative system of Tokyo and the historical legacy of government manipulation of neighborhood organizations during the Second World War, focusing on the way these shape contemporary attitudes toward neighborhood-government relations. Third, I outline the roles assigned to neighborhood associations in the present-day administrative framework of the ward government. And, last, I examine the ward government's efforts to create a new sense of local community through its policies of *machi-zukuri*, or "community-building." The attitudes and expectations revealed in such a survey show a neighborhood fundamentally—even if now quiescently—at odds with the government over its own significance as a social arena. This implicit opposition reflects the force and meaning of locally held sentiments of community, belying simple characterizations of neighborhood social organization as either a political machine or an administrative appendage.

Miyamoto-chō and the Local Politician

The fabric of urban Japanese political organization does not come precut in bits the size of Miyamoto-chō. The neighborhood is only a tiny fragment of much larger electoral districts, and so there are neither elected officials nor formal political organizations that claim to represent Miyamoto-chō and Miyamoto-chō alone. As a political unit Miyamoto-chō—like most urban Japanese neighborhoods—goes unrecognized in the laws and regulations that govern the apportionment of elective offices and the structure of political and administrative institutions.

Nevertheless, politics interweaves throughout neighborhood social life in Miyamoto-chō as elsewhere. The full array of contemporary Japanese political parties is active there: the Liberal Democratic Party, which has controlled the national government since the party's founding in 1955; the Kōmeitō, the Clean Government Party affiliated with the Sōka Gakkai; the Socialists; the Democratic Socialists; the Communists; and several splinter parties of the right, left, and center. Each party has members in the neighborhood who serve as local organizers and vote canvassers; often a party's active supporters will post a sign on their home or store identifying it as one of the party's *renrakujo*, or liaison offices. On walls and fences throughout the neighborhood, party activists maintain bulletin boards displaying announcements of speeches, lectures, and study clubs, as well as glossy photos of their leading local champions.

But the activities of the parties—with one major exception—do not become a direct part of community life; they touch the neighborhood only in so far as contacts among politically like-minded residents create bonds within the neighborhood that might not otherwise exist. The exception is a small splinter party, a little to the right of center, that left the Liberal Democratic Party in the middle 1970's over the issue of corruption at the national party level. During my research in 1979–81 this party stood apart in Miyamoto-chō because its local spokesperson—Tsurumi-sensei—served as a member of the ward assembly. His position in the assembly both trumpets the political cohesion of a neighborhood able to mobilize itself to support a local candidate and provides a central institutional pillar around which the neighborhood can organize and identify itself.

Tsurumi-sensei is a middle-aged professional politician who has lived in the neighborhood for over 20 years, since marrying into a politically prominent local family. Before his first election to the ward assembly in 1979, he had served as president of the chōkai, an office he held again in 1983–87. He has also served as president of the PTA for both the junior high school and the elementary school. He is an honorary adviser (*komon*) to many other Miyamoto-chō organizations, as was his father-in-law, who in a long and distinguished career as a local political leader filled many positions before retiring as a member of the Tokyo metropolitan assembly. Tsurumi-sensei has a strong ally in his wife, a youthful and vivacious woman. As a lifelong resident of Miyamoto-chō she knows and is known by many residents in and around the neighborhood. Mrs. Tsurumi enthusiastically joins in the activities of many local associations, but even as a leader in her own right she tactfully avoids asserting herself or flaunting her husband's position. Through her connections and by his own efforts, Tsurumi-sensei maintains an impressive range of contacts throughout the neighborhood and throughout the ward. With his affable and self-effacing manner and his strong local ties, he easily wins the goodwill (and the political support) of many local residents.

Tsurumi-sensei could not survive without the political support of Miyamoto-chō, a political base he represents but did not create; at the same time Miyamoto-chō would not consider itself so much a community if it could not elect a representative to the assembly. If Tsurumi-sensei did not provide a focus for the neighborhood's political impulses, the inventory of groups and individual ties that contribute to the neighborhood's organizational structure would be far poorer, and Miyamoto-chō would lack one of its central symbols of community identity. Charming, friendly, hardworking, dedicated, and well respected as Tsurumi-sensei is, his appeal does not center by and large on his personal qualities. For many residents the important thing is that he is from the neighborhood; Miyamoto-chō has someone it can and does elect to represent it.

Since members of the ward assembly are elected at large, in principle they do not represent specific districts. But of course candidates for office and sitting assemblymen alike rely on their personal bases of political support, their informal constituencies: labor unions, trade associations, religious groups, or neighborhoods. Because Tsurumi-sensei lives in Miyamoto-chō and draws the core of his support from there, the neighborhood in effect possesses its own assembly member. He is a community resource, an accessible and effective channel through which residents may influence government policies. He provides access to the government both for the neighborhood as a whole (through organized interest groups such as the chōkai, the shopkeepers' guild, and the PTA) and for individual residents with business to transact with the ward administration. Since there are 48 seats in the assembly and over 120 distinct (and both officially and popularly recognized) neighborhoods in the ward, a neighborhood that has its own assembly member regards itself, and is perceived by other neighborhoods, as highly advantaged in dealings with the ward government.[1]

The local politician is thus an important community asset, valued for his role as a broker with extremely useful ties to the ward administration and other institutions, as well as to politicians, businessmen, and other influential people outside the neighborhood. Furthermore, he symbolizes neighborhood unity and solidarity; residents comment on this using arguments that can be paraphrased as, "Since we are a community, we work together, and look, we are able to elect our own representative," or the obverse, "Look, we can elect our own representative, unlike other neighborhoods, and that must mean we work together for the common good, so we must be a community."

But Tsurumi-sensei does not merely symbolize local unity; his presence in the community and his campaign activities (throughout his term, not just before elections) add greatly to the proliferation of formally organized groups, informal ties, and opportunities for social interaction in Miyamoto-chō.

The Kōenkai

Tsurumi-sensei's *kōenkai* (or supporters' club) is his most visible contribution to the neighborhood's inventory of organizational forms.[2] This loosely organized political club provides a focus for Tsurumi-sensei's supporters, many but by no means all of whom live in and around Miyamoto-chō. Although the club's officials and members tend to be people active in neighborhood affairs, "members" participate for various reasons. Some non-neighborhood residents belong because of personal or business ties to Tsurumi-sensei. And some Miyamoto-chō residents who are totally indifferent to local politics belong because they find it a pleasant way to take inexpensive trips with their friends.

A couple of dozen block captains (*renrakuin*) appointed by

Tsurumi-sensei help keep him in touch with his supporters. They distribute fliers and posters, maintain political bulletin boards, line up participants to attend occasional public speeches and "study sessions" sponsored by Tsurumi-sensei or his party, and keep Tsurumi-sensei informed of significant events in the families of his supporters: births, weddings, successful completion of school entrance exams, or funerals. Of course, when elections roll around, Tsurumi-sensei's captains go to work to bring out the vote.

Tsurumi-sensei keeps file cards on the households of supporters throughout the ward, listing their names, addresses, special interests, the nature of any personal connection—such as alumni ties with Mrs. Tsurumi who graduated from the local elementary school, joint involvement in local festival organizations, or common membership in local chambers of commerce—and notations about the level of gift-giving he should maintain with the household through funeral offerings or seasonal gifts. The information on these cards is crucial for the kind of personal politics that wins elections in Miyamoto-chō, and Tsurumi-sensei relies on his block captains to help keep him abreast of the several hundred households he courts.

The block captains are all old friends of Tsurumi-sensei's, and most of those from the neighborhood have served with him as officials in one or another of Miyamoto-chō's associations. A dozen or so of them also belong to a loosely organized travel club. Every month each of the club's members pays 3,000 yen into a kitty to finance an annual outing, usually a weekend trip to a hot springs resort.[3] The group formally calls itself the Wakamono Shinbokukai, the Young Men's Friendship Association. Although most of its members now constitute Tsurumi-sensei's kitchen cabinet, the club long predates his electoral career. It was formed in the early 1960's, when the men were all in their twenties or thirties, and over the years the membership has remained fairly constant, with occasional additions of younger drinking buddies and occasional defections by men whose wives no longer approve of the group's hard-drinking, hard-playing image.

During my research the group included Tsurumi-sensei; Mr. Yamamura, a successful contractor whose father moved to

Miyamoto-chō in the 1920's; Mr. Kataoka, a self-employed professional who was then the president of the chōkai; Mr. Nakajima, a skilled construction worker and festival aficionado, whose family shares a home on a back alley near the shrine with his father and brother, a retired craftsman and a skilled blue-collar worker, respectively; Mr. Izumi, the adopted son-in-law of a family that owns a thriving factory; Mr. Kobayashi, who runs a laundry that he inherited from his father and who is among the few Edokko (third-generation residents of Tokyo) in the neighborhood; Mr. Hirota, a moody tradesman who runs a paper supply business and is a leader of the volunteer fire brigade and has obvious ambitions—too obvious to be successful—to become the chōkai president; Mr. Seto, an artisan whose father established a construction business in Miyamoto-chō before the war; Mr. Asanuma, an engineer and inventor who works for a large corporation and, who, with his wife, runs a tiny snack bar on a back street near the old river; and Mr. Baba, the heir-presumptive to a successful hardware store still run by his father, with whom he does not get along well. Some members have known each other all their lives, having attended the local elementary school together; others—like Tsurumi-sensei, Mr. Asanuma, and Mr. Izumi—came to Miyamoto-chō as young men when they married into local families;[4] still others moved to the neighborhood as adults simply because it seemed a good place to practice their trades.

The club was formed by a group of young men from locally prominent families who had political ambitions but were too junior to lead in either the chōkai or the political organization of Motofuji-sensei, the now-retired owner of a tiny factory near the shrine who preceded Tsurumi-sensei as Miyamoto-chō's ward-assembly representative. As Tsurumi-sensei and his cohort came of age in the generational politics of neighborhood life, the group advised him through his tenure as PTA president and leader of the chōkai, as well as through his first campaigns for public office. Today its members continue to be Tsurumi-sensei's innermost circle of local supporters, and when—as during much of the early 1980's—Tsurumi-sensei and his allies do not directly control the chōkai, this group serves as something of a shadow cabinet in opposition. For its members, the Wakamono Shinbokukai still provides chances for yearly outings and for nights of drinking several times a month, but it also serves as a base for their political interests. They have aged, their political sights have broadened, and they now lead many of the organizations from which they once felt excluded. Their club now serves also as the central core of leadership for Tsurumi-sensei's larger political support group, his kōenkai.

Although Tsurumi-sensei's lieutenants in both the Wakamono Shinbokukai and the kōenkai are men, women are the key to his electoral success. Not only do they vote at slightly higher rates than men in Miyamoto-chō, but they usually have more time and energy for political activity in the neighborhood. If Tsurumi-sensei (or one of his political mentors at a higher level) needs leaflets distributed, or box lunches made, or word-of-mouth information spread, he is much more likely to find willing and available hands among his women supporters than among his male buddies.

Paradoxically, the importance of women in local politics stems from their domesticity. More women than men spend their days at home in the neighborhood, and in various ways their roles are more likely to include a strong component of community involvement. At the minimum a married woman with children has established local contacts through the school's PTA and through her shopping; many commuting white-collar male residents know even their closest neighbors only by sight. In addition most women are involved in a variety of local groups and networks, based on schools, on hobbies, and on friendships established with neighbors over the years. These contacts are much more likely to be purely local than are male networks, and within the limits of local social variation, women's ties are likely to transcend class and status barriers in ways that the men's cannot. In a place like Miyamoto-chō the wives of corporate executives and the wives of greengrocers are far more likely to interact than their husbands. Thus women can provide Tsurumi-sensei with entry to networks that cross-cut all levels of local society in a way that his male kitchen cabinet is unequipped to do. He therefore carefully courts female support, and women outnumber men on the trips his kōenkai sponsors.

The kōenkai is serious business for Tsurumi-sensei, but for most residents of Miyamoto-chō it simply offers opportunities for recreation cloaked in an aura of civic responsibility. A good measure of the quality and quantity of attention residents generally focus on political matters is found in the kōenkai's excursions—outings that give 150 to 200 residents an excuse for a weekend trip to a hot springs resort or a famous temple. The politician heavily subsidizes these semiannual trips; participants have only to pay a modest fee and to listen attentively to a few minutes of gentle political speechifying.

One such trip—about midway through Tsurumi-sensei's first term—took four busloads of supporters, friends, and neighbors off to a hot springs resort on the Izu peninsula, a few hours' drive south of Tokyo. Participants each paid 15,000 yen for their travel, room, and board: an incredible bargain that Tsurumi-sensei (or his political party) clearly subsidized.

At the assembly point Tsurumi-sensei and his wife formally welcomed each busload of travelers. Tsurumi-sensei cracked a few jokes at his own expense and turned the microphone over to Mr. Izumi—the wealthy factory owner who is one of Tsurumi-sensei's most important backers. Mr. Izumi earnestly requested everyone's continuing support for Tsurumi-sensei in superbly formal Japanese, interspersed with sotto voce wise-cracks in his native southwestern dialect that kept the first few rows of grandmothers giggling for the remainder of the formalities.

The buses were off: down the expressway to Hakone for lunch and quick boat rides on the lake under the crest of Mount Fuji, then over a "skyline drive" cut across the ridges of otherwise scenic mountains, to the hot springs resort, where they arrived in midafternoon. The 160 excursionists quickly dispersed to their assigned rooms—10 or 12 to a large tatami suite. Roommates had signed up together, or were grouped by the trip's organizers on the basis of personal interests and ties. One suite had been reserved by several women from the old people's club of Miyamoto-chō led by old Mrs. Yano, a slender chain-smoking woman in her seventies who leads many women's activities in the neighborhood. Another was occupied by Ta-chan, the stylish young owner of a tiny cabaret near Miyamoto-chō that Tsurumi-sensei patronizes, who recruited some of his other patrons to come along for the trip. Still another was assigned to Mrs. Hara, an elegant teacher of traditional dance, and some of her students from Miyamoto-chō, all of whom Tsurumi-sensei carefully courts with his joking attentions. One suite contained Tsurumi-sensei, his chief lieutenants, and the anomalous anthropologist. Since the suites were sexually segregated, husbands and wives who came on the excursion together were separated off into their separate *nakama*, or circles of friends. But because of household or occupational responsibilities, few couples in fact made the trip together; as elsewhere in Japan husbands and wives in Miyamoto-chō rarely pursue recreational activities together. In any event the point of this trip was to create group sentiment focused on Tsurumi-sensei, not to provide individual couples with a chance to get away together for a quiet weekend.

After settling into their suites, many excursionists changed into the light cotton yukata provided by the management. Some then wandered off to the baths, filled with water piped in from a nearby volcanic hot spring, as others set out for a stroll along the banks of a rushing torrent next to the hotel.

In the evening the group assembled in the hotel's banquet hall for an elaborate dinner featuring many courses of local seafood and oceans of *sake*, beer, and orange soda (the "proper" beverage for women drinking in mixed company and one that men often assume women prefer). As the trays were cleared away, Mr. Izumi stepped forward to the microphone to welcome everyone once again. He read congratulatory telegrams from other politicians and local notables, and introduced several respected elder statesmen of the neighborhood, who gave brief speeches praising Tsurumi-sensei.

Old Mr. Kataoka—a jovial former chōkai president, retired government bureaucrat, and father of the current chōkai president—talked for 20 minutes, stressing Tsurumi-sensei's many contributions to the local well-being and pointing out his rapid rise to prominence in the ward assembly even so early in his first term. The speaker touted Tsurumi-sensei's support of education and his success in getting the ward to build a new nursery school in Miyamoto-chō (next to the shrine). Thanks to

Tsurumi-sensei's efforts, he said, Miyamoto-chō's stature was assured as the ward's *kyōiku no miyako*—its "capital of education"—a reference to the fact that there are also public elementary and junior high schools in the neighborhood. Other speakers focused on Tsurumi-sensei's accomplishments in ward finance and administrative reform. Motofuji-sensei presented a short toast to his fine successor. Tsurumi-sensei returned to the microphone, again thanking everyone for coming and discussing in extremely general terms some of the issues that would be facing the ward assembly in the next few months. A few more rounds of formal welcomes and expressions of thanks, and the evening's entertainment was set to begin.

Talented supporters of Tsurumi-sensei now took their turns on the stage: troupes of folk-dancing matrons led by their local teachers, grandmothers playing *shamisen*, middle-aged factory owners acting in comic mime, dance teachers performing elegant solos, men and women singing sentimental ballads from their home provinces, and almost everyone joining in the electronic sing-along karaoke contests. The performances ended as the hotel's house band came on stage to play music for ballroom dancing. Couples in yukata began to twirl and spin to 1940's dance tunes, until the band departed for the hotel's nightclub. The party then split into smaller groups—some heading off to the nightclub to continue dancing to the pop trio, others retiring to their suites to sing, to dance in more subdued traditional styles, and to drink. Until late into the night troops of Tsurumi-sensei's happy supporters prowled the halls of the hotel, bearing bottles of beer and bags of *senbei* (rice crackers), inviting themselves into one suite after another to listen to a shamisen balladeer or to join a group of folk dancers.

Late the next morning everyone assembled in the hotel's courtyard for the obligatory *kinen shashin*—the group photograph that commemorates all such outings—before setting off for a huge greenhouse in a nearby town that featured an elaborate orchid garden. After a two-hour stop for strolling through the gardens, the group traveled on to a factory that processes *sansai*—mountain vegetables, a local speciality—and then to a famous shrine to soak up a bit of culture and history. At each stop most excursionists bought *omiyage*—souvenirs in some way typical of the place visited—for families, neighbors, co-workers, and friends. By the time the buses returned to Miyamoto-chō, the luggage racks and aisles of the buses were full to overflowing with potted orchids, packages of sansai, boxes of local senbei, amulets from the shrine, and bottles of *sake* brewed on the Izu peninsula.

As people took their seats on the buses for the last leg of the excursion, they found they had been given several pamphlets outlining the policies of Tsurumi-sensei's party on the national level, as well as a sheet or two of information on what Tsurumi-sensei had accomplished for residents of the ward. Tsurumi-sensei himself boarded each bus to thank everyone for coming, and as the buses got under way for the four-hour drive back to Tokyo, one of his lieutenants on each bus urged everyone to read the pamphlets carefully and to share them with their families and neighbors. A few excursionists briefly scanned the material, but most tucked it away politely with their omiyage and went to sleep.

Gathering Support

Through events such as these Tsurumi-sensei builds support by providing people with an opportunity for a bit of communal merrymaking. In turn whenever an election approaches, whether Tsurumi-sensei is up for reelection to the ward assembly or other candidates from his party are running for prefectural or national office, he can mobilize many local residents to provide volunteer labor for the campaign. He relies on these volunteers to solicit votes from their families and neighbors, as well as to canvass their personal networks of friends, colleagues, patrons, and clients throughout the ward.

Miyamoto-chō possesses in Tsurumi-sensei not an abstract symbol of access to power, but someone who comes from the local community, who interacts face-to-face with many of its residents every day, and who knows and is known by at least one person in many, if not most, of its households. His advice, his contacts, and his offers to intercede with the local bureaucracy, which he gracefully dispenses with seeming casualness, are clearly accepted with great appreciation as valued favors; the interchange between Tsurumi-sensei and Mr. Ikeo, with which I introduced this chapter, is but one example. By such means Tsurumi-sensei easily garners support.

Such support is not automatic, however. For one thing, although party affiliation does not play a decisive role in ward elections, Tsurumi-sensei's party lacks strength in the ward as a whole. He is affiliated with a small reform-minded conservative group, which broke away in the 1970's from the Liberal Democratic Party, the party that holds a majority not only in the Diet, but also in the ward and metropolitan assemblies. He cannot necessarily count on the unwavering support of those residents who still staunchly back the Liberal Democratic Party or on those who identify with other parties, such as the Kōmeitō, the Socialists, or the Communists.

But even if he had their undivided support, the Miyamoto-chō vote is not large enough to elect him. In recent elections candidates have generally required a minimum of 2,000 votes to assure their election to the ward assembly; Miyamoto-chō has only about half that number of registered voters.[5] To ensure a stable (and sizable enough) political base, Tsurumi-sensei must court potential voters both inside and outside Miyamoto-chō. He therefore constantly strives to maintain a high profile in local affairs throughout the four-year interval between ward-assembly elections.

He does this not only through his supporters' club, but through his own involvement in most local events and organizations. At local gatherings he is always accorded a seat of honor. Invariably he is introduced as "Miyamoto-chō's own Tsurumi-sensei" (though everyone in the audience knows him) and is asked to say a few words to open or close the event. He can be found at nearly every local funeral. Like politicians everywhere, he does his best to help his constituents solve their problems with the local government, and on their behalf he constantly intercedes with—or simply provides introductions to—the appropriate bureaucrats in the ward government. Residents call on him to help with school admissions problems, minor tax matters, inadequate garbage collection, noise from public facilities, construction permits, and a hundred other complaints and sources of red tape that urban politicians throughout the world routinely untangle. He does his best to act on even the most tangential requests, and so serves as a broker, providing local residents with connections not just to the ward government, but to businessmen and other influential people he knows, to politicians at higher levels of government, and to a variety of public and private institutions with which he may have influence.

As an active leader of the chōkai, he plays a central part in most of its activities and frequently appears in roles where he can be seen working for the good of the community. Thus one summer afternoon just before a Diet election in which his party's candidates were running for office, Tsurumi-sensei went around the neighborhood as part of the chōkai's pesticide spraying crew, and made a point of greeting everyone he met and thanking them for their support; in doing so he narrowly skirted the legal prohibition against house-to-house visits by electoral canvassers.[6] Lest too cynical an interpretation be attached to this, let me add that he *always* joins the spraying crew, which from repeated personal experience I know to be a hot, sweaty, smelly, and widely underappreciated chōkai job.

In addition to such visible activities and whatever personal ties he can exploit on his own, Tsurumi-sensei depends on his supporters to mobilize their own networks of relationships on his behalf—their own *tsukiai*, the ties of mutual obligation, the "connections," that are the stuff of business, political, and social interaction throughout the neighborhood. He assiduously cultivates the support of other local leaders—in the shōtenkai, the chōkai, the volunteer fire brigade, the travel clubs, and even the traditional folk-dancing groups—and will call on them to get in touch with their own followers, friends, acquaintances, and students when election time draws near.

One supporter, whose wife worked part-time in a day care center, told me how before a recent election he had phoned each of the 200 households whose children attend the center asking them to support Tsurumi-sensei. It was clear from the man's account that he believes his efforts made possible Tsurumi-sensei's victory in an extremely close election; in his view Tsurumi-sensei is therefore under great obligation to him. Whether the votes he gathered were really crucial is not important; the significant point is the debt he believes Tsurumi-sensei owes him for the victory.

Gathering support through the tsukiai of others is thus a two-way street, and the successful local politician who bases his campaign on a strategy of exploiting ties in an informal local constituency must be solicitous of his supporters both before and after the election. Indeed, he must probably be far more solicitous than those candidates who run on ideological platforms, supported by labor unions and issue-oriented political committees (as are Socialist and Communist candidates) or religious sects (as are Kōmeitō candidates).

Furthermore, tsukiai does not necessarily equal or guarantee support. Supporters may become disaffected, and both Tsurumi-sensei and old Soeda-sensei—a retired politician from an adjoining neighborhood who capped a long career as a local doctor with 20 years of service in the ward assembly—agreed that between any two elections officeholders can count on losing at least 25 percent of their supporters, for any number of reasons. Voters become dissatisfied with a politician's performance, they move out of the ward, or they succumb to competing claims for their support. A given household may receive appeals from many different sources, all with equally valid social claims on their support, and all perhaps emanating from candidates with essentially similar political platforms. Exploitable ties may be based on almost anything: working together in the PTA or the volunteer fire brigade; drinking together in the same bar or studying flower arrangement with the same teacher; having graduated together from the elementary school; pursuing the same occupation or practicing the same religion. All these relationships, and many more, are called upon to bolster claims for political support. The appeal can be based on the personal connections and shared attributes of the canvasser and the voter, or on the common interests (or affiliations) of the candidate and the voter's household.

Household support rather than individual preference often seems to be the critical factor behind the votes cast, and the allocation of a household's votes among several candidates may be a matter of household rather than individual decision. As both politicians and voters often told me, votes cast for different candidates do not necessarily reflect political disagreements among household members; they indicate a household's attempt to respond to and fulfill its members' social obligations to a variety of candidates and vote-canvassers who confront household members with competing requests for political support.

This vote splitting is encouraged by the system of proportionally representative multiseat constituencies in all legislative bodies. In elections for the ward assembly the winners are the top 48 vote-getters out of a field of perhaps 60 or 70 candidates. The Tōkyō-to metropolitan assembly divides the prefecture into 38 constituencies; Shinagawa-ku forms a single constituency with five seats. Tōkyō-to is divided among 11 constituencies for the Diet's lower house; Shinagawa-ku and Ōta-ku, an adjacent ward, along with a number of distant islands administered by Tōkyō-to, make up a single constituency with five representatives. In the Diet's upper house, Tōkyō-to as a whole is a prefectural constituency with eight seats, four of which are filled in any given election. One hundred seats in the upper house are reserved for a national constituency, and half these seats are filled every three years by the top 50 vote-getters in a nationwide campaign.

In legislative races, at whatever level in the political system, politicians are never in head-to-head contests that produce single victors, and voters are never confronted with a situation where votes cast for competing candidates necessarily cancel each other out. Consequently, when households allocate their votes, they can parcel them out to several candidates knowing that they will help each, harm none, and meet their own obligations.

Even in the small political realm of Miyamoto-chō, therefore, support for Tsurumi-sensei is hard to gauge. In any given election, household voting strategies mean that support for him need not translate into actual individual votes, and people whose votes go to other candidates may nonetheless consider themselves firm supporters of Tsurumi-sensei. Further complicating calculations of the percentage of local residents who support Tsurumi-sensei is the probability that from one election to the next some backers will defect, move away, or die. Even just after an election no local vote counts are available; since the polling district itself is not any sort of constituency, the election office does not provide local vote breakdowns.

But the local character of Tsurumi-sensei's base of support became quite visibly evident during a Diet election in the summer of 1980, because of the unique fact of his membership in a minor political party. When Tsurumi-sensei decided several years ago to leave the Liberal Democratic Party for the new splinter party, he took many of his local supporters with him. Few were consulted about the party switch beforehand—and indeed Tsurumi-sensei may have had little to say about a shift in allegiance determined by his mentors much higher in the metropolitan and national political hierarchy. Some of Tsurumi-sensei's local supporters still grumble a bit about giving up their lifelong ties to the Liberal Democratic Party, but most now wholeheartedly support the entire splinter-party slate.

In 1980 Tsurumi-sensei was the only elected officeholder in the ward who belonged to the splinter party. Throughout the Diet election campaign Miyamoto-chō conspicuously stood apart from surrounding areas by its profusion of banners and posters advertising the party and its candidates. Splinter-party advertisements far and away outnumbered those of all other parties combined in Miyamoto-chō itself, but were almost nowhere to be seen only a couple of blocks away in surrounding neighborhoods. The geographical range of support for the party therefore appears to extend not much beyond Miyamoto-chō, with the density of support for it (and presumably for Tsurumi-sensei himself) tapering off rapidly in all directions beyond the immediate neighborhood.

The circumstances surrounding this display of support were unusual, yet even if Tsurumi-sensei belonged to a larger party, the underlying relationship between his supporters and his party would not differ. It simply would be less starkly visible. That is, even if Tsurumi-sensei represented a more powerful party, he would mobilize and offer the backing of his local supporters to that party's candidates; the limits of his backing would be obscured, however, in overlapping circles of support generated by other local politicians from the same party. In this instance, where Tsurumi-sensei stands as the single local pillar of support for his party, the geographically constricted coattails of a ward assembly member are clearly visible.

Alone or not, the case casts in sharp relief the close relationship between a local politician and a neighborhood base of support. This relationship is important for several reasons. Tsurumi-sensei's political organization is generally informal— at least in the sense that he has no patronage system at his command or any way to gain preferential treatment for supporters in the letting of government contracts. Still, he provides a means for local residents to contact the ward government through channels that are at once more open and more responsive than the bureaucratic paths normally traversed by individuals approaching government agencies (as we shall see in the following sections). But Tsurumi-sensei also plays other crucial roles in the life of the neighborhood as a whole. Although his overt appeal is to political conservatives and moderates, his political organization and the activities he sponsors add to the sum of institutions and ties that link residents to one another regardless of their political leanings. In the largely apolitical stance that most residents take toward ward affairs, Tsurumi-sensei's real importance is as a symbol of the neighborhood's collective unity. Its success in electing him lends weight to Miyamoto-chō's view of itself as a politically independent, autonomous unit, a view not shared by the ward government.

The Context of Neighborhood Autonomy

Scholars frequently assume that neighborhood associations are little more than appendages of the government itself; conflict or disagreement between them and the government therefore presumably occurs only in times of crisis. In the pages that follow I will show that this is not the case by examining the administrative roles of Miyamoto-chō and its chōkai, as well as some of the broader historical and contemporary institutional factors that create an inherent tension and the potential for conflict over the roles and definitions of the important units of local community life. In response to the ambiguity of its status, Miyamoto-chō asserts its autonomy and pushes its claims to its own identity by manipulating and accentuating traditionalism in its internal activities, a subject that the next chapter will examine more fully.

Tokyo Metropolitan Prefecture and Tokyo's Wards

There is no single, separable city of Tokyo in any legal, political, or administrative sense. There is, instead, a Tokyo Metropolitan Prefecture (Tōkyō-to), established in 1943 when the national government merged the City of Tokyo (Tōkyō-shi) and the Prefecture of Tokyo (Tōkyō-fu). Currently Tōkyō-to includes the 23 wards (ku) that are conventionally considered the city of Tokyo—the area of Tōkyō-shi as it existed from its expansion in 1932 to its disappearance in 1943. Tōkyō-to also includes 26 suburban cities (shi), five towns (machi), and one village (mura) on the mainland, as well as a string of small islands that stretch from the Izu peninsula to the tiny volcanic islet of Iwo Jima, over 1,000 kilometers from the main Japanese island of Honshū. At the end of 1982 Tōkyō-to's population totaled 11.68 million. About three-quarters of these people (8.34 million) lived in the 592-square-kilometer ward area (27% of Tōkyō-to's total land area)—for a population density of 14,104 people per square kilometer (Tōkyō-to Tōkei Kyōkai 1982: 1, 19, 26).

In several ways it is significant that there is no city of Tokyo, "no governmental unit, embracing only the urban core of the metropolis and intervening between it and the metropolitan [prefectural] government" (Steiner 1965: 149).[7] Under present Japanese law the rights, responsibilities, and obligations assigned to the prefectural administration of Tōkyō-to and to Tokyo's 23 wards are divided differently from those of all other systems of prefectural and municipal coordination in Japan. This arrangement affects more than merely the conduct of municipal affairs; it also illustrates fundamental attitudes of the central government toward local autonomy, particularly the autonomy of the citizens of the nation's capital and largest urban concentration. Both in the day-to-day details of administration and in official attitudes toward local autonomy, Tokyo's administrative system has consequences for the development and the functioning of neighborhood-level institutions such as chōkai.

The legal complexities of Tōkyō-to's prefectural government and in particular its relationship with the 23 wards do not require great elaboration here, but a brief explanation may be helpful. National legislation designates the 23 wards as *tokubetsu ku* ("special wards"). Special status brings no benefits; throughout the modern period the national government's special treatment of Tokyo and other large cities "was not to give these cities a greater degree of self-government but to put them under stricter control" (Steiner 1965: 178). The special wards possess far more limited powers than those enjoyed by ordinary cities (shi). In fact they are more tightly controlled than any of the other units under Tōkyō-to's jurisdiction. In short "the special wards . . . have less self-government than the ordinary public entities on the municipal level, that is, cities, towns, and villages" (ibid., p. 149).

The Tokyo Metropolitan Government handles all matters affecting the 23 wards as a group or requiring "comprehensive planning and coordination, uniformity of execution, or technical expertise" (Steiner 1965: 195). Post-Occupation changes in 1952 reduced many of the powers first given the wards only a few years earlier by the original postwar local autonomy law. They were left with only limited rights to administer a specified range of institutions, including elementary and junior high schools, parks, playgrounds, recreational areas, libraries, public halls, and some roads. In principle, other municipal functions may be granted under the prefecture's bylaws, but because the wards lack the independent power of taxation, their ability to carry out additional functions is severely limited. The only tax they can collect under those bylaws is a ward residents' tax, which citizens pay in lieu of a prefectural residents' tax. Even so they must depend on the prefectural government for regular subsidies. Municipal governments elsewhere in Japan may rely on various forms of taxation (such as a local property tax to raise funds for city planning programs); in Tokyo all such taxes are collected by the prefectural government (TMG 1978b: 88).

Special wards exist only in Tokyo. Other large cities, including Yokohama, Kobe, Nagoya, Osaka, and Kyoto, are also divided into ku, or wards, but these do not possess any of the features of self-government that give the special wards of Tokyo at least a limited degree of autonomy. They are merely "jurisdictional areas of the branch offices of the city administration," not legal "local entities like the special wards in Tokyo" (Steiner 1965: 198). On the other hand, thanks to their ordinary municipal governments, residents of those cities possess a greater direct voice in municipal affairs than residents of Tokyo's wards.

Each of Tokyo's 23 wards is governed by an elected unicameral ward assembly (*kugikai*) and an executive branch headed by a *kuchō*, a mayor or chief executive officer. The same legislation of 1952 that limited the wards' functions also deprived residents of the right to elect the kuchō, reversing another of the Occupation reforms. Instead, ward assemblies were to select kuchō, subject to the final approval of Tōkyō-to's governor. The residents' loss of their right to directly elect kuchō set the special wards apart from all other such entities in postwar Japan, creating a bone of contention between Tokyo and the national government that lasted for over 20 years. Finally, with the revision of the national Local Elections Law in 1975, the right of direct election of the kuchō was restored (Shinagawa-ku 1980: 10).

Persistent themes of official antipathy to local autonomy and strong tendencies toward the centralization of control and decision-making run throughout the Japanese system of local administration. These features of Tokyo's present-day administration significantly affect the nature and operations of chōkai in several ways. Functional divisions of responsibilities among many agencies at different levels in the prefectural and ward administrative hierarchies contribute to the sense among chōkai leaders, in Miyamoto-chō at least, that they are inundated by almost constant, yet uncoordinated requests and demands for their cooperation in government projects. But this division of functions also means that the government agencies with which the chōkai has the closest connections and the most influence—those of the ward government—are often powerless to make decisions, to take independent action tailoring programs to local needs, or to solicit residents' views. Lastly, in the postwar years as during the prewar period, the attitude endures at all levels of government that the lower, more local institutions do not exist as autonomous entities: lower levels are seen as existing to serve the needs and meet the demands of the higher strata of administration. Civil servants therefore see chōkai—the lowest institutions to which responsibilities are delegated (despite their legal standing as independent citizens' groups, not arms of the government)—as agents of the government's making and under its control, there to do the government's bidding.

The Ward Office and the Chōkai

Attitudes on both sides of the issue are colored in part by the lingering memories of relations between the government and neighborhood organizations during the Second World War. As we have seen, at the end of the war chōkai, the subordinate household clusters called tonarigumi, and similar institutions had been discredited because of the role they played in the wartime mobilization. As a result local leaders, anxious to maintain an image of their organizations as voluntary groups of local citizens as well as to preserve their associations' autonomy, try to avoid both the appearance and the actuality of close entanglements with the government. Government officials for their part seek to have chōkai and other local groups carry out many aspects of local administration, but frequently have to do so through circuitous means.

Despite the reluctance of chōkai leaders to be seen as agents of the government, liaison with ward offices is today a major part of the responsibilities of Miyamoto-chō's chōkai leaders and occupies much of their time and effort. The closest and most frequent contacts are with the shutchōjo (the ward government's branch office), which is located in the neighborhood. As mentioned in the previous chapter, the ward's system of branch offices was established in the late 1940's to handle rice rationing, but has since expanded its functions to encompass most contacts between the municipal government and local groups.

Connections with the government and cooperation in government programs do not constitute a single, identifiable segment of the chōkai's sphere of responsibilities; interaction with the government pervades its structure, its ethos, and its activities. This diffuse relationship causes continual complaining among chōkai leaders. They grumble that the ward government shifts the burdens of office from paid public servants to unpaid citizen volunteers. They complain that the government's demands on the chōkai strain its human and financial resources. They resent the way in which requests come from many sources with little or no coordination, with little thought of the difficulties they might cause the chōkai, and with little consideration of whether local residents might find the programs and campaigns necessary or desirable.

Many of the government agencies that take an interest in the welfare and well-being of local residents, or in the administration of local affairs, contact the chōkai directly to make their requests and demands. National, prefectural, and ward agencies are all involved; the local office of the national tax agency; the prefectural police, fire, sanitation, public health, and public works departments; and the ward offices concerned with social welfare, education, nutrition, social discrimination, disaster preparedness, building standards, economic development, and housing.

To the government officials who directly contact chōkai leaders, this may appear to be an efficient method of launching programs. But to local leaders who must respond, the uncoordinated system is counterproductive. It often results in what chōkai leaders see as torrents of demands made with little or no thought of the net effects on the neighborhood as a community and the chōkai as an organization. Leaders feel that the resources they and their organizations can command—the time and labor of local residents, and the social capital required to mobilize them—are exploited by the government; occasionally they complain of their lot as the government's *shitauke*, comparing themselves to industrial subcontractors whose one-sided exploitation by prime contractors is a notorious feature of Japanese society.

Although the general direction of communication between government agencies and the chōkai is downward, the chōkai does act as an advocate for local community interests, lobbying the ward government on issues that concern the neighborhood as a whole. The premier example local activists cite when discussing the chōkai's skills and strengths in negotiating with the ward office is getting the traffic bypass built over the river. Here

Miyamoto-chō's success resulted from long and concerted lobbying by chōkai leaders and the use of the neighborhood's political influence through elected officials.

The chōkai will intercede with the authorities on much more
trivial matters as well. One minor problem it solved concerned
the noise and congestion caused by mothers waiting to pick up
their children outside the public nursery school near the shrine.
Neighbors complained among themselves and finally appealed
to the chōkai leaders; the chōkai asked the nursery school to ban
mothers from riding bicycles to deliver and pick up their children, and from waiting (and socializing) in the street outside the
gate. The nursery school agreed and issued the ban. The problem
subsided.

Both upward and downward communications can involve direct contacts with the relevant agencies, but the ward government relies primarily on its branch office as its major interme-
diary with the neighborhood. The branch office, housed in a new
building across the street from the elementary school, serves ten
contiguous neighborhoods (including Miyamoto-chō) with a total population of about 27,000 residents in 11,000 households
(Shinagawa-ku 1979: 54). The branch office handles a wide range
of bureaucratic matters for individual citizens; its 13 officially
designated responsibilities are as follows (ibid., pp. 50–51):

1. Registering and certifying household residence
2. Registering and certifying personal seals (*inkan*)
3. Registering dogs
4. Handling requests for nutritional assistance through the
ward's mother and infant health program
5. Registering residents for rice-rationing purposes (not cur-
rently in force)
6. Accepting tax returns for the ward and prefectural residents' tax
7. Managing the ward-run residents' meeting halls
8. Accepting registration forms and other documents for the
national health insurance plan (Kokumin Kenkō Hoken)
9. Accepting registration forms and other documents for the
national pension plan (Kokumin Nenkin)
10. Sponsoring local activities for young people

11. Providing residents with information about the ward government

12. Conducting surveys on various matters

13. Handling other matters as directed by the kuchō

Although not specifically enumerated among these responsibilities, liaison with neighborhood associations is undoubtedly among the most important of the branch office's functions. Not all requests to chōkai from the ward go through the branch office, but its staff keeps in almost daily contact with local leaders on a wide variety of issues. The branch office's major mechanism for communications with the individual chōkai within its jurisdiction is a federation of the neighborhood associations. The branch office staff holds regular meetings for the chōkai presidents and for other chōkai officers who deal with specific tasks. Through the federation and these meetings, the ward secures chōkai participation in and coordination of public health projects, recreational programs for children, quasi-public charity drives, disaster preparedness campaigns, pesticide sprayings, and many other government efforts, including the annual Kumin Matsuri (Ward Residents' Festival). At these meetings the chief of the branch office and other officials explain ward policies, make requests for cooperation in specific projects, and give at least modest opportunities for chōkai leaders to discuss and perhaps criticize ward plans. However, since these ward officials serve largely as a conduit for requests and declarations made by a disparate array of agencies and offices, the chances that the staff can act on the local leaders' views and objections are slight.

Requests to leaders as individuals—rather than to their organizations—for aid in such things as compiling the biennial national census of businesses and industries or the quinquennial national population census also flow through the branch office. For these censuses and other surveys, local leaders are deputized as official enumerators—complete with badges and identification cards—to gather the information from local residents. As official census takers local leaders swear to maintain the confidentiality of the forms they collect; they are usually assigned to canvass an area some distance from their homes (although within their neighborhood).

The ten neighborhoods in the chōkai federation under the branch office's jurisdiction are grouped together—based on geographic contiguity and compactness—by government decision and for the government's convenience, not because each of the ten is linked to all the others by other ties. The branch office's federation ignores and cuts across other existing constellations of neighborhoods generally seen as significant by the neighborhoods themselves, such as those formed around shrine parishes, elementary school districts, or consortia of merchants' associations covering neighboring shopping areas. Thus, the branch office's federation is but one among several competing institutional frameworks in which interneighborhood coalitions may be formed; the federation does not reinforce the unity or identity of an otherwise existing group of neighborhoods, all of whom cooperate or share common interests along other dimensions of interneighborhood affiliation.

On the contrary, the ten neighborhoods variously belong to three distinct shrine parishes, participate in several separate coalitions of merchant groups, and fall into five elementary and four junior high school districts; each of these parishes, commercial federations, and school districts includes other neighborhoods outside the jurisdiction of the branch office. Miyamoto-chō itself shares its complete inventory of links— through parish, merchant federation, and school districts— with only two other neighborhoods in the branch office's block. With one neighborhood in the block, Miyamoto-chō shares no ties other than their common membership in the branch office's federation. With six other neighborhoods it shares at least one additional strand of affiliation. On the other hand, of the thirteen neighborhoods to which Miyamoto-chō has an institutional tie, only four do not belong to this branch office's block. Miyamoto-chō is thus rather centrally positioned in the network of interneighborhood ties that the branch office coordinates, and there is a relatively large overlap among the various sets of neighborhoods to which it belongs. (See Table 7 and Map 3.)

But other neighborhoods among the ten block members are not so fortunate; some have few if any connections to the other neighborhoods in the group beyond the connection provided by

TABLE 7
Neighborhood Coalitions

Neighborhood[a]	Federation of chōkai under shutchōjo	Shrine parish[b]	Federation of shōtenkai	School districts[c] Elementary	School districts[c] Junior high
Yanagi 1-chōme			x		
Yanagi 2-chōme	x		x[d]		
Yanagi Chūō-chō	x	x	x[d]		x[e]
Yanagi 3-chōme	x	x	x	x	x
Yanagi Miyamoto-chō	x	x	x	x	x
Yanagi 4-chōme	x	x	x[f]	x	x
Uehara 2-chōme	x				
Uehara 3-chōme	x	x			
Uehara 4-chōme	x	x		x	
Uehara 5-chōme	x			x[e]	x
Uehara 6-chōme	x				x[e]
Hirota 4-chōme	x				
Ogawa 6-chōme				x[e]	x[e]
Otani 1-chōme					x

[a] Neighborhood names are those established by chōkai. In most cases chōkai adopt names that reflect the system of *chōme* (blocks used for addresses) even when chōkai-recognized boundaries do not correspond to the ward's chōme system.

[b] The shrine parish corresponds to the old hamlet and is coterminous with the volunteer fire brigade, which forms another institutional strand of interneighborhood alliance. All neighborhoods indicated participate in the shrine's festivals, but there is a further link among Yanagi Miyamoto-chō, Yanagi Chūō-chō, Yanagi 3-chōme, and Yanagi 4-chōme, which coordinate their festival processions.

[c] The schools themselves are major institutional connections among residents of different neighborhoods, as are their corresponding PTAs and alumni clubs.

[d] In addition to the two shopkeepers' associations that represent Yanagi Chūō-chō and Yanagi 2-chōme separately, a third shōtenkai (which also belongs to the federation) straddles the boundary between these neighborhoods and extends into parts of Uehara 2-chōme and Uehara 3-chōme.

[e] Only a part of the neighborhood falls within the school district.

[f] There are two shopkeepers' associations in Yanagi 4-chōme, only one of which is affiliated with the federation of shōtenkai.

the branch office. For these neighborhoods, the overlap between these administrative ties and other affiliations of shrine, school, or commerce is low, and the neighborhoods' attentions are divided among a number of only slightly intersecting coalitions of neighborhoods.

The ward government's federation therefore cuts across clusters of neighborhoods organized around other kinds of links, and this suggests something of the discrepancy between the meaning and importance attached to local units by the ward government on the one hand and by chōkai on the other. These diver-

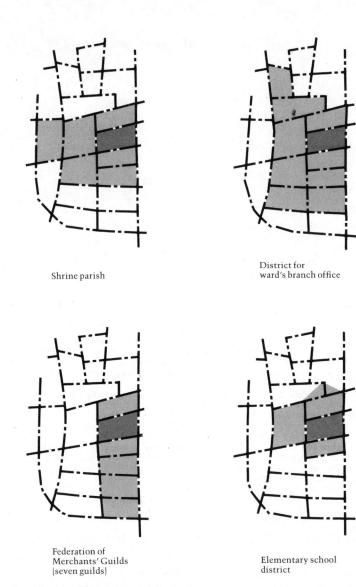

Shrine parish

District for
ward's branch office

Federation of
Merchants' Guilds
(seven guilds)

Elementary school
district

MAP 3. Neighborhood coalitions, 1979–81. The dark-shaded area is
Miyamoto-chō. The chōkai boundaries are shown schematically.

gent views color assessments of the legitimacy both of constellations of chōkai organized around some common interest and of individual neighborhoods themselves. The ward government sees the groupings of the neighborhoods centered on each branch office as the fundamental units, or blocks (*burokku*), on which local social organization should be built or rebuilt (Shinagawa-ku 1978: 25–28). But chōkai consider this government-sponsored federation merely one among several important groupings and federations. Even at the semantic level there is disagreement; the ward government and the branch office refer to the ten chōkai together as a "burokku" under its leadership, whereas the chōkai see themselves as constituting a *"rengō"* (a federation), for which the branch office provides staff support.

Machi-zukuri: The Ward's Community-Building Policies

Disagreement over which sorts of groups constitute the significant units of local life and who legitimately should represent those units is an underlying source of tension in the relationship between the chōkai and the branch office (and hence the ward government). Both administratively and socially the ward's policies seem to have as one goal shifting the focus of local social life to institutions of the government's making, away from chōkai and other "parochial" local organizations. The chōkai leaders accept the administrative roles of the branch office (though they wish that the government would assume more of the responsibility for actually executing its policies, instead of delegating them to unpaid chōkai officials), but they are less sanguine about the social aspects of the ward's policies. Yet chōkai leaders usually do not overtly oppose the government's efforts; their resistance is revealed instead in their attitudes toward the government's role in many essentially nonadministrative activities and events.

A good example of how the chōkai and the branch offices jockey for position as the primary institution of local social life can be seen in the ward's *machi-zukuri* (community-building) policies, a program intended to rejuvenate local community life (Shinagawa-ku 1978: 25–28; 1979: 27–35). These policies are apparently aimed at gradually supplanting the chōkai as the local institution with which residents identify and through which local administration is most effectively carried out (see Falconeri 1976).

In this relatively recent development, the ward's branch offices have expanded their functions beyond coordinating administrative affairs to include the support of community activities centered on the blocks of chōkai in their jurisdictions. As part of this effort they sponsor many essentially social and recreational events for, and nominally organized by, local residents. Leaders of the chōkai under a branch office's jurisdiction serve as members of advisory boards and recruit participants from their neighborhoods, but the planning and the execution of events are done by salaried government employees, who spend considerable time, effort, and tax revenue on them. These events often duplicate those put on by the neighborhoods themselves, but as one would expect, the official ones seem quite spectacular next to anything the unpaid and often harried chōkai leaders can put on for their own separate neighborhoods. In conversations with me, and presumably among themselves, chōkai leaders voiced complaints about being upstaged by the larger and more lavish events the branch office can produce.

One machi-zukuri effort is a recreational program for children. Each summer, as part of its mandate to promote the social welfare of children, the branch office sponsors a one-day "day camp" along the ward's waterfront, where landfill has created a huge artificial island with a large park, an enormous apartment complex, and container-handling facilities for the Tokyo port. At the day camp local children (accompanied by an almost equal number of chōkai and fujinbu officials) play baseball, fish in canals—carefully warned not to eat the catch—and cook a midday meal of curried rice over open campfires. Another activity is a summer field trip to a park or other site of interest in the outskirts. On one of these trips the children visited the cliffs and beaches of the Miura peninsula, a two-hour train ride from Miyamoto-chō. Another summer 100 or so children and a like number of adults spent the day at a park that featured an elaborate obstacle course with log bridges to clamber over, mud to slog in, tunnels to crawl through, walls to scale, and rope swings to negotiate.

Each October 10, on Sports Day (a national holiday), the branch office sponsors an *undōkai*, or athletic field day, for residents of all ages. The undōkai rotates each year among the playgrounds of the three elementary schools within the branch office's territory. Teams from each of the ten chōkai compete with one another; the five adjacent chōkai from Yanagi along the river (including Miyamoto-chō) and the five chōkai from Uehara on the plateau are also grouped together in competition. The day's events feature relay races, throwing contests, three-legged races, and other similar contests. Almost all of the contests are between groups and are designed to reward teamwork rather than individual effort. Everything is carried out with the sort of punctilio that marks many such events in contemporary Japan, including formal opening and closing ceremonies, small children representing the group to take pledges of good sportsmanship, and awards (every participant goes away with a prize, even if only a box of tissues). Marching to and from the undōkai, the residents of each chōkai walk together as a group, following the lead of the chōkai banners; at the playground these banners mark each chōkai's assigned position around the field, where mothers spread out picnic lunches and cheer their kids on.

Activities such as these do not arouse much opposition from local leaders, even when they duplicate (but on a grander scale) neighborhood programs. Events like the Ward Residents' Festival (Kumin Matsuri), however, are real bones of contention. The Kumin Matsuri, first held in the summer of 1979 on a huge ward playing field a few blocks from Miyamoto-chō, is modeled on the customary Bon Odori, or summer folk-dance festivals, held in July or August throughout Japan. For years each neighborhood in the area has staged its own Bon Odori. As a folk-dance festival, the Kumin Matsuri differed from a neighborhood Bon Odori simply in scale, with dance troupes from dozens of neighborhoods performing on a large, multi-tiered drum tower in the center of the field, surrounded by rings of hundreds of residents joining in as the spirit moved them. But in addition to dancing, the first ward-wide festival lavishly featured rides on a miniature steam railroad, children's sumo tournaments, fireworks displays, pony rides, and innumerable other attractions. In a related part of the effort to foster community identification, the ward had commissioned a new "folk song" in 1978—the "Shinagawa Ondo"—with an accompanying "folk dance," and these too were prominently featured at the Kumin Matsuri. The ward

government distributed records of the song, commercially produced by a professional popular singer in an acceptably pseudo-
traditional style, to neighborhood organizations and other
groups throughout the ward, along with printed lyrics and instructions for the dance steps.[8]

Taken together, the scale and extravagance of this first Kumin
Matsuri aroused enough ill-will among local leaders in Miyamoto-chō and elsewhere that the following year each of the
ward's 12 branch offices separately held much scaled-down versions for the neighborhoods they serve. But these events were
still far more elaborate than the neighborhoods' Bon Odori, and
chōkai leaders continued to complain both about the "cooperation" they felt compelled to lend the effort and about the ward
government's unnecessary duplication of events they themselves had been putting on for decades for the enjoyment of
neighborhood residents. Though local leaders still serve on the
advisory panel organized by the branch office to help with planning the Kumin Matsuri, at least for the second annual festival,
Miyamoto-chō and the other nine neighborhoods in the branch
office block withheld some sorts of cooperation, such as lending
their equipment for the event.

Such incidents may appear to be nothing more than trivial examples of the antagonisms that from time to time enter the relationship between chōkai and the branch offices, but given the
ambiguity introduced into that relationship—by the postwar legal disestablishment of the chōkai, and by the machi-zukuri policies that seem intended to overshadow the chōkai in a role their
leaders feel is rightfully theirs—the relationship is ripe for mis-
understanding and conflict. Occasionally dramatic breaks occur.

One came in the mid-1960's, when the ward government (responding to national and prefectural policies) tried to redraw the
boundaries of Miyamoto-chō and other neighborhoods and
amalgamate them into larger units. The ward authorities tried
to couch their case in terms of increasing the efficiency of local
government through such reforms. The drive began a few years
before the 1964 Tokyo Olympics, Japan's first major postwar international showcase event. As part of general campaigns to
spruce up Tokyo for international scrutiny, national, metropol-

itan, and ward officials argued that the old units and street-address system were "feudal," "irrational," and "confusing to foreigners" (Shinagawa-ku n.d.: 1).[9] Their arguments did not impress local leaders. They resisted as best they could, arguing that to combine neighborhoods would vitiate local traditions and destroy the fabric of local social life.

The neighborhoods were not entirely successful in their opposition. The address system was revamped and on maps, at least, the boundaries were redrawn. Up to then the name Miyamoto-chō had not been used. The neighborhood had existed since the early 1940's as Yanagi-chō 5-chōme. Under the government's new scheme, the old fifth and sixth chōme of Yanagi-chō were combined into a new unit called Yanagi 4-chōme (see Map 4).[10]

Local leaders adamantly refused, however, to combine their neighborhood organizations. Miyamoto-chō's chōkai officially changed its name from the Yanagi-chō 5-chōme Chōkai to the Yanagi Miyamoto Chōkai, but to residents of this and surrounding areas the neighborhood is simply Miyamoto-chō and the association is called the Miyamoto-chōkai. When Miyamoto-chō's residents now talk of 4-chōme, they mean the old sixth chōme of Yanagi-chō, whose neighborhood association calls itself the Yanagi 4-chōme Chōkai, not the new 4-chōme (combining the old fifth and sixth chōme) of which Miyamoto-chō is now officially a part. To this day the neighborhood associations and the boundaries they recognize have remained unchanged, a fact that undermines whatever benefits of increased efficiency might have resulted from the reforms. And at this point even the ward government itself generally ignores the new boundaries of its own creation, because to work with the various chōkai and rely on them to carry out its many tasks it has had to accept the boundaries observed by the still-intransigent local leaders.

The government, in its desire for "administrative efficiency," misjudged (or chose to ignore) how important local traditions and community symbols are to the residents of Miyamoto-chō and the surrounding neighborhoods. The subject came up one morning in a casual conversation in the shop of my landlord. Mr. Takahashi, who is something of an amateur local historian, and Mr. Hasegawa, an elderly man with a sometimes intimidating

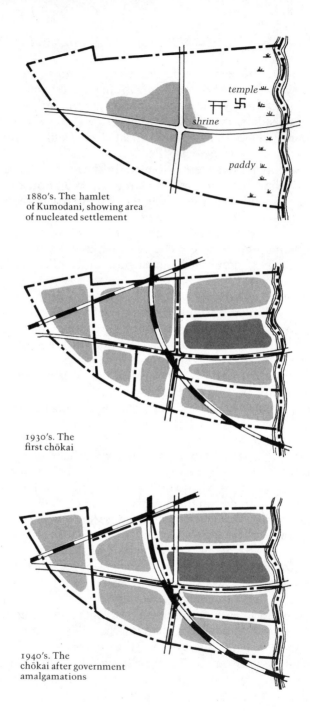

1880's. The hamlet
of Kumodani, showing area
of nucleated settlement

temple

shrine

paddy

1930's. The
first chōkai

1940's. The
chōkai after government
amalgamations

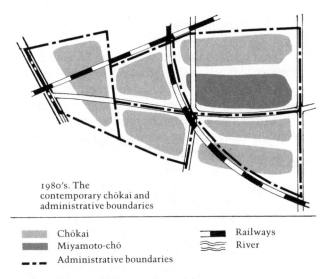

1980's. The
contemporary chōkai and
administrative boundaries

Chōkai   Railways
Miyamoto-chō   River
Administrative boundaries

MAP 4. Neighborhoods and administrative boundaries from the 1880's to the 1980's. All boundaries are shown schematically.

air who is as close to being a *yūryokusha* (a "local boss") as anyone in Miyamoto-chō, explained the neighborhood's resistance as a means of preserving the distinct traditions and different ways of doing things in the communities affected by the proposed merger. Each neighborhood prides itself on its customary ways of organizing local activities—their methods of collecting donations for the annual festival, the relationship that has been established between their chōkai and their shōtenkai, the ways they select representatives from each *kumi* (household cluster, a unit that we will return to in Chapter Five). The leaders of each chōkai felt (and continue to feel) that their methods are best suited to the needs of their own neighborhood and to their community's unique traditions and identity. No one was willing to compromise or to give these up.

Furthermore, the property owned by each of the neighborhoods was at issue. Not only were such objects as mikoshi (portable shrines) involved, but in Miyamoto-chō there was the neighborhood hall, at the time the only one in the area. In the eyes of the Miyamoto-chō leaders, sharing ownership of what was at best a tumbledown building was not the real issue; the issue was relinquishing a crucial symbol of Miyamoto-chō's recent history and of the development of its spirit of community identity.

The hall dated back to the last year of the Second World War, when the households along the railway line were forced to raze their homes for the government-ordered firebreak. Built on land leased from the Buddhist temple, it was constructed from the roof tiles and lumber salvaged by the men and boys from the chō-kai who helped dismantle those homes. Even in the 1960's it was an aging relic; compared with halls built in recent years by adjacent neighborhoods, Miyamoto-chō's was very small and ill-equipped. Nevertheless, it was the center of community activity, and for residents Mr. Takahashi's age or older, it was an important symbol of the neighborhood as a community. This symbolism, more than the building itself, was what Miyamoto-chō had no desire to share with the partner proposed for merger. Opinions about the neighborhood hall changed in subsequent years, and one faction of local leaders (including Mr. Takahashi) came to favor building a modern hall with more space, providing room for ground-floor shops and third-floor apartments that would generate needed income for the chōkai.[11]

Yet the point remains; the neighborhood consistently seeks to preserve its sense of autonomy in the face of government efforts to merge what are seen as "parochial" loyalties into a more "modern" sense of citizenship focused on institutions of the government's own making. Furthermore, the neighborhood seeks to preserve its autonomy through conscious appeals to its own unique traditions and the manipulation of symbols that imply the legitimacy of this tradition.

As the next chapter will show, these efforts paradoxically are most apparent in the projects the chōkai undertakes within the neighborhood, mainly at the request of the ward government itself. But the chōkai's self-consciously traditional activities and its goals of identity and autonomy must be understood against the backdrop of the sometimes strained relationship between the neighborhood and the ward government, as well as against Miyamoto-chō's perception of itself as an informal but nonetheless effective political bloc.

The sociologist Hachiro Nakamura (1980a) has criticized the concern with *komyuniti* ("community") and machi-zukuri that became popular in policy-making circles in the early 1970's. The policies to which this concern gave rise, he feels, are based on misconceived stereotypes that portray chōkai and other traditional community organizations as undesirable and "feudal." Furthermore, he argues, those policies assume that urbanization inevitably leads to forms of social breakdown that must be reversed through government-inspired community-building campaigns. Such policies fail to recognize the positive contributions made by chōkai and similar organizations to creating and maintaining the fabric of local social life. In a related vein the sociologist Susumu Kurasawa has commented that government community-building policies would better bolster community life if they supported the construction of more *sentō* (public baths) and fewer "community *sentaa*" (community centers or auditorium complexes, frequently built on a lavish scale). In other words the government should encourage the informal institutions that have always sustained community life.[12] Many residents of Miyamoto-chō would agree with Kurasawa; the jockeying between neighborhood and ward government over the independence and autonomy of the neighborhood (and the community's resistance to the plans of presumably well-meaning bureaucrats) are at the root of Miyamoto-chō's efforts to sustain its self-identity through the activities of its chōkai.

CHAPTER FOUR

Community Services and Neighborhood Events

THE SLIGHT MORNING CHILL of what will soon become a hot Sunday in July nips a sleepy group of men standing outside Yamamura's construction office. Ku-chan the carpenter quietly nurses a hangover and puffs on a cigarette. Mr. Kitayama, who runs a kimono-dyeing workshop, swaps jokes with Narita-sensei, the master of the abacus academy. Mr. Kataoka, the chō-kai president, stands ignoring Mr. Meguro, the young owner of a tiny dry-cleaning shop whose obvious wish to be accepted as a neighborhood leader makes him a target for good-natured ribbing in public and mild belittlement behind his back. A dozen men await Tsurumi-sensei, the local politician, and Mr. Nomura, a government employee who lives up by the tracks; the two of them have gone to the municipal office to pick up a couple of gasoline-powered compressors used for pesticide spraying.

The men are gathered for the least pleasant job the chōkai undertakes. One Sunday each month from late spring through early autumn, the chōkai's public health and sanitation division sprays the entire neighborhood with pesticides to control mosquitoes and other insects. The dozen or so men who regularly turn out wonder among themselves why they do it; they are probably driven more by peer-group pressure than anything else, and by a perverse sense of pride that comes with the realization that if they do not do the job, no one else will.

With a throaty, stuttering roar, the compressors turn over, and the men set off in two groups, one headed for kami ("uphill"), and the other for shimo ("downhill"). Each compressor is mounted on a small handcart, along with a tank that holds about 50 liters of pesticide mix. Mr. Kitano, a jack-of-all-trades craftsman, has fashioned a couple of large sheet-metal funnels that attach to the compressors, enabling the crew to add pesticide and water without getting drenched. Half a dozen men accompany each compressor, to handle the two 15-meter spraying hoses, to maneuver the carts through tight places, to fetch and carry water, to pour pesticide concentrate, to grumble together about what a lousy way this is to spend a Sunday morning. It is a hot, sweaty, smelly, muddy job. Men wear their oldest work clothes, and swathe their heads with cotton towels. Up and down the back alleys they trudge, pausing every few minutes for a cigarette break or to refill the tank.

For hours they slog along, spraying every manhole cover and drain pipe, every shrub and potted plant, every shuttered storage shed and dank cul-de-sac. The crews carefully cover every corner of the neighborhood. If they did not, leaders comment rhetorically, skipped households would complain that they were missing out on chōkai services and would question why they pay their chōkai dues. At the old wells behind Mrs. Maki's snack bar, next to the Tsunodas' shop, and across from the police box, the men stop long enough to pump up a tankful of water and mix more spray. As the roaring compressors wreathed in a foul white mist approach, some housewives react with alarm, quickly bringing in the hanging wash and slamming their shutters; others run into the alley urging the work crew to pay special attention to their potted azaleas or asking for a few cups of pesticide to sprinkle inside. None ever volunteers to do more than get the crew a bucket of water or move a bicycle blocking a path. And strangely, on those Sundays the spraying crew works, Miyamoto-chō is almost devoid of other able-bodied adult males. The pesticide crews continue their rounds encountering few offers of assistance. Since it is always difficult to recruit crew members, the work falls on the inner circles of the chōkai leaders; as in all chōkai tasks the participants receive no pay.

By the early afternoon both crews have completed their areas.

They meet back at Yamamura's office to hose off the equipment. A pair takes the machinery back to the ward office; the others return home to shower and change. A few minutes later all gather at the chōkai hall for a meal. The chōkai budget pays for a modest spread, but donations from individual householders make it a small banquet. Mrs. Endo, a schoolteacher living near the shrine who always directs the sprayers into her tiny garden, may call the Watanabes' sushi shop to have a large platter delivered for the men's lunch; Mr. Fukutake, the owner of the Chinese restaurant across from the chōkai hall, may bring over a huge platter of fried noodles; Mrs. Sakuma, with the large trellis of morning glories, may ask Yokokawa-ya, the liquor store, to send over half a case of beer; the Inoguchi household up by the elementary school may leave on their doorstep a *daruma*, a bottle of scotch.[1] After a couple of hours of eating, drinking, and talking local politics, the crew splits up to return home to watch television, to nap, to while away the few remaining hours of Sunday afternoon.

Miyamoto-chō's political roles—as a voting bloc usually capable of electing one of its own to the municipal assembly and as a quasi-official administrative unit, recognized and utilized by the ward government—are key elements in the neighborhood's self-definition. But activities such as the pesticide spraying give real life to the neighborhood as something that exists apart from its political or administrative persona. Through the pesticide spraying and a dozen similar projects, the neighborhood can provide some of its own services, more or less on its own terms. The chōkai's ability to offer such services is seen by both leaders and ordinary residents as a measure of its worth and of the neighborhood's integrity as a self-sustaining social unit. In addition to the instrumental ends that such services may meet, the organizational efforts they require add to Miyamoto-chō's inventory of interlocking social ties, and the activities themselves offer ample opportunities for creating or elaborating the symbolism of neighborhood identity.

Of course, Miyamoto-chō's residents and leaders recognize the neighborhood's political and administrative roles as important. For government officials who deal with Miyamoto-chō,

The shopping street, ca. 1950

Shopping street storefronts, late 1970's

Top: The urban landscape

Middle: The women's dance troupe

Bottom: A backstreet in *shimo*

The volunteer fire
brigade on New Year's
Eve, 1980

Summertime pesticide
spraying near the shrine

Chōkai leaders at the shrine, ca. 1935

The children's *mikoshi* charging a liquor store

Festival contributions
posted outside the
chōkai hall

Miyamoto-chō's new *mikoshi*

these roles *are* the fundamental features of this or any other neighborhood. And for many political scientists and sociologists who contemplate the nature of urban Japanese neighborhoods, the political and administrative roles of chōkai are the bedrock of a community's existence, creating both its form and its content. Without the government's active promotion of chōkai as administrative devices, and without the territorially organized political impulses of shopkeepers and other local elites of the old middle class, neighborhoods as any form of community—as any systematic structuring of local social or political organization—would simply not exist. Or so this point of view would have one believe.

Undeniably, it is in great measure because of these political and administrative roles that the something called Miyamoto-chō exists, in the eyes of the wider world and even in the eyes of many of its residents. These roles do create an identifiable unit and a convenient set of geographical and social boundaries that delimit Miyamoto-chō. Yet Miyamoto-chō is more than simply the sum of these roles and boundaries. Even as the neighborhood carries out projects and activities to further its political ends or to fulfill government requirements, it provides services to residents, elaborates ties among them, and promotes a sense of identity—all of which confirm to local activists their view that the chōkai and other local groups are organizations of, by, and for the people of Miyamoto-chō.

In this chapter I focus on the community services and neighborhood events that local organizations sponsor, in particular on those activities that punctuate the flow of daily life as major but only periodically undertaken responsibilities. The chōkai delivers most of these services and organizes most of these events, but the women's auxiliary, the old people's club, the merchants' association, and the volunteer fire brigade take charge of some. (The formally sponsored projects and programs by no means exhaust the repertory of local community services. Many community goals are met through the informal, almost unselfconscious cooperation of individual residents; those aspects of community service are discussed in Chapter Six.)

Many community services and local events are mandated by

government agencies, but others are purely neighborhood matters; in either case the chōkai and other groups pursue their own
goals. Although the chōkai's ends may coincide with the government's, to Miyamoto-chō's activists the two sets of goals are
conceptually independent. The neighborhood agenda is to provide necessary services and at the same time to promote a spirit
of local sociability and cooperation, elaborate the neighborhood's sense of identity, and maintain Miyamoto-chō's sense of
communal autonomy, separate from and not controlled by the
actions and policies of the ward government. In furthering these
goals, neighborhood projects—even the most mundane services, such as providing minimal protection against crime and
fire or promoting public sanitation—can come to be viewed as
proof of Miyamoto-chō's heritage of communal cooperation and
self-sufficiency, an image of local organizational life that is en-
hanced by the aura of "tradition" that often hovers around neighborhood activity.

The Chōkai's Community Services

The chōkai's constitution—written in 1966 and similar to
the constitutions of neighborhood associations throughout the
ward—outlines the association's aims and its intended activities to meet those goals (see Appendix B for the text). The two
pertinent articles are worth quoting in full:

ARTICLE FOUR: This association shall be dedicated to contributing to the advancement of the public good through neighborly cooperation for mutual aid, self-government, crime prevention, and fire prevention.

ARTICLE FIVE: To fulfill the goals set forth in the preceding
article, the association shall act upon the following matters:
  1. Fire and crime prevention
  2. Traffic safety
  3. Public health and sanitation
  4. Festivals and support for the local tutelary deity
  5. Activities for women and youth
  6. Expressions of condolence
  7. Other issues that may become important

The constitution provides no details on how these goals are to be met. It also ignores some areas of activity that now occupy a major place among chōkai programs: maintaining liaison with the ward government, encouraging awareness of earthquake dangers, creating local channels for disseminating information, and sponsoring recreational activities. The constitution also omits, of course, the narrower goals of such local groups as the shopkeepers' association. Several important neighborhood activities and functions—some mentioned in the constitution and others not—actually take place outside the organizational framework of the chōkai or other local groups. Abstract aims such as encouraging mutual aid, promoting social welfare, and maintaining social order are often met largely through the informal interactions and ties among neighborhood residents. And some activities, such as the neighborhood's annual festival and other religious matters, are not a part of the chōkai's ordinary day-to-day functions. Yet despite its fragmentary and incomplete listing of local activities, the constitution sketches a general picture of the neighborhood association's perception of its official duties and responsibilities.

Many chōkai programs address matters of public safety and health, such as crime and fire prevention, disaster preparedness, traffic safety, and sanitation. These programs reflect the chōkai's concern with maintaining or improving Miyamoto-chō's living environment, but are also strongly stimulated by ward and prefectural government agencies. Frequently the chōkai coordinates its programs with ward, prefectural, and national campaigns, and government offices often provide the chōkai with minor subsidies for a particular event or campaign. But though government agencies may encourage and at times mandate these mundane, utilitarian activities, for the chōkai even the most seemingly instrumental of functions offers much latitude for expressive elaboration, which promotes its standing in the eyes of the residents and adds lustre to the idea of Miyamoto-chō as a community. In short, these programs assume importance for the neighborhood as a means of fostering identity, solidarity, and camaraderie within Miyamoto-chō, quite apart from whatever material ends the activities may serve for local residents or for the government.

Crime and Fire Prevention

Crime and fire prevention is the major item on the chōkai's agenda. During the period between the official abolition of chō- kai and similar organizations by the Occupation forces in 1947 and the mid-1950's, when chōkai once again began to function openly, the chōkai of Miyamoto-chō existed as a "Crime Pre- vention Association." Though, in recent years at least, the main responsibility for these matters falls to police and fire depart- ments and the volunteer fire brigade, the chōkai and other local groups still play a role by helping to maintain public safety and local stability, and by establishing an atmosphere of trust and cooperation between the police and fire departments and the lo- cal community. Crime and fire prevention, as a major focus of chōkai activity, inevitably also provides opportunities for ex- pressing and developing symbolic values of communal solidar- ity that institutionally bolster the chōkai's standing and pro- mote the neighborhood's sense of identity.

Crime Prevention

As its major current contribution to crime prevention, the chōkai maintains streetlights on dark back paths and alleys. For these *bōhantō* (anticrime lights), the chōkai receives a modest subsidy from the ward to partially defray the monthly electricity bills and other costs of upkeep. The ward government erected and maintains streetlights along the paved roads, and the shō- tenkai takes care of the fancy fixtures along the shopping street; the chōkai is responsible only for the 50 or so light poles along the narrow unpaved paths. Because the chōkai's crime preven- tion program consists of little more than inspecting and repair- ing the lights, Mr. Yamamura, a local electrical contractor, has headed the anticrime division for a decade or so.

In addition to maintaining the lights the chōkai cooperates with the police by distributing public service announcements— notices warning people to lock their doors or asking them to call a special hotline if they observe gang violence. This is often done as part of the national campaigns that the police sponsor several times a year to focus public awareness on some particular social or criminal problem. Occasionally police representatives appear at special chōkai meetings to make similar pleas personally.

The police rely on the chōkai as a convenient medium for communicating with local residents, and they hope for the cooperation of citizens on an individual basis. They make no overt efforts, however, to co-opt the chōkai into serving as a police auxiliary, whether by apprehending suspects, enforcing laws, observing the behavior of local residents, or attempting to maintain local order. Most local residents would of course use the *kōban* (local police box) to report anything suspicious or illegal, but they would be acting as concerned citizens rather than as chōkai members or officers.[2]

One obvious reason for the chōkai's low level of activity in this domain is that, like most of Tokyo, Miyamoto-chō is almost crime free.[3] The only crime of any consequence that occurred in the neighborhood during my two years of fieldwork was an arson case, a fire in the teachers' office at the local junior high school that was apparently set by a disgruntled student. The arson shocked the neighborhood and was the subject of gossip and speculation for days, but for residents it was only indirectly a neighborhood matter. Although the school stands in the center of Miyamoto-chō next to the Shintō shrine, residents did not see the crime as a smirch on Miyamoto-chō's reputation, nor did the crime and fire prevention divisions redouble their efforts in the fire's aftermath. To the extent that local opinion assessed blame for the incident, people held the school responsible: the school's night watchman for failing to prevent the arson, and the school's principal for allowing so bad a situation to develop that one of his students could even consider, let alone carry out, such an act. The principal was transferred to another school at the end of the term, and local residents agreed that his career—abruptly and irreversibly—would go no further.

No other crimes worthy of the name occurred in Miyamoto-chō during my research. Occasionally advertising posters were vandalized, and once in a while the shopping street would be the scene of a late-night scuffle between drunks, quickly broken up by the patrons of Mrs. Maki's snack bar and by the sharp tongue of Mrs. Maki herself. The most serious disturbances were the infrequent midnight forays of hot-rod gangs (bōsōzoku). Sometimes on a hot summer night a pack of between 10 and 30 young men in small cars or on motorcycles and mopeds—none with mufflers—would suddenly appear, storming down the street, yelling and waving the banners of their car clubs. In a large circuit of Miyamoto-chō and the surrounding neighborhoods, the pack would race down the entire two kilometers of the shopping street and then return up the paved-over river. Through several circuits, the roar of their vehicles rising and receding in the distance would be followed by the sirens of police cars attempting to head them off, until the police succeeded in intercepting them or the gang dispersed. Although noisy and offensive to most residents for their disrespect of the police, of traffic laws, and of social mores in general, the bōsōzoku who roared through Miyamoto-chō seemed harmless and to my knowledge caused no injuries or damage.

Fire Prevention

Fire represents an ever-present danger to all of Miyamoto-chō's residents, whose densely packed homes are built almost entirely of wood. Indeed, fires have been so constant a scourge in Japanese urban life that they were once known as *Edo no hana* ("the flowers of Edo"). But romantic bravado notwithstanding, in a wooden city fire is a horrifying danger. Many Miyamoto-chō residents lived through, lost relatives in, and vividly recall the fires that devastated Tokyo in the wake of the two great disasters of this century, the Kantō earthquake of 1923 and the American bombings of 1944–45.[4]

The danger is greatest during winter months, when the use of portable gas, kerosene, and electric heaters in homes and apartments built of wood, their interiors filled with tatami mats and paper partitions, creates the potential for disaster. Almost nightly during those months fire sirens can be heard somewhere in the distance, and once or twice a winter a fire breaks out in Miyamoto-chō or an adjacent neighborhood. No matter the time of night, the streets quickly fill with residents. Some are merely fire buffs, but most residents tumble out of their futon with serious purpose. Though the professional fire department arrives on the scene in a matter of minutes, fires can spread quickly and far in tightly packed neighborhoods such as these. People who live near the fire may have to help less fortunate neighbors evacuate their threatened homes, take in friends and neighbors for the night, or flee their own homes on short notice. News about the extent, the cause, and the extinguishing of a fire travels quickly, and the clusters of residents dressed in their night-clothes who gather on street corners blocks away quickly form opinions about the nature of the problem, the cost of the damage, and the culpability of the structure's occupants, all without having to visit the scene of the blaze itself.

The primary responsibility for firefighting of course falls on the professional, highly trained, and well-equipped prefectural fire department, which responds promptly and efficiently to all alarms. The volunteer fire brigade—the *shōbōdan*—assists. But the relationship embodies respect and deference for each other's areas of expertise. The professionals know they must depend on the volunteers to direct them to underground cisterns and wells hidden in the warren of back-street wooden homes. Equally, only the volunteers can direct the professionals to the homes of the elderly and the bedridden, or alert them to the tiny work-shops and factories that may contain highly flammable paints, oils, or gases. The professionals acknowledge their respect for the volunteers' skills (at the same time instilling esprit de corps among brigade members) by taking the brigade seriously; at drills and reviews throughout the year, brigade members are put through many of the same paramilitary maneuvers that the firemen go through and are expected to comport themselves with professionalism when donning the uniform of the shōbōdan.

The shōbōdan draws its members from throughout what was once the old hamlet of Kumodani, now the shrine parish encompassing Miyamoto-chō and six other neighborhoods. About half a dozen members live in Miyamoto-chō, nominated to the unit by the chōkai and other local groups. Shōbōdan duty is inconvenient, hard, and sometimes dangerous, but members feel it is a great honor and important community responsibility. Not surprisingly, given the prestige of the job, members are not young men, but middle-aged men chosen for their community-mindedness (though of course physical vigor is important as well).

Among the Miyamoto-chō members is the engineer Mr. Asa-numa. He is unusual among Miyamoto-chō's white-collar males in being willing (and able) to devote much of his free time to neighborhood service. In addition to belonging to the fire brigade, he can be counted on to pitch in whenever the chōkai needs an extra hand or a bit of mechanical engineering skill. Mr. Hirota, the quiet and somewhat brooding tradesman who is a member of the inner circle of chōkai leaders, also serves as a volunteer. On the other hand, Mr. Urata, who with his adult son runs a trucking service, is well respected in Miyamoto-chō as an active member of the volunteer fire brigade, but plays almost no role in chōkai affairs. Motofuji-sensei, Tsurumi-sensei's predecessor in the ward assembly, is the senior member of the Miyamoto-chō contingent. Although far past the age when he can lift a hose or pull a cart, he holds a high honorary rank in recognition of his many years of service. When a fire is being fought, the captain of the professional squad seems invariably to consult closely with Motofuji-sensei, probably out of a mixture of deferential courtesy and respect for his unsurpassed knowledge of the local terrain.

In principle members of the brigade must turn out for fires within about half a kilometer's radius of their homes, but in practice they are permitted to miss some, since they cannot be expected to be on constant call. They are trained in first aid and basic firefighting techniques. The brigade's major piece of equipment is a gasoline-powered pumper mounted on a hand-cart that can be pulled by two or three men. It is stored next to the elementary school in a shed that was built in 1981 to replace a tiny wooden hut in one corner of the temple precincts behind the chōkai hall.

In general the volunteer fire brigade helps with crowd control and lends the professional firefighters and police officers its intimate knowledge of the neighborhood. The brigade members not only know all the twisting back paths; they know who's who, and can help the police prevent looting or apprehend arson suspects by pointing out unfamiliar faces among the bystanders. And since most water for fighting fires comes from old wells and cisterns rather than hydrants, their help in directing firefighters to such sources is crucial.

The volunteer fire brigade also plays a symbolic role in the community. Among all local organizations it alone can trace a connection back to the days of the old hamlet. The area covered by the brigade corresponds to that of the shrine parish, and monuments dedicated to or by the fire brigade dot the shrine's grounds. When a festival or some other special event is held there, the fire brigade sends a uniformed honor guard. Solemn occasions call for paramilitary khaki twill, but for more light-hearted events the members wear heavy cotton *happi* or *hanten*, the coats customarily worn by construction workers and the firefighters of Edo.

The Fire Watch

The chōkai plays no direct part in fighting fires: its role is limited generally to informational and educational efforts—often largely symbolic. Through it the fire department distributes notices—how to prevent fire hazards, how to fight fires in the home, and what emergency equipment no home should be without—to the kumi, and for the chōkai's bulletin boards. The chōkai also allows the fire department to use its hall to present films on fire prevention and earthquake precautions in the home. Several dozen housewives and chōkai leaders attend the films and stay for question-and-answer sessions with two or three firefighters. The information distributed often seems simplistic and the presentations heavy-handed, but the national campaigns of which they form a part appear to be very effective in keeping public awareness of fire and earthquake dangers at a high level.

The chōkai sponsors fire-watch patrols that are nominally intended to aid in heightening this public awareness and to inspect the neighborhood for potential hazards. The patrols, however, are largely symbolic: they reflect a carefully nurtured aspect of "traditional" community life more than they represent a pragmatic strategy for fire prevention. The fire watch is conducted only on the last two days of the year and is seen as a customary part of the preparations and events leading up to O-Shōgatsu—the New Year, Japan's most important holiday.

Around eight in the evening on December 30 and December

31, men of the chōkai, mostly younger leaders or would-be leaders, gather at the chōkai hall, which for the occasion has a large sign hanging on the door proclaiming it the Yanagi Miyamoto-chō Guard Headquarters. Inside they sip tea as they huddle around a gas stove in the otherwise unheated building, waiting for enough members to show up to begin the patrols. When 10 or 12 men have appeared, they divide into two teams and agree on which group will patrol kami and which shimo, the upper and lower halves of the neighborhood. Narita-sensei, the former chōkai president and current leader of the fire-prevention division, stays at the hall to receive any visitors who might drop by to pay their respects, and with him remain a couple of other men who can serve as messengers to contact the two patrols in the unlikely event some emergency arises.

In their groups of five or six, the men set out carrying powerful flashlights and candle-lit paper lanterns. The lanterns do nothing to dispel the gloom, but they are emblematic of official chōkai activity; chōkai leaders carry and display them on this and other official occasions. One member of each group carries a pair of wooden clappers joined by a long cord looped behind his neck. The wooden clappers are a crucial part of the patrol. Every few yards the bearer of the clappers beats out a distinctive and customary rhythm—CLAP! CLAP! clap-clap!—and calls out in a deep, long-drawn-out voice, "*Hi no yōjin*," "Take care with fire!"

For many residents the rhythmic clapping and the cry are as important a part of the holiday feeling as the sounds of Christmas carols are for most Americans. My first winter in Miyamoto-chō I joined the patrol on its rounds. With Mr. Izumi, Mr. Yamamura, Tsurumi-sensei, my landlord Mr. Takahashi and his seven-year-old son, Akira-kun, and two or three others, I trudged the dark, cold alleys of Miyamoto-chō. At some point during the evening the wooden clappers were passed into my hands. For a block or two I took charge of beating out the rhythm and sounding the cry. A simple task, and having listened carefully to the deep bass of Mr. Izumi and the others all evening, I was confident that I could duplicate both the rhythm and the cry in passable fashion. All went well, and after 10 or 12 minutes I passed the clappers on to someone else. Not until the next day did I begin to hear that people in one small area of the neighborhood had been puzzled the evening before because the rhythm had been distinctly off; I had made the half-beat pause between the last two staccato claps too short, and to the ears of those who were listening for the familiar rhythm it was all wrong. My companions in the patrol, of course, had been too polite to point out my mistake at the time, but by the following evening it had become an amusing anecdote for them to pass around the chōkai hall as they rested between patrols.

On cold winter nights, particularly just before the New Year, the streets are almost deserted; the patrols meet only a few pedestrians staggering home from *bōnenkai* (lit., "forgetting-the-year parties"). As the patrols walk the boundaries of Miyamoto-chō, they often meet a patrol from an adjoining neighborhood and pause to shout quick greetings and commiserate about the cold.

Once in a while they cross paths with groups sent out by the volunteer fire brigade, which patrols throughout the shrine parish's seven neighborhoods. As our patrol passes the fire brigade's shed on the corner of the school grounds, the men of the two groups banter back and forth. Of course several chōkai stalwarts from Miyamoto-chō also belong to the brigade, like Mr. Asanuma, the engineer, and Mr. Hirota, the tradesman, who on this evening have chosen to put service to the fire brigade above the camaraderie of the neighborhood association. Members of the fire brigade—officially commissioned by the fire department—cannot take a drink on duty, but members of the chōkai's patrol are free to warm themselves with *sake* between circuits; much of the joking between the groups consists of mock offers of a drink and equally mock outrage that anyone would think of such a thing.

As the Miyamoto-chō group passes the police box, the officers on duty salute the patrol and formally thank them for their trouble.

The patrols go down every path and alleyway, crying out warnings of the dangers of fire and the need for people to lock their doors at night. They check each of the chōkai's four dozen streetlights for burned-out bulbs and loose connections. In a pattern repeated in many other chōkai activities, the patrols carefully trace their way through all corners of the neighbor-hood—and not merely to be thorough in their inspections. By patrolling all the neighborhood's outer boundaries and thread-ing through all its paths and alleys, the fire-watch patrols sym-bolically maintain and reaffirm the integrity of those boundaries and the communal unity of those who live within them. Mr. Ki-tano, the jack-of-all-trades craftsman, reiterated these seem-ingly abstract sociological points to me several times as we walked shivering down the back alleys to the most obscure cor-ners of Miyamoto-chō.

Two or three times on the patrol's rounds a shutter opens noisily, and a householder beckons them over for some quick re-freshment. At the Ikeda home, Mrs. Ikeda, a cheerful woman who with her husband—a retired government official—takes charge of liaison between the chōkai and the residents of their corner of the neighborhood, produces steaming lacquered bowls of thick, sweet redbean soup. The patrol members accept this holiday delicacy politely and drain the bowls quickly, but they are much more pleased when several blocks away, at the Naka-jima house, Grandfather suddenly hails them and thrusts at them a tray with half a dozen large tumblers of hot *sake*.

One round of either kami or shimo takes a patrol about an hour, and the two groups arrive back at the hall at about the same time. One or two other men, unable to make it for the patrols' first circuit of the evening, await their return. With them are Motofuji-sensei, the elderly retired politician, who on this cold night has forsaken the volunteer fire brigade to stay in the warmth of the chōkai hall, and Mr. Mizuno, the head of the shop-keepers' association, who have come by to express their thanks to the patrol members. As the men return they compare notes on burned-out streetlights, on which other patrols they encoun-tered, and on which homes were passing out *sake*. For an hour or so they sit around and talk, drinking *sake* and whiskey and munching snacks the leader of the fire-prevention division, Narita-sensei, brought from home. At some point during the two nights of patrols, moderately high-ranking officers from the local headquarters of the police and fire departments will drop by to thank the men formally for their efforts and to leave some small gift of appreciation, such as a box of cakes or crackers.

After warming themselves and relaxing, the patrols set out for their second and final circuit of the evening. The two groups trade routes, so that during an evening each patrols the entire neighborhood. The patrols follow the same routines on both nights, the only notable difference being that on December 31 the men are clearly much preoccupied with the traditions of New Year's Eve.

Some traditions are creations of the age of mass communications—the New Year's Eve broadcasts of the song-of-the-year contest and the Kōhaku Uta Gassen, a competition between teams of the year's leading male and female stars of *kayōkyoku* (a genre of popular music). These contests routinely capture most of the national television and radio audience, and their outcome is the subject of small talk for days beforehand. As the patrols make their rounds, Ku-chan the carpenter listens through an earphone to a pocket radio to keep the other members abreast of the happenings. When the patrol arrives back at the chōkai hall, Mr. Yamamura brings a color television set out of his father's appliance shop so the men can watch the shows as they eat and drink between patrols. The detailed level of knowledge almost all adults possess about the careers of popular television stars and recording artists ensures that the men's banter about the shows rarely lapses. When the programs drag a bit, however, local politics offers itself as a topic sure to keep a lively discussion going; it was at one such late New Year's Eve session that I got my first inkling that behind-the-scenes discussions, or *nemawashi*, and even covert campaigning had begun in earnest over the election of a new chōkai president—an event almost five months away.

But the modern "traditions" of New Year have by no means displaced more venerable ones. At the end of the second patrol, around 11:00 or 11:30, an apprentice from Kato's noodle shop delivers large bowls of *toshikoshi soba*, the extra-long noodles one should eat at the New Year for good fortune during the coming year. The noodles eaten, the men formally exchange New Year's greetings and hurry off to their homes for whatever private rituals their households observe at the juncture between one year and the next. Mr. Izumi rushes home to change into formal kimono to exchange greetings, prayers, and cups of *sake* with the members of his family, following established household customs that (according to Mr. Izumi) have been observed for generations.

At the Tsunoda house the family gathers to put up a special amulet to ensure the prosperity of their rice shop during the coming year. Grandfather Tsunoda purchases the amulets each year at a distant shrine, but no one in the family really knows much about them, and everyone crowds around the instruction sheet trying to decide where the amulet should be mounted this year (for its ideal position varies from year to year, according to arcane principles of geomancy and formulas that take into account the family's fortunes during the previous year, all of which are outlined in the amulet's instructions).

The members of the fire patrol cannot afford to linger long over these family observances, however. Changing hurriedly out of their domestic finery, they regroup within a matter of minutes at the Shintō shrine, where as befits the patrol from the *mi-yamoto*—the seat of the shrine—they informally take charge of crowd control, oversee the festivities, and show the chōkai's colors by hanging its official lanterns in prominent places on the stone *komainu* (dogs) that guard the approaches to the shrine.

Miyamoto-chō's patrol exchanges greetings with officials of neighboring chōkai and members of the volunteer fire brigade, who have also come a bit early. It is not long before about 200 parishioners have queued up, and some of the patrol members keep them in line, while others help ready the bonfire that will be ignited at midnight. For several days beforehand, parishioners have brought to the shrine the year's accumulation of ritual paraphernalia from their households: ornaments from their household shrines, amulets purchased from this and other shrines during the preceding year, last year's New Year's decorations, and charms such as Daruma figures on which both eyes have been painted, signifying the accomplishment of a wish or goal. Amulets and other ritual objects retain their efficacy only for a given year, and so all will be set ablaze under the shrine's supervision precisely at midnight.

At the stroke of midnight signaled by the final toll of a distant temple bell completing *joya no kane*, a sequence of 108 peals, the crowd surges forward, hurling coins at the offering box on the altar, and people struggle up the crowded steps to clap their hands and say a quick prayer. Off to one side of the steps, in a small wooden booth temporarily erected for the occasion, the priest and his wife, son, and daughter-in-law pour each parishioner a small saucerful of *o-miki* (sanctified *sake*), distribute small charms, sell larger, more elaborate amulets, and accept donations to the shrine. Several of Miyamoto-chō's patrol members stand over the fire pit, tossing in armloads of amulets and keeping small children from getting too close. By 1:00 A.M. or so the crowds have largely dispersed, and the bonfire has died down to a few embers. The members of the patrol exchange a final round of greetings and disband, their duties finished for another year.

Disaster Preparedness

In the 1970's, as part of a widespread government effort throughout the Kantō region (centered on Tokyo) to prepare the populace for the inevitable recurrence of a major earthquake like the one that struck Tokyo in 1923, the ward government started to urge local chōkai to form disaster-preparedness teams. The authorities offered financial incentives: one-time grants for equipment and continuing subsidies at the paltry level of 35 yen for each household in the neighborhood. Since concern over the effects of a major earthquake is justifiably widespread, Miyamoto-chō's chōkai was sympathetic with the government's goals, but it resisted forming a team. The leaders objected to the drain on the chōkai's finances that would be entailed, given the meager government subsidies. They also complained about the strain it would put on the chōkai's human resources—on leaders who already feel overburdened with government requests for their participation in campaigns and drives of all sorts, and with the task of repeatedly mobilizing residents in support of the many government-promoted projects.

Miyamoto-chō continued to resist despite years of intense prodding from the ward's disaster-planning office and was among the very last neighborhoods in the ward to agree to the plan. At a chōkai meeting in the spring of 1980, after showing films on earthquake safety, an official from the disaster-planning office (who also happened to be a resident of

Miyamoto-chō) gave an impassioned speech urging the chōkai to form a team as quickly as possible. He ended with an emotional personal plea, explaining what a source of great embarrassment it was to him, as an official responsible for organizing these teams, that his own neighborhood—the place where he had grown up and the neighbors he had known all his life—refused to join in such a manifestly worthwhile program. Bowing to intense lobbying, from this and other official channels, the chōkai leaders finally agreed to establish a team. By September 1—the anniversary of the 1923 earthquake and the date for a myriad of public relations events sponsored by the national, prefectural, and ward governments to heighten awareness of the inevitability of another great quake—Miyamoto-chō had a contingent ready to participate in the ward government's drill and review of neighborhood teams.

The disaster-preparedness campaign's principal goal is to familiarize housewives, and others who remain in the neighborhood most of the time, with what they should do when a major quake hits. The chōkai formed its team by the simple expedient of creating a new suborganization under the chief of the fire-prevention division; most of the members are officials of the women's auxiliary. On September 1, the team members—some two dozen housewives, a half dozen male chōkai officials, and I—held a brief practice session on the fundamentals of bucket brigades and of tossing water at plywood targets (both familiar to many from their civil-defense training as children during the war). We then gathered in front of the volunteer fire brigade's shed at the elementary school grounds, where leaders distributed the equipment supplied by the government: several dozen plastic safety helmets inscribed with the chōkai's name. With the chōkai banner in the lead, and a handcart carrying buckets and other equipment bringing up the rear, the team set out in a group for a public playground a 15-minute walk away.

At the playground government disaster officials had erected rows of canvas awnings, and each of the 30 or 40 teams had its assigned place. The team members spread out plastic sheets, took off their shoes, and positioned themselves to watch demonstrations of firefighting techniques by members of the fire department and teams from the large optical-equipment manufacturing plant next to the playground. After watching these techniques—and sipping tea, nibbling on box lunches, and chatting with one another—the teams from each chōkai were given a chance to show their skills. Under the watchful eyes of fire department officials and a reviewing stand of local dignitaries, the team members attempted to put out small fires with hand-held extinguishers. Pulling the handcarts in a relay race, each team rushed out to pick up "injured" members and transport them back to safety. Using well-honed bucket-brigade techniques, team members attempted to throw water accurately through the cut-out portion of a plywood target as members of the fire department carefully measured the amount of water that actually got through the hole into a collection pan behind.

As these competitions ended the fire department announced its scoring of each team's performance. Officials then made what seemed to be a few closing remarks and abruptly told the large crowd that had gathered to watch to go home: the review was over. Hearing this, the chōkai teams began to pack up their belongings when suddenly, to everyone's surprise, the government officials announced that all the teams should immediately present themselves front and center, in formation, on the field before the reviewing stand.

Reluctantly, the teams complied, lining up in the middle of the shadeless playing field. There they stood as government officials, some of them wearing uniforms similar to those of the fire department, barked commands from the reviewing stand: "Attention!" "Parade rest!" "Form ranks!" Team members and leaders exchanged glances of irritated disbelief as the commands—issued in the impolite imperative forms of address used in elementary school assemblies and in the old Imperial Army—came down from civil servants addressing adult civilians. As the teams stood in formation in the sun, the disaster-preparedness officials launched into a series of speeches commending the day's performance and urging redoubled efforts in the future. The crowd grew increasingly restless, and with each new speaker there were audible groans, a few cries of "enough," and a few defectors from the back ranks. Finally, one perceptive bureaucrat whispered something to the next speaker, who wound things up immediately.

At long last the teams were dismissed. As we walked home, members of Miyamoto-chō's team complained bitterly about the day's experience and about the arrogance of public servants treating concerned citizen-volunteers like conscripts or schoolchildren. Although the ward office successfully cajoled Miyamoto-chō into forming a team, the drill and review showed how badly they bungled in getting willing cooperation. It reconfirmed in the eyes of most chōkai leaders the idea that the government and its requests should be kept at arm's length.

Traffic Safety

Traffic-safety campaigns, like most public services, receive strong backing from government agencies, but as in most things the chōkai agrees to do for or with the government, the neighborhood pursues its own agenda as well as that proposed by the government.

Most organized traffic-safety activities fall into two ten-day periods, one in the autumn and one in the spring, coordinated with nationwide campaigns sponsored by the police. During these periods the chōkai erects an awning in a vacant lot along the shopping street, and chōkai leaders, enlisted for the occasion as traffic observers under the direction of the head of the traffic-safety division, watch the flow of traffic. By encouraging local leaders throughout the nation to sit conspicuously by roadways, the police apparently intend to show potentially errant drivers that the eyes of concerned communities are upon them. It seems to work, for cars do slow perceptibly as their drivers catch sight of the chōkai's outpost.

In addition, during the safety drives, which fall roughly at the beginning of the two terms of the elementary school year, the leaders of the traffic-safety division, along with officials from the PTA, temporarily join the crossing guards posted at major intersections. These guards, all women, are employed by the school, and not only stop traffic for schoolchildren, but also instruct the younger ones in the rudiments of pedestrian safety along the narrow streets.

As in much else, the chōkai leaders have their own ideas about the aim of the traffic-safety campaign. For the full ten-day stretch of the fall 1980 campaign, chōkai traffic spotters kept careful track of the numbers and types of vehicles that passed down the main shopping street, every hour, every day, rain or shine.[5] This information was not compiled out of idle curiosity or to provide me with additional data. The chōkai leaders wanted to document their case for a long-cherished goal: getting the main shopping street's traffic diverted to other routes.

This idea especially appeals to the local merchants, who recognize that the cross-town traffic funneled down the narrow street hinders efforts to develop Miyamoto-chō into a more prosperous shopping district. They look with envy on the good fortune of nearby neighborhoods that are able to block off traffic during high-volume shopping hours to create what are called "pedestrian paradises" or even to permanently close off traffic to create covered shopping arcades. It is hard to imagine that Miyamoto-chō can successfully get all the traffic diverted, but the chōkai and the shopkeepers' association (together with their counterparts in adjacent neighborhoods) hope eventually to convince the authorities that the bypass built over the former river should be turned into a two-way road to carry the burden of cross-town traffic.

Persuading the government to make such a drastic change, which would necessarily involve the entire two-kilometer length of the shopping street and would require the widening of the road over the river, seems a tall order, but hardly an impossible one. Falconeri's study (1976) of a chōkai's disintegration in the face of its inability to shape or participate in decisions affecting traffic flow would suggest otherwise, but in Miyamoto-chō the neighborhood association has a long history of successfully lobbying for a no less important change. The river's diversion underground and the construction of the traffic bypass over it in the early 1970's culminated 20 years of campaigning by the several chōkai and merchants' groups in the neighborhoods lining the stream. The federation of the seven shopkeepers' associations along the entire length of the shopping street was formed in the mid-1950's largely to press this issue. The federation was involved in another successful cause as well, helping to push through a controversial project to build a new railway station at a point where a freight line converted to commuter passenger service crosses the shopping street.[6] But heavy traffic along the shopping street and through the neighborhoods continues to be a major issue for both the federation and the traffic-safety divisions of the affected chōkai.

Less far-reaching matters can also draw attention. The head of the traffic-safety division, Mr. Takeuchi, is the owner of a bicycle sales and repair shop, and is regularly helped by Mr. Shigemori, one of the chōkai vice-presidents, who owns a motorcycle shop. Not surprisingly, under the circumstances, Miyamoto-chō's traffic-safety campaigns feature free bicycle inspections and free adjustments and minor repairs of brakes, horns, and other safety equipment; children receive little lectures about safe riding habits as well. Mr. Takeuchi and his assistants also direct traffic at neighborhood events. When a large sale sponsored by the shopkeepers' group disrupts normal traffic, they guide cars and buses around the crowds. When a festival procession makes its rounds, they steer the mikoshi bearers and try to keep traffic flowing safely. When a funeral is held in Miyamoto-chō, they keep the mourners out of the streets, divert traffic, and clear a path for the hearse.

Recycling

Under the rubric of public health and sanitation, the chōkai co-sponsors an array of services with government agencies. Most are fairly cut-and-dried. The federation of local chōkai organized around the ward's branch office coordinates blood drives, tuberculosis tests, and free examinations by doctors from the government's public health department. With guidance from the prefectural sanitation department, the individual chōkai announce schedules for garbage collection. From time to time the chōkai passes on public health pamphlets and fliers from government agencies to local residents.

Only two programs require much effort. The summertime pesticide spraying is undoubtedly the hardest, dirtiest, and most arduous of any chōkai activity, and among the loudest and most visible. As a santitation and public health strategy, the spraying's long-term effects may be questionable, but in the short term chōkai leaders consider it extremely effective. They see it as one of the chōkai's most useful services, perhaps because both the immediate results and the efforts the leaders make on residents' behalf are so obvious to even the most critical local resident.

The recycling program is equally important to the chōkai and to its women's auxiliary, maybe less for its contribution to local health and sanitation than for its contribution to the organization's finances. In 1979–80 recycling brought in a total of 252,000 yen, equivalent to 15 percent of the chōkai's annual budget. But this income is not used for the chōkai's yearly expenses; one-quarter goes to the women's auxiliary, since it is the housewives who must make the recycling program work, and the remaining money sits in a special reserve fund. (See Appendix B for the chōkai's financial statement.)

Because of the money it brings, because of the obvious (and correct) image of doing good for the community it spreads, and (one might cynically note) because women do most of the work, local leaders enthusiastically support this government-inspired program. In the early 1970's, during the general awakening of environmental consciousness and the shattering effects of the oil shocks, the prefectural sanitation department began to encourage recycling both to conserve resources and to limit the problems of solid waste disposal; suitable landfill sites are scarce, and much of Tokyo Bay has already been filled in with the city's refuse. The prefectural sanitation officials, who from time to time arrange for local leaders to tour waste disposal facilities so as to hammer home the need for limiting solid wastes, also stress to leaders and ordinary residents alike that recycling saves taxes by reducing the expenses of waste collection and disposal. Not surprisingly, this argument is popular. The recycling program, in Miyamoto-chō as throughout Tokyo, is a success, although it is limited to paper, cardboard, cans, and other scrap metal.

At the small hut next to the chōkai hall that serves as a recycling center, residents and shopkeepers deposit large bundles of newspapers and flattened cardboard cartons throughout the month. In addition a sanitation department sound truck prowls the neighborhood one day each month announcing that today is recycling day; housewives scurry out to leave bundled paper and sacks of carefully washed and sorted cans at curbside collection spots scattered around the neighborhood. The private scrap dealer who collects the material from the curbsides and from the hut pays the chōkai a fee based on the weight of the materials collected.

The chōkai does very little to promote its program, content merely to maintain the recycling hut and to announce each month how much money it received from the scrap dealer. Some nearby neighborhood associations are more aggressive, including one in which (I was told in shocked tones) members of the women's auxiliary inspect the refuse neatly piled at collection points on ordinary garbage pick-up days, and carefully remove any cans, bottles, or bundles of newspapers they happen to discover. This, I was assured by my neighbors in Miyamoto-chō, was going too far. Perhaps because Miyamoto-chō does not make an all-out effort in its recycling program, the neighborhood is a fertile ground for private enterprise that competes with the chōkai. Throughout the month scrap dealers slowly crawl through the neighborhood in small trucks piled high with bundled magazines, newspapers, and flattened cardboard boxes. Through tinny loudspeakers cassette tapes endlessly repeat, "Chirigami kōkan de gozaimasu" (loosely, "Toilet paper exchange, at your service"), offering to redeem newsprint, old telephone books, or cardboard for toilet tissue, other household paper products, or cash. They do a thriving business, and between these free-lance scrap dealers and the chōkai's program, recycling is a widespread and highly visible part of everyday life in Miyamoto-chō.

Distribution of Information

Government officials and chōkai leaders alike view communication as one of the association's most valuable functions. The chōkai possesses a variety of formal and informal means for distributing and collecting information quickly and cheaply: bulletin boards, circulating message boards, a complex system of liaison officers, informal word-of-mouth communications, and a detailed directory, published every four or five years, listing all neighborhood households, including the name, address, telephone number, and occupation of each household head.

The chōkai's most thorough communication system is the *kairanban*, circulating message boards that pass from house to house within each of Miyamoto-chō's 50 or so household clusters. Braibanti (1948) called the kairanban the sine qua non of the wartime system of neighborhood associations; even today kairanban and chōkai are so closely linked in most people's minds that on a word-association show I saw on TV, a contestant prompted with one term responded with the other.[7] To spread information most effectively and widely, the chōkai relies on the kairanban and the tiers of liaison officers linking the chōkai leadership to the household clusters. In theory the system can pass information to or collect responses from all 750 households in a couple of days. But in practice kairanban often do not circulate to apartment dwellers. The responsibility for informing them of neighborhood events is left to the landlord or manager. As a result the chōkai's messages often bypass these people, which both confirms and further reinforces their status as less than full-fledged neighborhood residents.

The chōkai maintains seven bulletin boards (*keijiban*) scattered around the neighborhood—at intersections, at the entrance to the shrine, across from the police box, and in front of the neighborhood hall—on which officers post notices of children's outings, recycling schedules, announcements of shrine observances, and the death notices the chōkai posts whenever any resident dies. The black-edged death notices list the name, address, and age of the deceased, the date of death, and the time and place of the tsuya (wake) and the *kokubetsushiki* (the final rites performed as the body is taken from the home for cremation and burial), so that friends and neighbors may pay their final respects.

The kairanban and the keijiban transmit news only about internal neighborhood matters: announcements of upcoming chōkai, women's auxiliary, and old people's club meetings, trips, banquets, outings, and other activities; information on chōkai services such as recycling and pesticide spraying; solicitations for the charity drive; notices of the election of officers and the acceptance of a new budget; news of the festival and other shrine-related affairs; and the somber announcements of deaths. Following the chōkai's principle of purchasing goods and services in Miyamoto-chō whenever possible, local businesses produce internal chōkai notices and posters. Ordinary notices are reproduced by a *garibanya*, a craftsman who makes mimeograph-like copies using handwritten stencils on a simple slate-lithographing contraption. Official lists of chōkai leaders and notices about the annual festival are typeset and printed by a shop on the main street. Death notices are printed forms with appropriate blanks left to be filled in by Mr. Takahashi, the chōkai's senior vice-president, who handles this unhappy duty.

The kairanban and the keijiban occasionally carry notices from the local offices of the prefectural police, fire, public health, and sanitation departments, and from the ward's tax, social welfare, pension, and disaster-preparedness offices. But the chōkai tries to reserve its system for internal communications and resists what it sees as government efforts to overburden it with government messages. The chōkai also prohibits the use of the kairanban and the keijiban for private messages, political announcements, and commercial advertising (although it allows local businesses to donate plastic kairanban clipboards embossed with advertisements). The chōkai leaders do not allow notices not directly related to the activities of the chōkai and its affiliates. They tear commercial advertisements and political posters off the bulletin boards and try to discourage government agencies from putting up notices without going through chōkai channels.

Because the chōkai guards its communications system closely, other organizations, even local ones such as the merchant's association and the elementary school's PTA, have their own roughly parallel systems for distributing information quickly, with the result that similar, seemingly redundant channels crisscross Miyamoto-chō. Political clubs and local party branches erect small bulletin boards on every wall or fence where the homeowner gives them permission, and some four dozen political bulletin boards dot the neighborhood. The shōtenkai erects special signposts when it sponsors a sale, and local merchants put up posters on every available light pole. The ward government has also erected its own set of street-corner bulletin boards, on which it posts public service notices the chōkai does not distribute: posters advertising such things as a ward-wide contest for the most successfully remodeled retail shop, a show-ing of educational movies about discrimination against out-castes, or a special sale of pork jointly sponsored by the ward butchers' association and the ward's nutrition office.

Augmenting these formal channels of communication and playing a more important role are the almost constant informal exchanges of information among the chōkai's upper leaders. Mr. Takahashi's grocery store is one of the central points for the in-formal flow of news. As the chōkai's senior vice-president, Mr. Takahashi handles much of the association's record-keeping and holds the keys to the chōkai hall a block away. His store stays open until 10:00 or 11:00 each night, 364 days of the year, and people stream in and out throughout the day. Most, of course, come to make small purchases, but many residents drop by daily, or more frequently, to pass on or find out new bits of in-formation about local happenings. Mrs. Maki's nearby snack bar (sunakku) is also a favorite hangout for neighborhood leaders, both male and female, and after most meetings many of the par-ticipants retire there to discuss the day's events. Other, less pub-lic exchanges of information vital to the running of the chōkai take place in the offices of several businessmen active in neigh-borhood affairs, where local leaders stop from time to time dur-ing the day to sip tea—or in the evening to sip whiskey—and swap information.

The Promotion of Local Business

Among all the groups that make Miyamoto-chō the focus of their attentions, the shōtenkai has the most circumscribed membership and range of functions. All but a few of its mem-bers are retail merchants or the proprietors of service businesses along the main shopping street. The shōtenkai's primary goal, of course, is to promote local business.

The shōtenkai has three classes of members: retail and ser-vice businesses; other commercial enterprises, such as manu-facturing companies and the soroban (abacus) academy; and households that front the shopping street but do not operate any business. Only a handful of members fall into the last two cat-egories. In the past, before the growth of automobile traffic firmly established the shopping street as the major thoroughfare through Miyamoto-chō, and before the sophistication of the shōtenkai's public-address system and streetlights reached a point where it became uneconomical to extend them beyond the main shopping street, merchants with businesses on side streets were shōtenkai members. Today, however, only enterprises and residents whose property directly abuts on the shopping street belong.

Although the shōtenkai includes people who are not merchants, their membership is incidental and does not deflect the organization from its primary purpose. As the neighborhood's chamber of commerce, it instinctively devotes itself to local boosterism. Almost all its public activities aim in one way or another to attract additional shoppers to the shopping street and to upgrade the street's image.

Local merchants are fully aware of the competition they face from the large shopping district surrounding the Otani station, with its major department store and a huge discount supermarket, as well as from similar neighborhood shopping areas nearby in all directions. A few blocks up the shopping street, an area that calls itself the "Thursday Street," for its coordinated weekly sales, attracts hordes of shoppers and is the envy of Miyamoto-chō's merchants. They candidly admit they cannot compete; although they can offer many of the nonspecialized goods and services people use routinely, the neighborhood lacks in particular the great concentration of food stores needed to draw a high volume of shoppers.

Miyamoto-chō's shōtenkai, as part of the federation of seven business districts along the shopping street, played its part in lobbying for the station that was built a few blocks away to serve the new commuter line. But Miyamoto-chō's merchants gloomily concede that the new station will probably not do much to help their business. A new shopping district will almost certainly grow up around the station, offsetting whatever gains Miyamoto-chō might make by the increased number of people passing through the area.

The shōtenkai focuses its efforts on making the shopping street as appealing a place as possible for shoppers, and on making neighborhood residents feel that they can get special service and attention by patronizing the shops of their neighbors and friends. More fundamental issues confronting small-scale retailers in the present-day Japanese economy, such as inadequate credit, cumbersome distribution systems, unfavorable wage differentials, and the inability to match the economies of scale of larger competitors, are obviously not things the shōtenkai can hope to change, and none of its activities aim in these directions.

Attempts to upgrade the shopping area's image and make it a more pleasant place to shop are largely cosmetic. Often the shōtenkai's actions respond to some similar effort in a nearby shopping area. In the autumn of 1979 the merchants' association for the adjoining stretch of the shopping street erected a new set of ornate streetlamps with distinctive globes and lighted signs; within six months the Miyamoto-chō shōtenkai had followed suit, installing an equally fancy new system, with frosted glass cubes stacked on one another above small signs that proclaim the two blocks to be the "Yanagi Miyamoto-chō Shopping Street." Before my fieldwork had ended the shōtenkai in the neighborhood on the other side had also erected a new streetlight system. Like the concentric circles from a stone dropped in a pond, one can imagine rippling lines of new streetlights, changing in style and configuration every few blocks, quickly spreading down the entire length of the shopping street and gradually covering the ward.

The usefulness of an earlier, less-expensive improvement project—the installation of the public-address system that played taped music every afternoon during the peak shopping hours—is questionable. One wonders whether the music can even be heard over the din of traffic. But the shopowners along the street are satisfied that the music helps to make the shopping area more pleasant, or at least more identifiable.

Throughout the year the shōtenkai creates other opportunities to attract and keep customers. Once or twice each year it sponsors a special sale with merchandise donated by local merchants or purchased in large quantities at a discount. The organization advertises the sales through blaring loudspeakers and through leaflets inserted in the newspapers delivered by the three newsagents who serve Miyamoto-chō and two or three adjacent neighborhoods. By presenting a leaflet, the shopper can buy some household staple, such as sugar, soy sauce, or milk, at a nominal price. One sale, held a few weeks before I left Miyamoto-chō, attempted to harness (or create) tradition by holding the sale on the day of the Buddha's birthday (April 8). For this event, the Buddhist temple, in a rare gesture of cooperation, opened its gates to the shoppers and brought out a small statue of the Buddha over which people could pour dippers of sweet *sake*, a customary part of the observance of this Buddhist holiday. The temple's participation was a first, and merchants happily credited the event's success to the imagination and progressiveness of Mr. Ueno, the owner of a successful boutique (and in 1981, the newly elected shōtenkai president, succeeding Mr. Mizuno).

Twice a year the shōtenkai sponsors a lottery, or *fukubiki*. With each purchase from a participating local merchant, a shopper receives one or more tickets redeemable at the lottery headquarters in the chōkai hall for a chance to win a prize ranging from the simplest household staples—toilet paper, salt, cooking oil, or soy sauce—to a moped. The lotteries parallel the constant efforts by individual merchants to woo and retain customers by giving them some small item when they make a larger purchase, called *o-make* (a "knockdown") or *saabisu* (from the English word "service," but used here to mean a small gift or extra portion). Thus, a stationer may make a great show of presenting a customer with an extra ballpoint pen, a *sake* dealer may give a regular customer a small bottle of cooking *sake*, or a butcher may throw a few extra grams of meat on the scale and say in a stage whisper, "Ahh! This is *o-make*, but don't tell anyone else about it."

On a larger scale the shōtenkai tries to reverse the local economic circumstances that thwart business growth. As mentioned, the shōtenkai participates in the campaign to have traffic diverted from the shopping street, with the distant hope of eventually turning the street into a traffic-free shopping mall. It also supported the drive by the local federation of shōtenkai and chōkai for the new rail station despite the merchants' pessimism about gaining any advantage from it.

The shōtenkai is not the only institution concerned with local mercantile life. The ward government maintains several small offices that continually conduct surveys on local economic conditions and advise local businesses on how to improve their operations. In addition to issuing reports on the existing situation in various lines of business, these offices offer workshops and lectures on how to run a small business, sponsor competitions among shopowners and associations for the best ideas on how to spruce up a shopping area, and try to provide introductions to potential suppliers, sources of credit, and officials in other government agencies.

Neighborhood merchants are also helped by the local branches of several *shin'yō kinko*, a type of banking institution roughly analogous to a credit union that specializes in serving small business. These branches provide the normal array of financial services as well as statistical reports on local trade, counseling for business-related problems, and so forth. Since the *shin'yō kinko*, now government-chartered, are descended from merchants' mutual credit associations that were amalgamated into larger financial institutions in the 1930's and 1940's (see Rohlen 1974: 7–8), they maintain close connections with the merchant community. The *shin'yō kinko* play high-profile roles in neighborhoods like Miyamoto-chō, and at least once each day one of their representatives will visit each client in the area to collect deposits, to deliver supplies of change, or simply to talk. Because so much of the credit unions' business depends on local merchant goodwill, they donate heavily to neighborhood events, such as local festivals. When Miyamoto-chō was purchasing a new mikoshi for the festival, for example, one of the local *shin'yō kinko* was willing to make a loan of several million yen to the endeavor, secured of course by the assets of several wealthy businessmen in Miyamoto-chō.

In many lines of business local entrepreneurs belong to *dōgyōkumiai*, or "same-trade associations." Because these associations bring together business people who are both colleagues and competitors, they do little to aid individual entrepreneurs, but they do represent collective interests before the ward assembly and other agencies. In some cases, such as the dōgyōkumiai for *sake* dealers, they regulate competition by setting standard store hours and enforcing agreements about the placement and hours of operation of beer-vending machines. Several trade associations have established fixed nonbusiness days for their members. Some have picked a standard day of the week; others have chosen to retain the old-fashioned system of three dates a month, say, on the third, the thirteenth, and the twenty-third, or the seventh, seventeenth, and the twenty-seventh. Most trade associations also have an active recreational component, and the year-end banquets and overnight trips to hot springs they sponsor are for many busy entrepreneurs among the few chances they or members of their families have to get away from the store.

Most dōgyōkumiai are organized at the ward level, or divide the ward into Ebara and Shinagawa branches that cover the areas of the two old wards amalgamated in 1947. Some have even more localized branches, like the *sake* dealers, who organize themselves into blocks of about a dozen nearby shops. No matter what the scale of the local units, all dōgyōkumiai are affiliated with higher-level federations that link ward and prefectural groups into nationwide trade groups. At the higher levels these trade associations play an important political role, lobbying prefectural and national government agencies and supporting political candidates. Thus shopkeepers are often called on to canvass for Diet candidates endorsed by the national leadership of their trade association. Rarely, however, do such political stances play a part in local politics.

A business group that is more inclusive in its membership is the Aoiro Shinkokukai, a taxpayers' union for the self-employed. Unlike wage-earners, who have their taxes automatically deducted and often do not have to file tax returns, the self-employed are required to fill out and submit so-called "blue forms" (*aoiro shinkoku*). This organization provides information and assistance to entrepreneurs in dealing with the tax officials, and most merchants in Miyamoto-chō belong.

The activities of the shōtenkai remain distinct from those of this and the other economically oriented institutions and organizations, just as they remain distinct from the activities of the chōkai and other local groups. Although the prevalent image of neighborhood social organization in urban Japan strongly suggests that local merchant elites firmly control neighborhood organizations and manipulate them to their own ends, in

Miyamoto-chō, at least, the chōkai and the shōtenkai are not only separate organizations; they are also separate in their leadership and their core of most active members. Many chōkai leaders are shopkeepers or other self-employed business people, but entrepreneurs from the shopping street do not dominate the chōkai's leadership. By the same token several shōtenkai officials have (or have had) leading roles in the chōkai, but the shōtenkai and its activities attract the participation of many local merchants who have no interest in and play no role at all in chōkai affairs.

Of course, local merchants have a strong self-interest in playing active roles in local affairs. Since their livelihoods depend on attracting customers from the immediate area, their participation in local activities has an obvious advantage in creating networks of tsukiai—contacts or connections buttressed by a sense of mutual obligation. Merchants are quite conscious of these ties and pay careful attention to reciprocity. The Tsunoda family, for example, will purchase nothing from the Mizutanis' clothing store right across the street, because the Mizutanis never purchase rice from the Tsunodas' store. The Tsunodas will go several blocks away to a shop in another neighborhood run by the Noguchis—competitors of the Mizutanis—both because Mrs. Tsunoda went to elementary school with Mrs. Noguchi's younger brother and because the Noguchis' daughter is one of the Tsunodas' regular customers.

Merchants' local social networks, whether created by institutional ties or by personal social relationships, have a major impact on the stability of local retail and service businesses. Tsukiai is so important an element of the business environment that shops have no incentive to move to "better" locations if they are a success, and have every reason to stay. Those shopkeepers who leave Miyamoto-chō, therefore, are most often people who are retiring from business altogether or are in a business that does not depend on local tsukiai. For example, the Kita family had lived in Miyamoto-chō for about ten years, establishing a thriving wholesale business in dried mushrooms imported from Mr. Kita's home province in Kyushu. Although the Kitas were a gregarious family who had been active participants in local affairs, when the business prospered Mr. Kita moved his

family and his business out to the suburbs of Tokyo; for him location did not matter much, and local tsukiai was not a factor
in his volume. Few other merchants in Miyamoto-chō are in this
position.

Local tsukiai is valuable as well when retail merchants
branch out into other economic pursuits. For the sizable minority of Miyamoto-chō's merchants who have become landlords
since the Second World War, maintaining small apartment
buildings above or behind their shops, local tsukiai plays a crucial role in matching tenants and landlords (as was the case
when my wife and I found our apartment). For at least some of
the shopkeeper-landlords, it is probable that their major source
of income is from their properties, not from their retail businesses.

Beyond the very localized social ties that merchants maintain
throughout Miyamoto-chō, their leadership in neighborhood organizations has the benefit of creating networks of ties extend-
ing far beyond the neighborhood. Several local leaders commented on this as a particularly advantageous aspect of leadership positions: the chance to meet and develop contacts with
local leaders throughout the ward as well as with government
officials and other influential people who may at some time
prove to be of some aid. Some merchants active in local organizations appear to be content with the tsukiai inside Miyamoto-chō they accrue from their participation, but others appear to use service in local organizations as a springboard to
wider circles. In either case merchants' roles in local groups—
both in the specialized shōtenkai and in more general organizations such as the chōkai—reflect the importance to them of
localized networks that can be turned to their economic advantage.

Social Welfare and Recreation

Many of the social welfare functions that the chōkai and its
affiliates pursue—such as mutual aid, assisting the elderly, and
expressing condolences at funerals—are in practice met more
through the personal actions of individual residents than
through activities of the formal organizations. Most of the chō-

kai's official activities aimed at promoting social welfare (carried out under the heading of aiding women and youth) or encouraging local tsukiai turn out to be recreational.

Children's outings are frequent and tend to be enjoyed by adults as much as by children; adults often go on the excursions with no child in tow. Each summer the chōkai's youth division organizes a trip to a public swimming pool an hour's bus ride away, and 30 or 40 children plus two dozen or so adults make a day of it. The division also plans a more elaborate summer outing—one year an all-day trip to visit an aquarium and hike along the scenic seashore two hours from Tokyo, another year a trip to a huge "wilderness" park on the outskirts of Tokyo for a day of swinging across ravines and falling in mudholes.

The midsummer Bon Odori, one of the few joint projects of Miyamoto-chō's chōkai and shōtenkai, provides another major recreational opportunity. This popular event, held for two nights each July on the playground of the elementary school, attracts about 300 children and adults each evening for several hours of folk-dancing to recorded music. Children seem to prefer the Western-style folk tunes they learn in school, but local dance troupes of middle-aged women perform more old-fashioned dances on a wooden stage, which men from the two associations erect in the center of the playground. The "sale" of plastic lanterns—about 150 of which are hung around the stage and in long strings from the stage to the outer edges of the playing field—pays for the Bon Odori and usually earns a small surplus for the chōkai and the shōtenkai. Local merchants buy one or more small lanterns with their shop names painted on them for a contribution of 1,000 yen per lantern; larger lanterns, bought primarily by local politicians and local bank branches, cost the donors 10,000 yen apiece. The plastic lanterns are reused (and resold) from year to year, so the Bon Odori's major expenses are the electricity for the lanterns and the public-address system, and the hundreds of ice cream bars chōkai leaders distribute to throngs of clamoring kids at the end of the evenings.

Other activities planned more particularly with adults in mind include an annual New Year's party at the chōkai hall in early January. The women's auxiliary serves the banquet (the dishes themselves are prepared by a local restaurant), and afterward talented (and sometimes not-so-talented) residents play the shamisen, display their dancing abilities, or sing sentimental folk songs into "microphones" fabricated for the moment by balancing an inverted *sake* cup on the end of a chopstick.

The annual O-hanami (cherry-blossom-viewing party) sponsored each spring by the women's auxiliary provides a much more rollicking time. Sixty or 70 local residents travel to a park several stations away on the private train line, where—along with several thousand other people, most of whom are there with similar-sized groups from their companies, their schools, or their neighborhoods—they spread out mats and eat, drink, dance, and sing for several hours.

In the past the chōkai and its women's group also sponsored parties for elderly residents on the national holiday, Keirō no Hi (Respect for the Elderly Day, September 15), but in recent years they have stopped holding the parties because poor health prevents so many of the old people from attending. Instead, to try to benefit all the elderly, the chōkai and the fujinbu now present a gift to every resident over the age of seventy; one year they gave sets of underclothing sewn by the fujinbu women, along with amulets from the local Buddhist temple to protect against incontinence.

Until the middle 1970's the chōkai put on a coming-of-age party for all young people in Miyamoto-chō who were celebrating their twentieth birthday (the age of legal majority) during the year. That event was discontinued owing to the apparent lack of interest on the part of the young people themselves. Most clearly preferred to mark the milestone with friends on the national holiday in their honor (Adult's Day, or Seijin no Hi, January 15), attending one of the many large public ceremonies sponsored by the ward government and showing off their adult finery (especially the young women, dressed in gorgeous kimono) at a major shrine or temple.

Twice each year the women's group sponsors outings for its members: one is a daylong trip to some scenic attraction near Tokyo, and the other is usually a three-day, two-night excursion to the ward government's hostel at a hot springs resort on the Izu peninsula, several hours by train from Tokyo. For many women such excursions may be their only chance during the year to put aside their domestic responsibilities for a day or two, and (according to my wife, who accompanied them on several outings) the several dozen women who do go make the most of it. The women quickly shed the quiet, restrained, somewhat subservient demeanor they generally display at events in Miyamoto-chō; women who would not publicly drink anything stronger than orange soda back home produce from their hand-bags bottles of whiskey that are quickly consumed. Freed from the constraining presence of their husbands and other neigh-borhood men, some women dispel the prevalent stereotypes of Japanese feminine behavior; many become assertive, boister-ous, argumentative, or even drunk.[8]

Another activity, far more restrained and designed with the formal obligations of neighborly etiquette in mind, is the Mei-shikōkanshiki (exchange-of-greetings ceremony) that the chō-kai sponsors at the Shintō shrine on January 2. Bundled against the dry chill of a Tokyo January, local leaders and a handful of other residents gather at the shrine in midmorning. Mrs. Horie, Mrs. Tsurumi, and other women dress in their finest kimono, and most of the men wear darkly formal, padded winter kimono as well, perhaps for the only time during the entire year. A few men arrive in dark Western business suits, and Mr. Iwao, a tailor whose shop stands near the elementary school, subtly advertises his skills by donning an elegant morning coat of the type cur-rently favored by the fathers of the bride and groom at a fancy wedding. After the informal greetings and banter have died down, the two dozen or so residents who assemble for the event formally toast one another with *sake*. The entire group files quickly into the main hall of the shrine, where the priest offers a brief prayer for everyone's good health and prosperity during the coming year. As they leave they assemble on the shrine steps for a group photograph before hurrying back to the warmth of their homes and the other social obligations that await them throughout the holidays.

The Meishikōkanshiki, which had been held in Miyamoto-chō until sometime in the late 1940's or early 1950's and had reentered the repertoire of local custom only a year before I be-gan my fieldwork, enables local residents to easily discharge their obligations to make formal New Year's greeting calls upon at least some of their neighbors. In the new—actually newly revived—custom, people may offer their best wishes to one and all collectively, before spending much of the rest of the New Year's holidays making formal calls on business associates and others to whom they feel obligated. Local leaders who had taken the lead in reintroducing the Meishikōkanshiki explained to me that they saw themselves drawing upon old customs and creating new elements of local tradition that evolve in response to the changing needs of the community.

Quite apart from the wide array of practical as well as recreational ends that local activities meet, they promote an image that Miyamoto-chō holds of itself as self-reliant (if not self-sufficient) and to a degree autonomous from the local government. Whatever the nominal, expressed goal—fighting crime, providing recreation, or preparing for disaster—all the various sorts of organizationally sponsored activities bolster a spirit of community, at least partly through the opportunities for tsukiai they create for residents. Both the institutions and the ties that ramify from them help inculcate a sense that residents interact with one another within an established, enduring framework of local life.

Images of self-reliant autonomy and of durable social relations both bolster and are themselves bolstered by the notion that Miyamoto-chō is shaped by a self-sufficient local tradition. Local social life is seen as occurring within an established— even if often only recently established—body of local custom and tradition. Whether tradition is old or new, consciousness of it is carefully cultivated through many of Miyamoto-chō's essentially recreational events, as well as through its more instrumental activities, helping to create and maintain a sense of local identity. The camaraderie and sense of purpose that develop through the chōkai's activities underscore the contention of leaders and residents alike that Miyamoto-chō exists apart from whatever governmental purposes it serves, and that this existence in part reflects the strength imparted by adherence to local tradition. Miyamoto-chō's traditions may not have a long local ancestry, but the neighborhood's partisans see them as things developed in response to the needs and desires of the community. Even though the customs themselves may not be unique, their particular configuration in the neighborhood and the perception of even widespread customs as somehow embodying a local tradition foster community spirit and mark—to the residents' own satisfaction—Miyamoto-chō as a unit distinct from others.

CHAPTER FIVE

Formal Hierarchies of Participation and Power

IN THE AUTUMN OF 1979, a few months after my arrival in Miyamoto-chō, workmen began to erect new lampposts along the shopping street. Elaborate towers of frosted glass cubes replaced spindly, now-rusting lamps put up in the 1950's. Upon the completion of the project, its sponsor, the shōtenkai, and the chōkai held a joint celebration, a *kagami-biraki* (opening a keg of *sake* to commemorate a triumph). The neighborhood was flooded with announcements inviting everyone to sip *sake* and to participate in a special lottery to celebrate the new streetlights.

The empty lot owned by the temple, down the street from the chōkai hall, was draped with festive red-and-white bunting to serve as the site of the kagami-biraki. The chōkai and the shōtenkai erected awnings under which would sit a dozen dignitaries: the aged senior advisers of the neighborhood association and its affiliates, the managers of local bank branches, politicians from the ward and metropolitan assemblies, and the secretaries of Diet members. Another awning was set up to house a receptionist's desk.

At the appointed time dozens of residents congregated at the site. Members of the merchants' group and the invited dignitaries were dressed formally; the passing shoppers, attracted by a chance to win a motorbike and have a sip of *sake*, were dressed in the normal array of daily clothing. With great fanfare the head of the merchants' group called on Tsurumi-sensei to smash open the caskhead with a large mallet to start the *sake* flowing. The lights were turned on, and the shōtenkai's loudspeaker system began to play the ward's folk song. The shoppers surged forward to the lottery booth and lined up for *sake*. A steady stream of visitors stopped at the receptionist's desk to pay their respects. It was they who particularly attracted my attention.

As a newcomer to the neighborhood, watching one of my first public events, I found it fascinating but bewildering. Particularly confusing were the distinctions that seemed to be drawn between people who, with my then-limited knowledge of local status, I had thought to be roughly equals. Standing near the receptionist's desk, I watched as dignitaries, members of the merchants' group, officials of the chōkai, and a few other residents who fell into none of the other categories presented congratulatory donations of cash, discreetly enclosed in decorated envelopes. As soon as the envelopes were presented, the cloak of discretion vanished; one of the receptionists wrote the amount and the donor's name in bold brush strokes on a sheet to be posted on a nearby signboard. I wondered, Why were some people giving large amounts and others small? Why were some of them giving anything at all? Why was Mr. Hasegawa, a retired business executive in his seventies, who lived a couple of blocks away from the shopping street and who certainly did not belong to the merchants' group, directing shōtenkai officials and supervising the recording of donations? Why did the members of the merchants' group array themselves with such care as the commemorative group photograph was taken? Why were some who gave donations invited into the chōkai hall to join a festive banquet? Why did others—like Mr. Iwao, the tailor up the hill, and Ku-chan the carpenter—only get invited to stand near the *sake* keg and nibble at some trays of sushi that had been put out on a table?

In my eagerness to participate and to see what was happening inside at the banquet, I hurried home to get a suitable festive envelope and returned to offer a modest donation. With great patience and tact, I was rebuffed. Mr. Hasegawa hurried over to explain that it would be inappropriate for the merchants' group to accept my donation, but would I like to join Mr. Iwao and Ku-chan over by the *sake* barrel for a bit?

It was a frustrating and confusing day, but it was also my first chance to watch social hierarchy in action. What was particularly fascinating was to note, first, that people used various criteria to sort out and classify residents into some sort of ranked continuum, and, then, to see how some residents tried to manipulate the criteria, such as the amounts of their donations, to achieve a status other than the one their neighbors had intended for them. Of course, my attempted manipulation was an abject failure, but others were clearly more skillful than I in playing the game. Although this celebration had centered on the merchants' group, as I traced out the day's events and observed dozens of similar public displays over the next two years, again and again in the activities of all local groups I came to focus on the common interaction of principles of hierarchy and differential access with the neighborhood's publicly stated norms of communal solidarity and equality.

The overt view of the chōkai and other local groups, constantly although subtly expressed through activities sponsored by Miyamoto-chō's several associations, is that local organizations are of the people, by the people, and for the people of Miyamoto-chō. In emphasizing this "us" versus the "them" of the ward government and even of society in general, local leaders strongly imply that Miyamoto-chō's "we" are all just plain folks, unified in the solidarity of a self-defined community in which all are nearly equal. Although residents readily acknowledge that by the standards of society at large, there are marked status differences among them, they often cite these differences, paradoxically, as proof that such considerations have no bearing within the neighborhood. Residents point out examples of highly placed government bureaucrats, teachers, and symphony orchestra members cooperating in community affairs with carpenters, retail merchants, and day laborers; status in the outside world, they insist, does not intrude into local affairs. Yet against the backdrop of this ethos of communal egalitarianism, neighborhood activities are planned and carried out in organizations that are elaborately structured hierarchies.

This chapter will describe the formal structure of Miyamoto-chō's major set of institutions—the chōkai, the women's auxiliary, and the old people's club—and the hierarchical principles that shape them. Some hierarchical features reflect general ordering principles of Japanese culture: trajectories of status and authority linked to normative ideals of behavior deemed appropriate to a person's age and gender. Others are inherent in the structures of the organizations themselves; of course these structurally determined hierarchies reinforce general cultural expectations.

In their elaborate organizational structures, their complex chains of leadership with almost innumerable specialized offices, and their intricate territorial subdivisions, these groups are fundamentally similar, closely paralleling one another at most levels. For that reason, they are best discussed together, though I shall place primary emphasis on the chōkai. In examining the formal organization of local institutions, I shall outline the ways in which their hierarchical structuring affects participation in neighborhood activities and differential access to power over local groups. I shall also discuss the ways in which power or control is centralized in a cluster of leaders who set chōkai policies through various informal consultations and channels of decision-making that underlie but are not explicitly part of the formal structure of local institutions.

Membership

Households, not individuals, are members of the chōkai, and in principle membership is both voluntary and universal. Chōkai leaders say that no one is forced to join, while noting that no households refuse to belong. Both statements are probably true.

The household membership fee is 200 yen a month for those living in houses or in *manshon* ("mansion," used to describe larger, more modern, better appointed, and more expensive apartments) and 100 yen a month for households living in other apartments (*apaato*) or rooming houses (*geshuku*).[1] Once a month, upon the payment of its dues, each household receives a receipt certifying it to be a member in good standing.

For residents who may not wish to belong or who object on principle to such associations, it is probably simpler to pay the trifling monthly sum than to fly in the face of established neighborhood custom and raise the issue with their neighbors, one of whom—as the chōkai's representative—collects the dues. Furthermore, those who probably feel least compelled to belong—apartment residents—are enrolled as members through their landlords, from whom the chōkai representative collects their dues.[2] Only a few old people living alone do not pay chōkai dues; for elderly residents financially unable to pay even the minimal fee, a chōkai representative may waive it semiofficially (or pay it out of his or her own pocket).

As the term fujinbu ("wives' division") suggests, the women's auxiliary does not exist separately from the chōkai, and women belong not as individuals but as members of households: as wives not as women.[3] Fujinbu membership is not distinct from household membership in the chōkai, and there are no separate fujinbu membership fees. Membership in the old people's club, or rōjinkai, however, does not automatically accompany chōkai affiliation. Instead, households with eligible members pay separate dues of 100 yen a month. This fee, like the chōkai fee, may be semiofficially waived if an old person living alone cannot afford it. Many households whose older members do not or cannot participate in the rōjinkai nevertheless pay dues to the old people's club as a matter of course to support the idea of neighborhood activities for the elderly.

A person must be at least sixty years old to join the rōjinkai, but not everyone eligible for membership is active in it. Participation in the club implies one has retired from the workaday world and has withdrawn from active involvement in the affairs of the chōkai or the women's auxiliary. Many leaders and others who are still enthusiastic members of those associations therefore hold off active participation in the old people's club until their mid-sixties or later. And some people simply stay away because of poor health or lack of interest.

To a certain extent age determines people's interest and participation in the chōkai and the women's auxiliary, too. Despite universal household membership, men—if interested in chōkai affairs at all—do not generally become involved until their late twenties or early thirties, and only rarely does a man assume any position of responsibility until his late thirties or early forties. Women do not usually become active in the fujinbu until their late thirties or early forties, in part because the responsibilities of child rearing and other domestic duties limit their time for activities outside the home. When a woman's youngest child graduates from elementary or junior high school, she may begin to involve herself in the affairs of the women's auxiliary. In general the PTAs of the elementary and junior high schools are associations for younger women, and the fujinbu an association for older adult women whose major child-rearing duties are behind them.[4]

The distribution of responsibilities for particular local activities among the chōkai, the women's auxiliary, and the old people's club bolsters this informal age structure. Their different domains reflect and perpetuate conventionally stereotyped divisions of labor by age as well as by gender. For example, the functions of the women's auxiliary in many respects mirror the nurturing roles expected of Japanese females: the women of the fujinbu prepare food, wait on men, and clean up afterward at neighborhood events; sew garments for the local festival; make and distribute gifts to the neighborhood's senior citizens on Keirō no Hi (Respect for the Elderly Day); and sponsor charity drives for orphans and the widowed.

Similarly, the tasks of the old people's club mirror conventional expectations of the elderly. Since its members have by definition mostly retired from active participation in neighborhood affairs, no one expects them to be responsible for any public activities or functions outside those of the rōjinkai. Nevertheless, the neighborhood implicitly leaves certain ritual matters to them in a tacit acknowledgment that older people tend to be more concerned with religious matters than their juniors. Younger adult men therefore run the neighborhood's annual matsuri, whereas men from the old people's club take charge of the semiannual festivals for the tiny Inari shrine. The

Inari festivals in February and July are much smaller and more closely linked to the shrine than the much more boisterous, more secular, neighborhood-centered festival for the local tutelary deity held each September. Organizationally at least the old people's club does not distinguish along gender lines in assigning official positions and duties, and both men and women participate more or less equally in activities with little apparent regard for the differentiation of domains that characterizes the division of labor among younger generations.

But in general the implicit distinctions of age and gender that define the participants in these groups and the nature of their activities are hardly noticeable, if only because they so "naturally" blend into the prevailing norms that shape gendered and age-graded roles and statuses. In most instances the activities of the chōkai, the women's auxiliary, and the old people's club do not duplicate or parallel one another, but are integrated in a complementary, organic fashion.

Residence in Miyamoto-chō and payment of the monthly dues are the only requirements for membership in these organizations. Beyond this minimal obligation households and individuals may in principle freely involve themselves in any of the groups' activities as little or as much as their personal inclinations and circumstances dictate. Even members of households that choose not to join actively in general neighborhood affairs, however, usually participate in the lowest level of the chōkai's organization, one based on geographically defined clusters of households.

Members of the Tsunoda family, for example, are run-of-the-mill chōkai members: participants but not leaders. They maintain cordial relations with their immediate neighbors, and their primary institutional connections to the chōkai come every few years when they must represent their household cluster.

The elder Mr. Tsunoda, in his middle sixties, moved to Miyamoto-chō from a shitamachi district of central Tokyo with his wife and infant daughter shortly after the Second World War to open a rice shop on the shopping street. The family, which now consists of him, his daughter and her husband, and his three grandchildren, live in quarters above the shop as well as in a tiny apartment they rent a few doors away, down the alley behind their shop.

Mrs. Tsunoda, in her late thirties, grew up in Miyamoto-chō and graduated from the local elementary school, where she still spends much of her time as an enthusiastic officer of the PTA. She and her three children take advantage of almost every chō-kai-sponsored excursion but otherwise pay little attention to the neighborhood association. The three children belong to several clubs at the elementary and junior high schools—cartooning clubs, art clubs, music clubs—which together with schoolwork and preparing for the next round of entrance exams take up all their time. Like the younger Tsunodas, Mrs. Tsunoda's father enjoys the inexpensive recreation local groups provide—once or twice a year he goes off on a rōjinkai-sponsored weekend excursion to a hot springs—but he takes no other active role in local organizations.

Young Mr. Tsunoda—the family's *mukoyōshi,* or adopted son-in-law—is from northeastern Japan. After graduating from high school he moved to Tokyo to become an apprentice in a shop in the same line of business as the Tsunodas' store. Through his apprenticeship he met Miss Tsunoda, and a marriage was arranged; Mr. Tsunoda was adopted into the family, taking the family name and becoming heir to the family business, which he now runs. Young Mr. Tsunoda, now in his early forties, generally stands aloof from local associations—especially the chōkai—because he disagrees with what he sees as the authoritarian attitudes of some of the older leaders. As a local businessman he belongs to the shōtenkai and participates amiably in its activities, often serving as unofficial photographer for its banquets and parties. With much more enthusiasm he spends considerable time as an officer in the ward-wide dōgyō-kumiai, the trade association, for his business. He also actively participates in an informal photography club and in a ward-wide club of azalea fanciers (he raises several dozen potted plants on the roof of the Tsunodas' shop).

The Tsunodas are a friendly, outgoing family active in any number of organizations; on the occasions when I sat above their shop sipping tea, someone was always bustling out the door to a meeting or activity related to school, hobbies, or the family trade. But rarely do their attentions focus on the chōkai itself. When the neighborhood association offers a chance for recreation, the Tsunodas join in, and as their turn comes up to represent their household cluster in the chōkai and the fujinbu, they take the job as a matter of course, much as they contribute trifling sums of time and money toward sharing with their immediate neighbors the upkeep of a pump in the alleyway beside their home and shop.

Household Clusters and Their Representatives

For internal administrative purposes the chōkai groups neighboring households together into some 50-odd household clusters, or *kumi* ("groups" or "sets").[5] The average kumi has 13 households, but they range from as few as three to as many as 33. Larger clusters may include one or more apartment buildings; if apartment dwellers are excluded, the average number of households per kumi is nine. Most clusters, therefore, are small enough to enable close and frequent interaction among their households.

Kumi resemble the wartime *tonarigumi*, the neighbor groups that were banned under the Occupation in 1947 because they were seen as fundamentally undemocratic and tainted by their intimate links to wartime mobilization and social control. Though residents of Miyamoto-chō sometimes refer to kumi as tonarigumi, the kumi of today have none of the powers of coercion and control exercised by the wartime tonarigumi, such as collective responsibility for members' behavior, control over the distribution of foodstuffs and other basic necessities of life, and formal statutory links to the state apparatus.

Kumi are not corporate groups in any significant sense, nor do members meet together formally to make decisions or discuss neighborhood affairs. Each cluster has a minimally separate identity: each is numbered, and the chōkai directory (published every four or five years) lists households by clusters rather than by address or in alphabetical order. But people do not think of each other in terms of their kumi; even the most knowledgeable residents would have to consult the chōkai directory to locate the boundaries and members of specific clusters. Although groups of neighboring households along a single stretch of street or pathway informally interact with each other, offering various forms of mutual aid—keeping watch on each other's property, pitching in to clean and repair shared paths and wells, and helping out during funerals—these ties and the cooperation they foster exist outside the framework of the kumi as a structural element of the chōkai.

Kumi connect to the neighborhood's formal organization in two ways: each kumi has a *riji* (representative) who acts as the liaison between its households and the leaders and councils of the chōkai; and each has a corresponding liaison officer (renrakuin) in the fujinbu.

Each kumi has a single riji and a single renrakuin; typically the riji is the male head of the household and the renrakuin his wife.[6] But these liaison positions are household offices, not individual offices, and whichever household member is available at the moment performs the duties at hand. Most frequently all tasks fall to the wife, who in effect fills both the chōkai and the fujinbu positions.

The mild obligations and simple tasks liaison officers undertake for the chōkai define the formal organizational roles of the kumi. Once a month the liaison officers collect chōkai dues from each household and pass them on to higher levels in the association. Once or twice a month they start a kairanban on its rounds from household to household carrying various notices from the chōkai, the women's auxiliary, or other neighborhood groups. Occasionally they collect reservations and payments from cluster members for some local outing or banquet, or collect contributions for the semiannual charity drives of the women's auxiliary. They gather information on such things as the number of preschool children or senior citizens in each household to aid the planning of activities by the women's auxiliary. Liaison officers notify the chōkai when streetlights on back alleys need repair. And they should (but often do not) attend the chōkai's annual general business meeting and other occasional meetings to represent and report back to the residents of their clusters.

Riji and renrakuin serve one-year terms. Because the positions rotate in a set order from household to household within each cluster, in theory every household will hold the posts at some time or another. Serving as a kumi representative carries no great prestige or power, and, like all offices in local associations, it carries no salary. It is neither a stepping-stone to higher offices nor a strategically important post in which one can control resources—the flow of information, services, or access to important people—to one's own advantage. Rather, residents see the posts as a duty and an obligation, not so unpleasant or onerous as to warrant shirking them, but not anything to be coveted or sought.

With automatic annual rotation there could be a complete turnover of kumi representatives from one year to the next, but in practice this does not occur. The chōkai usually excludes apartment-dwellers from the rotation, and a household may ask to be skipped if its members feel incapable of carrying out the job for some reason, such as ill health, the demands of work schedules, or the unfamiliarity with the neighborhood felt by a newly arrived household. Nevertheless, the rotation system widely distributes office-holding at this lowest level, with almost nine of ten positions passing each year from one household to the next.[7]

Over a period of several years, then, most households play some role in the chōkai's formal structure, have frequent contact with all the neighboring households, and have regular dealings with other liaison officers and with higher-level chōkai leaders. During the five years between 1977 and 1981, there were 265 one-year riji slots available, and these were filled by 234 different households out of the roughly 750 living in the neighborhood at any given time. That is, within five years roughly a third of all households had held at least the lowest-level offices in the chōkai. Equally important, the system ensures that every household in Miyamoto-chō has contact a couple of times a month with the chōkai or the women's auxiliary through a close neighbor with whom its members may interact daily in a wide variety of other, less formal relationships.

At this level the neighborhood's structure tends toward the egalitarian, with responsibilities and access to power well distributed among residents. Above the kumi level, however, the chōkai's structure becomes progressively more hierarchical, with access and power less and less evenly allocated.

Intermediate Layers of Organization

Two layers of organization stand intermediate between the kumi and the chōkai leadership. Because both serve primarily as liaison between the top and the bottom of the neighborhood's formal structure, these intermediate levels are not marked by the same type of individual or household interaction as kumi.

Sections and Liaison Officers

The chōkai groups three to five kumi together into *bu* (geographical sections), of which there are 13.[8] Within each geographical section a *jōninriji* (permanent representative) for the chōkai and a corresponding *hanchō* (section leader) for the women's auxiliary handle liaison between higher and lower levels. Their duties are largely the same: passing notices, requests, membership dues, survey results, and other items of information up and down the chains of command within the chōkai and the women's auxiliary.

As the title implies, the position of permanent representative does not rotate automatically among households; the president of the chōkai appoints the jōninriji, and the chief of the women's auxiliary appoints the hanchō, with the expectation in both cases that the appointee will serve several terms. These officers do not represent a random selection of neighborhood residents; they are people both well known to association leaders and actively interested in the affairs of the chōkai or its women's auxiliary. Some permanent representatives are former leaders of those organizations who no longer wish to assume so prominent a leadership role because of age and poor health or family and business commitments. In a few cases they are up-and-coming leaders who lack the age, experience, or neighborhood status to assume higher posts. In most instances they are simply well-established residents of Miyamoto-chō who solidly support the organizations' goals and activities, but cannot or will not play the top roles in them.

Members of the Ikeda family have for many years been the permanent representatives for a geographical section of Miyamoto-chō near the traffic bypass above the old river. Mr. Ikeda is a retired government official, and his wife is a pleasant, friendly woman who can often be found chatting with her neighbors in the street outside their home. He serves as the chōkai's permanent representative, she as the section leader for the women's auxiliary. They live in a large, walled, older home, along with a married son, his wife, and their small children. The minimal duties of permanent representative for the chōkai and the women's group require little effort on the Ikedas' part. Mr. Ikeda most visibly plays a role in neighborhood affairs during the annual festival, when he pitches in with preparations at the chōkai hall—collecting and recording contributions and advising younger members on the proper assembly of festival paraphernalia. Mrs. Ikeda, an avid folk-dancer, practices weekly with members of the women's auxiliary as part of the dance troupe that performs at the neighborhood festival, the local Bon Odori, and the festival sponsored by the ward government. In alternate years she and the other women hand-sew the festival yukata (light robes of blue-and-white cotton) for themselves and some of the male leaders of the chōkai.

Although the permanent representatives nominally serve one-year terms, there is little annual turnover. In seven of the 13 geographical sections the same person remained permanent representative over the period 1977–81. In five other sections two people held the position during the five years. In only one bu did the position change hands every year. The corresponding women's positions followed a similar pattern. These positions differ from those of cluster representatives less in substance than in the method of recruitment. At this level office-holding shifts less often, and the posts are filled by individuals chosen for their special interest in neighborhood affairs, instead of through automatic rotation among households.[9]

In the old people's club the 13 section leaders—some men, some women—are the lowest-level officers. They have roughly the same duties as the permanent representatives for the chōkai and the fujinbu. Because the old people's club draws its members from only a fraction of households in the neighborhood, it does

not require representatives in each cluster of households. Moreover, the clusters' representatives for the women's auxiliary
handle routine communications for the old people's club as part
of the fujinbu's general concern with the care of the elderly.

Districts and Vice-Presidents

At the next level in the chōkai's hierarchy, the geographical
sections are grouped into three districts (*chiku*). Each district is
under a chōkai vice-president (*fukukaichō*), who maintains liaison between the chōkai leadership and the four or five permanent representatives in his district. Assistant division chiefs
(*fukubuchō*) hold corresponding positions in the women's auxiliary, as do vice-presidents in the old people's club.

These large districts have no special names or designation.
When residents use a name at all, they speak of "Mr. Shigemori's
district" or "Mr. Kobayashi's district," referring to whichever
vice-president comes from that district. These organizationally
expedient districts do not correspond to any recognizable social
units or boundaries. They are simply clusters of contiguous bu,
and this division of the neighborhood into districts ensures that
senior officers of the chōkai are not all drawn from a single area
within Miyamoto-chō. The districts overlap the "upper" and
"lower" regions of the neighborhood described in Chapter One.
One covers the bulk of kami and part of the shopping street; the
other two divide shimo, most of the shopping street, and a small
chunk of kami.

The vice-presidents, appointed by the chōkai president, form
a chōkai cabinet. There are five vice-presidents in all: the three
who in some fashion represent the geographical districts of the
neighborhood, a senior vice-president, who acts as the president's closest aide, and the head of the women's auxiliary, who
serves in an ex officio capacity. Together with the president
these five people plan and carry out almost everything the chōkai does. Liaison with the sections and clusters in the district
under them is only a small portion of their duties. Indeed the
vice-presidents' geographically defined tasks differ only slightly
from those of the sections' permanent representatives; they
have the additional minor duty of posting notices on the seven
chōkai bulletin boards scattered around the neighborhood.

During my research Mr. Kobayashi served as one of the chō-kai's vice-presidents. He grew up in Miyamoto-chō, where his father had established a laundry a year or two before the 1923 Kantō earthquake, just as the neighborhood was coming into being. Mr. Kobayashi inherited the business, located on a side street of shimo just beside the temple's entrance. Mr. Kobayashi, in his late forties, belongs to the "young" group of leaders who in the late 1970's attempted to dominate neighborhood organizations. He is an easygoing man with a long memory for local affairs and a somewhat cynical bent when discussing goings-on in Miyamoto-chō. As a vice-president of the chōkai, he has to spend many evenings each month debating current neighborhood matters in small meetings at the chōkai hall, but he holds no special responsibilities within the organization. He is simply the representative of his district and one adviser among the "kitchen cabinet" that sets chōkai policies. But his standing in leadership circles is strengthened by his position as the treasurer for the Wakamono Shinbokukai, the group of about a dozen "young" men that plays an important role in the campaigns of Tsurumi-sensei. This informal faction dominated the inner circles of chōkai leadership during 1979–81, but (as I discuss later) lost power in 1981 to an older, more conservative faction.

The Upper Echelons of Leadership

Above the three tiers of territorial clusters, sections, and districts, with their corresponding strata of liaison positions, stand several dozen chōkai officers who hold functionally, not territorially, defined positions. The chōkai constitution specifically mentions 13 upper-level officers, but defines their duties flexibly, allowing the chōkai to expand or contract the number of offices as circumstances warrant. Over the years, as the chōkai has started new activities or has taken on new responsibilities, it has added many new leadership positions: 34 upper-level officers appeared on the combined 1980 roster of chōkai and fujinbu leaders. (The roster, as well as the constitution, appears in Appendix B.)

The most important officer is of course the *chōkaichō*, the president of the neighborhood association. During most of my fieldwork the president was Mr. Kataoka, a taciturn self-employed professional whose home and office are a few feet away from the railway tracks at the boundaries of Miyamoto-chō. Mr. Kataoka, a man in his early fifties, was raised in the neighborhood and graduated from the local elementary school. Before becoming president of the chōkai he served as the president of the elementary school's PTA. He and his family—his wife, a daughter in high school, and a son in elementary school—live behind and above his office, and his widowed mother lives in the house next door. His father, a retired government official, had been president of the neighborhood association a decade and a half earlier; he continued to play a prominent role in local affairs as a respected elder statesman until his sudden death in 1980.

As president of the chōkai Mr. Kataoka spends part of almost every day on neighborhood affairs. In addition to semiformal meetings with other upper-level chōkai officers once a week or so, he spends many hours each week in Mr. Takahashi's shop talking over local matters with other leaders and residents who drop by to gossip. He receives numerous phone calls every day—from neighborhood residents seeking information about upcoming activities; from officials of the ward government asking him to attend a meeting or to arrange for Miyamoto-chō's participation in some government-sponsored campaign; and from leaders of nearby neighborhoods checking on how Miyamoto-chō plans to respond to some new government request. His presence is obligatory at every funeral in Miyamoto-chō; he is expected to deliver a few congratulatory remarks in the name of Miyamoto-chō at every ceremony sponsored by any local school attended by a neighborhood child; and he is invited to represent Miyamoto-chō at each and every event sponsored by other local organizations—the shopkeepers' association, the volunteer fire brigade, and the Aoiro Shinkokukai. The ward's branch office calls on him several times a month to attend advisory meetings, where government policies and programs are explained and the reactions of local leaders are solicited. A variety of federations of neighborhood associations, covering progressively larger parts of the ward, expect him to participate in meetings to discuss machi-zukuri programs. Since he sits on the board of governors of the Shintō shrine, he must attend all important ritual events. And of course at all events sponsored by Miyamoto-chō's chōkai—from summertime picnics for children and the cherry-blossom-viewing party sponsored by the women's auxiliary, to the pesticide spraying crews and the drills for the disaster-relief team—Mr. Kataoka is expected to visibly lead the neighborhood.

Only three of the chōkai's officers—the president and two auditors (*kaikei kansa*)—stand for election. The chōkai president appoints all other officers himself, after complex though informal consultations within the chōkai's inner circles of leadership—a behind-the-scenes process that also plays a major role in the nomination and election of the chōkai president himself.

The nonelective offices can be divided into three main categories. Most offices deal directly with the day-to-day affairs of the chōkai and are for set terms of one or two years. The vice-presidents, the treasurers, and the chiefs and assistant chiefs for the five functional divisions fall into this category.

The chōkai's functional divisions are responsible, respectively, for fire prevention, crime prevention, beautification and sanitation, traffic safety, and youth activities. Often, if a division's activities logically correspond to some occupation, the chōkai president will appoint someone with the appropriate expertise to head the division. We have seen an example of this in Mr. Yamamura, the electrical contractor who has long headed the crime prevention division, responsible for the upkeep of streetlights on back alleys. Mr. Yamamura's family moved to Miyamoto-chō just after the 1923 earthquake, and the family business his father established is now split into two enterprises—a contracting business run by the son and an appliance store run by the elder Mrs. Yamamura, with loose supervision from her much older husband. The younger Mr. Yamamura, now in his mid-forties, is a key (though behind-the-scenes) member of the young leadership faction of the chōkai. The small office of his contracting firm is a frequent hangout for leaders. Many evenings each month Mr. Izumi and Tsurumi-sensei, or Mr. Kobayashi and Mr. Nakajima, can be found there discussing neighborhood affairs and plotting strategies for the chōkai, before they set out for a nearby *sushi* bar or a cabaret for a night of drinking.

A smaller number of positions—seven in 1980—are advisory posts, filled by respected senior members of the community, who serve for unspecified, extended terms. In recognition of their community standing, they are appointed by seeming consensus—confirmed by the acclamation of the chōkai's general business meeting or by the agreement of the leadership council.

Finally, two pairs of offices—the parish delegates (*ujiko sōdai*) and the social welfare representatives (*minseiiin*)—are essentially chōkai appointees to other institutions; they have little to do directly with the internal affairs of the chōkai or its women's auxiliary. For example, Mr. Asakawa, a middle-aged greengrocer who has served for over a decade as the chōkai's parish delegate, attends every shrine event and plays an active role in Miyamoto-chō's annual festival, but does not visibly take part in any other chōkai affairs. By the same token Mrs. Uramoto, an older widow who serves as one of Miyamoto-chō's two minseiiin, can be seen almost daily visiting the homes of elderly shut-ins, but she rarely appears at any chōkai meeting, and her duties require consultations with ward staff far more than with neighborhood officials.

Most important for the chōkai's week-to-week functioning is the *shikkōbu* (executive committee or cabinet), made up of the chōkai president, the five vice-presidents, and the junior treasurer.[10] This group, which interacts informally almost every day and meets semiformally three or four times a month, makes most decisions and initiates most projects. One vice-president acts as the closest assistant to the chōkai president. He keeps most of the written records and handles the keys to the chōkai hall. During my research my landlord Mr. Takahashi filled this post. The *fujinbuchō*, or chief of the women's auxiliary, holds a vice-presidency, but in an ex officio capacity. The other three vice-presidents have no specific tasks beyond maintaining liaison with the three districts, but for all practical purposes, as part of the shikkōbu they run the chōkai, planning, supervising, and providing their own labor for almost all its activities. Similar inner circles of leaders play the major role in determining actions and policies for both the women's auxiliary and the old people's group.

The fujinbu, headed by Mrs. Horie, has four other officers—*fukubuchō*, or vice-division chiefs—who together form a similar cabinet for the women's auxiliary. Mrs. Horie, a smiling woman in her late fifties, and her husband run a small housewares shop across from the chōkai hall. The four fujinbu cabinet members are Mrs. Tsurumi, the wife of the politician; Mrs. Oshima, a gregarious woman whose husband is an official in a national government ministry, and whose father-in-law, now bedridden, once served as a chōkai president; Mrs. Abe, the wife of a sarariiman ("salaryman") with a large but not fancy home on the quiet street next to the shrine, a perpetually-smiling woman whose main hobby is the folk-dance troupe; and Mrs. Morita, a quiet woman, married to a construction worker, who lives on a back alley near the old river.

Mrs. Horie and her four assistants seemingly spend most of their evenings at the neighborhood hall, attending meetings or serving tea to male officers. None has small children to care for, but Mrs. Abe's and Mrs. Morita's children still attend the local junior high school, and both women are officers of the PTA. Mrs. Tsurumi and Mrs. Oshima have sons who are deep in preparation for the all-important college entrance examinations, and both have elderly parents in their households who require attentive care. And Mrs. Horie, who often has her infant grandson in tow, not only spends many hours each day working in the family's housewares shop, but pursues a side career as an instructor in the art of kimono wearing. All five women have obviously reached some careful compromise between neighborhood service and domestic responsibilities, for it would be unthinkable to relegate family duties to second place.

The fujinbu and chōkai cabinets are the two core groups of the organizational structure. The heads of the various functional divisions may not participate much in the chōkai's councils unless the association is planning projects that fall within their jurisdictions. These functional divisions—many of whose activities I described in Chapter Four—really consist of little more than the division chief and one assistant, who twist arms to gather the necessary work crew when the need arises. Though

the chōkai frequently selects a division chief because his occupation bears some relationship to the division's activities, his
general community standing and active interest in neighborhood affairs are important requirements.

At the top of the neighborhood's hierarchy of status are the
chōkai's honorary counselors and advisers—the *sōdanyaku* and
the *komon*. Although usually removed from the day-to-day running of the chōkai, they play extremely important roles in its
decisions, both in the informal councils, where the most important issues are decided, and in the lengthy discussions preceding the selection of new leaders. Mr. Hasegawa, the retired
business executive, was the most active komon in 1979–81; he
could be found at every event, standing off in the middle distance directing other officers or huddling in hurried conversations about the matter at hand. Some leaders, not entirely flat-
teringly, called him Miyamoto-chō's *kagemusha* ("the power
behind the throne").

Sōdanyaku during the same period included Tsurumi-sensei
and Mr. Mizuno, the head of the shopkeepers' association until
1981, both of whom had been recent chōkai presidents. As sōdanyaku each assumed a role of political strategist and planner,
Tsurumi-sensei more likely to speculate or advise on the chōkai's relations with the ward government, and Mr. Mizuno more
frequently calculating the internal political dynamics of a decision to be made or the appropriate response to the activities of
an adjacent neighborhood. Tsurumi-sensei and Mr. Mizuno
have different agendas, which also affects their roles as advisers.
Tsurumi-sensei is a central figure in the "young" faction of leaders, who seek to open up the chōkai and to get more residents
actively involved. Mr. Mizuno is a key member of the older,
more conservative faction, which sees no particular reason to
upset the established hierarchy of the organization or to change
the mix of chōkai events and activities.

The general roles of both the komon and the sōdanyaku are
crucial in part because few codified principles or written guide-
lines exist to govern the chōkai's activities. Instead, questions
about the properly traditional and traditionally proper ways of
doing things tend to be settled in consultations among leaders,
and in such consultations the greater experience (and prestige)

of the older men carries enormous weight. They base their opinions on their interpretations of chōkai precedent and tradition, not on the written constitution or other specified rules and regulations. Their authority extends beyond the chōkai organization per se, and they may be consulted about general issues or unexpected difficulties in local life. Therefore, not only the most important issues, but also seemingly trivial problems—such as deciding that I should be permitted to spend a particular Sunday in early September polishing brass ornaments for the upcoming festival with a group from the old people's club instead of spraying pesticides with a work crew from the sanitation division—are resolved in discussions with the advisers. Late in my fieldwork I confirmed that during the first several months of my research, my presence in Miyamoto-chō and the oddity of a foreigner wanting to study the neighborhood association raised frequent questions about my participation in local events. The private, informal deliberations of these senior honorary advisers resolved, or at least discussed, these issues.[11]

Of the two categories of advisers, komon are older and of higher status. The number of advisers is not set; during my research there were four komon and three sōdanyaku, and all seven of the men were past presidents of the chōkai.

The position of sōdanyaku is almost automatically bestowed on recent past presidents of the chōkai. All sōdanyaku had been chōkai presidents within the past ten years, and all chōkai presidents who had served within the past decade are sōdanyaku. The position of komon is not such an automatic honor; although all komon have been president of the chōkai, not all past presidents achieve sufficient stature to be elevated from sōdanyaku to komon . Unlike sōdanyaku, komon are considered to be retired from active leadership and so are not potential candidates for the office of chōkai president.

The sōdanyaku are all in their fifties or early sixties, and are thus roughly the equals of the current president in age as well as community standing. All are healthy and still active in chōkai and other neighborhood affairs, and any might be called on again to serve as president. Indeed Mr. Mizuno, a sōdanyaku in 1980, was elected chōkai president again in 1981, a few weeks before my fieldwork ended.

Mr. Mizuno, a retail merchant in his mid-sixties, had served two terms as the chōkai president in the 1970's before becoming a sōdanyaku. His shop is a large and successful one, the day-to-day management of which is left to his son, in his mid-thirties. Mr. Mizuno therefore has time for neighborhood leadership and other forms of social service; he is, for example, an officially appointed volunteer youth probation officer to whom the police and other government agencies send juvenile delinquents for guidance. One can easily imagine what effect a "good talking to" by the self-assured Mr. Mizuno might have on a young offender; certainly his commanding manner does not always sit well with other—particularly younger—residents of Miyamoto-chō.

The komon range in age from their late sixties into their eighties; some are no longer active in neighborhood affairs. Not all past presidents of the chōkai eventually become komon because the position recognizes a man's high standing and reputation in the community and his outside contacts and networks of influence; some chōkai presidents do not achieve the requisite regard beyond Miyamoto-chō's boundaries. Komon hold a position at once more honored and more honorary than sōdanyaku; they usually play much less important roles in the chōkai's day-to-day decisions and affairs. Unlike the sōdanyaku, who serve only for several years, sometimes then going on to be chōkai president again or to be elevated to the status of komon, a komon once appointed holds the position for life.

Mr. Hasegawa was the most active komon during my fieldwork. A retired business executive in his later seventies, he had lived in the neighborhood since the 1930's. He made his home with a middle-aged unmarried daughter in a well-kept older house on the flatlands near the traffic bypass over the river. Mr. Hasegawa played a prominent role in neighborhood affairs in the years immediately after the Second World War, and when the chōkai began to operate openly in the 1950's, he was one of the first presidents. He continued as a leading neighborhood official through the early 1970's, when he "retired" from office. In fact Mr. Hasegawa remained active as an adviser and supervisor of almost all neighborhood events. Most days he could be found in the back of Mr. Takahashi's store discussing the affairs of Miyamoto-chō, and when any event was being planned or launched, he was there to oversee it. Whether he was making on-the-spot decisions about festivities to celebrate the new street-lights erected by the shopkeepers' association, or plotting strat-egies for dealing with the ward government's disaster prepar-edness office, or supervising the uncrating of festival decora-tions, or advising the women of the fujinbu on how to properly sew cotton robes for the festival, no one ever publicly doubted that Mr. Hasegawa knew the answer.

The komon and the sōdanyaku, if no longer officially wield-ing executive authority, are near the pinnacles of actual power and have achieved the heights of the prestige that the chōkai can confer or confirm. They stand, therefore, not only at the top of a status or prestige hierarchy, but also at one pole on a contin-uum of leadership positions within the neighborhood.

Paralleling the progression from the smallest units to the largest and from the lowest positions to the highest in the or-ganizational structures of the chōkai and its women's auxiliary, the character of leadership positions varies along several con-tinua (see Table 8). At the most geographically limited and least powerful end of the scale, in the kumi or household clusters, po-sitions are not really filled by the particular people who nomi-nally hold them, but instead are simply allotted to households by almost automatic rotation. At the middle level of the geo-graphical sections, the positions become much more individual, assigned because of people's interest and involvement in the as-sociation's affairs, and their actual abilities and qualifications for the position, although the duties may be carried out by other members of the officeholder's household. At the most inclusive and upper levels, posts are assigned on the basis of personal char-acteristics and achievements. Here the positions are unques-tionably held by the individual; he or she alone discharges the duties and responsibilities of the office.

Bitter behind-the-back criticisms leveled at one woman whose husband held a high chōkai office underscores the im-portance of this distinction. Mrs. Tono earned the scorn of many residents because she presumed to have a voice in chōkai affairs, including the disposition of funds, and even attempted to give orders to other officials of the chōkai and the women's auxiliary because of her husband's position. Mr. Tono also came in for

TABLE 8
Characteristics of Officeholding in the Chōkai

Category	Selection method	Term[a]	Individual (I) or household (H)
Honorary advisers (komon)[b]	Acclaim	Permanent	I
Honorary counselors (sōdanyaku)[b]	Retirement (from presidency)	Indefinite	I
Parish delegates (ujiko sōdai)[c]	Appointment	Indefinite	I
Social welfare representatives (to ward govt.; minseiiin)	Nomination (to ward govt.)	Indefinite	I
The chōkai cabinet (shikkōbu)			
President (chōkaichō)	Election	2 years	I
Vice-presidents (fukukaichō)	Appointment	1 year	I
Treasurer (1 of 2; kaikei)	Appointment	1 year	I
Other upper-echelon officers			
Treasurer (kaikei)	Appointment	1 year	I
Auditors (kaikei kansa)	Election	2 years	I
Chiefs of functional divisions	Appointment	1 year	I/(H)[d]
Territorially delimited officeholders			
District (chiku) vice-presidents (3 of 5; fukukaicho)	Appointment	1 year	I/(H)[d]
Section (bu) representatives (jōninriji)[b]	Appointment	1 year	I/(H)[d]
Household cluster (kumi) representatives (riji)[b]	Rotation	1 year	H

[a] Officeholders with fixed terms of office can and do serve more than one term, but the one-year rotation is normally observed in the case of the kumi representatives.

[b] Officeholder may concurrently hold an equivalent position in the women's auxiliary or the old people's club.

[c] The chōkai president is an ex officio parish delegate.

[d] Although the office is an individual one, some duties may be performed by other household members.

criticism for failing to prevent her from overstepping herself. Although some of this carping may have been simply personality conflicts or jealousy, the criticisms essentially revolved around the theme, "How dare she think she has any position or power simply because of her husband's office!"

Selection of officers for their individual attributes, rather than as representatives of households, and the individual exercise of leadership, rather than having duties carried out by interchangeable household members, are increasingly stressed toward the peak of the hierarchical pyramid. And higher in the organization, fewer and fewer households have more than one member in a formal leadership position.[12]

Practical considerations, moreover, work against households holding dual leadership positions. These positions place great time demands on officers, as they often complain. It is impossible to say precisely how much time leaders spend on neighborhood affairs, but their formal or informal discussions of neighborhood business alone probably consume at least an hour a day. Beyond that, they are typically called on two or three days a week to attend a meeting, to lend a hand at some event, or to join a work crew. For most local residents the demands of family life or the responsibilities of a family business mean that a household can spare no more than one member to time-consuming neighborhood activities. In selecting leaders the chōkai and other local groups take into account the candidate's household and business obligations and the strains that an office might place on him or her (as well as the possibility that the organization might suffer by having a leader unable or unwilling to devote the necessary amount of attention to the job). Because neighborhood offices require flexible time and nearly full-time presence in the neighborhood, white-collar sarariiman and other wage earners employed outside Miyamoto-chō—even if they want leadership positions—are effectively excluded from them.

Decision-Making and Hierarchy in the Chōkai

Although leaders frequently reiterate that Miyamoto-chō's chōkai represents the neighborhood's residents, no one—neither leader nor ordinary resident—doubts the centralized nature of decision-making. Throughout the elaborate layers of organizational structure, decisions percolate from higher levels to lower ones, and though the informal ties among neighbors that link leaders to rank-and-file residents provide ample means for ideas to move up as well as down, both the formal power to make decisions and the implicit influence required to set the chōkai's agenda reside with its top leaders.

The chōkai's annual general meeting, mandated in the constitution, offers the one institutionalized setting in which individual members may formally express their opinions about the way the organization operates. Given the extensive informal consultations among leaders that often determine chōkai policies and activities, this annual meeting is almost pro forma. Leaders set the agenda ahead of time, though other matters can be raised from the floor. Ordinarily, only a few residents—other than those obligated by their leadership positions—come to the meetings. Not even all the kumi representatives or their wives attend; when they do, they bring proxies stamped with the personal seals of householders from their clusters signifying that they are duly empowered to act on the households' behalf.

The chiefs of each functional division—traffic safety, sanitation, youth activities, and so forth—report briefly on activities past and planned, but the neighborhood's finances are the meeting's major business. The treasurers present the past year's finances and the proposed budget for the coming year. The auditors formally certify the figures. Chōkai members carefully scrutinize and question this report; many members, themselves proprietors of small businesses, know the ins and outs of bookkeeping and are wary of financial reports. The chōkai's annual budget exceeds 1.8 million yen, most of which comes directly from chōkai dues (see Appendix B). Whether dues are adequate or should be raised is always a matter of hot debate.

Discussions swirl around the chōkai's current finances, as well as its meager property. Some chōkai in Tokyo own considerable amounts of extremely valuable real estate, ancient ritual objects, and other property; Miyamoto-chō has little. The neighborhood hall stands on land leased from the Buddhist temple whose graveyard it overlooks, and the chōkai shares ownership of the structure with the merchants' association. Beyond that, the chōkai's property consists of the furnishings and equipment for the hall and the assortment of festival paraphernalia kept in the storage shed by the shrine. But this very lack of property keeps property a hot topic; both at the general meeting and in informal discussions among leaders, the more modern and comfortable neighborhood halls of nearby chōkai are held up with envy, and somebody is always floating an idea about how

Miyamoto-chō could come up with the money to rebuild its own hall. In response, somebody else always points out the chō-kai's modest financial resources, and the discussion moves on.

In alternate years the general meeting selects the chōkai's three elective officers—the president and the two auditors. The outcome of this process is largely predetermined. Formally, a nominating committee of about a dozen men and women—cho-sen from among the chōkai members attending the meeting, in-cluding one or two from the inner circle—retires to the vesti-bule of the chōkai hall, where they discuss the candidates pre-viously agreed upon by the leaders through informal caucuses among themselves over the previous four or five months. After about ten minutes, the ad hoc committee returns and an-nounces that the members have agreed to agree upon the slate of candidates proposed. They put the now-formally nominated slate to the meeting as a whole, which accepts it by acclamation. A delegation then quickly departs for the homes of the new of-ficials, who (like candidates at American political conventions) stay away until their elections are sewn up. The new president immediately takes over as the presiding officer of the meeting and of the chōkai. Within a few days, after he has discussed po-tential candidates for the other offices with the komon and the sōdanyaku, and has paid formal visits to past and future office-holders, he announces the entire slate of new leaders.

The selection process may seem authoritarian, arbitrary, and totally under the control of a self-perpetuating oligarchy. Critics of the chōkai (who voice their criticism mainly by their absence) argue that these characterizations—not only of the selection process but of chōkai affairs generally—are correct. But chōkai supporters maintain that the lengthy rounds of discussion among leaders and other residents preceding these and most other decisions automatically provide checks and balances in the decision-making process. The term *nemawashi*, often used to describe the process, refers to gradually trimming the roots of a living plant so that it can be transplanted; colloquially, the word describes reaching a consensus by carefully laying the groundwork for a decision and meeting any outstanding objec-tions before any action is taken. Supporters argue that, through the lengthy process of nemawashi, residents have ample opportunities to air their opinions and raise any objections, and that the only ones who have no voice in such decisions are those who exclude themselves by choosing to abstain from chōkai affairs.

Although consensus is the ultimate goal, even within the leadership circles unanimity of opinion is infrequent on many matters, and agreement takes time. One example mentioned earlier—the chōkai election in the spring of 1981—produced sharp disagreement over the choice of a new president, and provoked heated private discussions as early as the New Year's holidays, if not earlier. An important issue revolved around whether the younger leadership faction (men in their late forties and fifties) would continue to run the chōkai or whether the older generation of leaders (then in their late fifties and sixties) would regain control. Younger leaders, at least, saw the decision to select Mr. Mizuno—the stern sōdanyaku in his middle sixties who had held the position for two terms in the 1970's before going on to serve as president of the shopkeepers' association—as a rejection of their tenure and a return to more staid and conservative practices.

On other matters, discussion may continue for years; once a group attains consensus, however, action may be almost immediate. One such instance was the enduring debate over whether the chōkai should try to raise money to rebuild its hall or should invest in a new portable shrine. On one side of the issue, proponents argued for a new multistoried building with shops on the ground floor, meeting rooms on the second story, and apartments on the third; revenues from the ground and third floors could finance the loans necessary for the reconstruction, they argued. On the other side, opponents urged that if the chōkai was going to embark on extensive fund-raising, its efforts should be devoted to buying a new mikoshi (a portable shrine) for the annual festival; this side argued that the mikoshi would strengthen the chōkai generally, by attracting the interest and ultimately the participation of a wider group of residents, especially young men. The two sides to the debate paralleled the factional split in the chōkai leadership, with the older, more conservative leaders who resumed control of the chōkai in 1981 supporting the reconstruction of the hall, and the younger leaders arguing for a new mikoshi.

In May 1982, after informal discussions had gone on for several years, the young leadership faction (now out of power) finally decided to purchase a new portable shrine. Institutionally, the decision was made outside the chōkai and the fund-raising drive was based in a separate organization expressly created for the purpose, but within a matter of weeks the group raised pledges of over ten million yen from 400 local households. Fast action, once consensus had been reached, meant that a new mikoshi could be commissioned, built, and delivered in time for the festival in mid-September. (The purchase of the mikoshi is discussed in detail in Chapter Seven.)

But even here, although many people may be mobilized into action by a decision, the important consensus that must first be reached involves only a small handful of leaders. The hierarchical character of the chōkai is most evident in the patterns of decision-making, but there is more subtle evidence of it as well. For example, at the chōkai general meeting and other events, the leaders' implicit hierarchies of status and prestige are spatially displayed. The interior of the hall becomes an arena for the expression of social meanings in which space is far from undifferentiated, though the meanings attached to distance and proximity may shift, recede, or reappear under different circumstances.

At formal meetings chōkai members and leaders distribute themselves without apparent thought or prodding into a clear although implicit spatial hierarchy. In general terms the back wall of the main room ranks more highly than the front (the street side), and the end next to the kitchen anteroom more highly than the end next to the main entry and the vestibule. Men generally take a seat along the back wall facing the street, and women invariably sit along the front wall facing them.

Metaphorically, one can think of the floor as sloping both front to back and side to side. Looked at from the perspective of the street, the front left corner would be at the lowest and the back right corner at the highest point on the slope. Indeed people sometimes use the terms *ue* and *shita* ("up" and "down") to refer to the different ends of the room, but the arrangement is not really that simple. The front of the room where the women sit and the back where the men sit are essentially separate domains, connected to one another because gender implies a status distinction but otherwise governed by somewhat different and unconnected rules. The continuum of status distinctions is less finely graded on the women's side than on the men's side, where the seating is complicated by the fact that prestige does not necessarily equal power; ranking systems based on different dimensions come into play simultaneously.

It is around the middle of the back wall that the most obvious and at the same time subtle jockeying for position takes place. To continue the metaphor of the sloping floor, each of the upper-echelon leaders attempts to defer to the man next to him, urging him to take a seat farther "up" the room. As things sort themselves out, the most prestigious (and usually the oldest) men sit in the back corner, and the slightly younger men who hold the real reins of power in the neighborhood—the sōdanyaku, the chōkai president, and other members of the inner leadership— sit just "below" them, about two-thirds of the way up the room from the vestibule. There the room's attention focuses on them, not on the nominal "top" of the room.

Early in my fieldwork I learned the importance of social geography. At the first formal chōkai event that my wife and I attended together, we sat down without too much thought in what I already knew to be a low-status position: against the front wall toward the bottom of the hall. It visibly startled people that husband and wife would sit together, and several people gently urged us toward separate spots. When we foolishly declined— not wanting to cause a fuss, of course—the elaborate gradations of status and the "immutable" division between the men's and the women's sides were suddenly rearranged around us. Our positions had created a new line of demarcation that saw all the seats to my left, between me and the bottom of the room, filled by medium- and low-status men, and all those to my wife's right, stretching up toward the kitchen, occupied by women arrayed with little attention to status but simply crowded by the male encroachment that had taken half their side of the room. After that we took care to sit separately; I on the men's side close to the vestibule at the bottom of the room, and my wife on the women's side or in the kitchen. Our only foray toward the top of the room came during the farewell party the chōkai held for us, when I sat in the place of honor next to two septuagenarians and my wife sat near the head of the women's tables along the front of the hall.

Sharp status demarcations occur at the sliding doors at each end of the room (or rather at the wooden-door tracks embedded between the tatami mats, since the doors are generally removed). The kitchen anteroom at the top of the room is unquestionably women's territory, where no man ever sits during anything even remotely resembling a formal occasion. The vestibule at the bottom is akin to outer darkness, and the only people I ever saw sit there were some workmen the chōkai had hired to erect festival decorations who had been invited into the hall for a quick bite to eat after the job was done.

These kinds of status considerations are displayed, in one form or another, in almost all the chōkai's events. Principles of hierarchy and differential status underlie virtually every aspect of its structure and activities, shaping the decision-making and election processes, the access to power, and the opportunities to express opinions or to influence neighborhood activities. If the chōkai and related groups represented the sum total of the social relationships that link residents of Miyamoto-chō to one another, only a minority of residents could be considered truly involved. There would be no question that the neighborhood's social organization was extremely "vertical."

Yet the chōkai acts in the name of an ethos of communal life that implies a certain degree of egalitarianism among Miyamoto-cho's residents. Lacking powers of coercion, the chōkai could not exist and function without the willing and voluntary cooperation of the mass of ordinary residents at the bottom of the hierarchy. For most rank-and-file residents the structural complexities of the upper echelons of the chōkai are often irrelevant, but the activities it fosters on behalf of the neighborhood are not. Seen apart from the vertical structure, the events and programs and opportunities for interaction with one's neighbors merge with or are an extension of the egalitarian ethos that characterizes other extra-institutional ties among neighborhood residents. The chōkai exists and, in a sense, can only do so against the backdrop of these other, more horizontal ties.

CHAPTER SIX

Friends and Neighbors

THE ACTIVITIES AND organizational structure of Miyamo-to-chō's formal institutions are naturally the most prominent manifestations of neighborhood identity. But these institutions encompass or create only a fraction of significant social relationships. A neighborly, harmonious community life, which local groups uphold as their goal, owes as much to individual, often informal ties among residents as it does to the formally structured activities local institutions sponsor.

The informal, elusive, extra-institutional side of community life flourishes in many things: in the *idobatakaigi*, or "well-side conferences," of local gossip outside a vegetable stall; in the aid neighbors give one another for funerals; in the social pressures exerted to close down a pornographic book store; in the patterns of friendship that develop among schoolchildren and are maintained throughout adult life. Such things as mutual aid, social control, sociability, friendship, and the simple satisfaction of knowing and being known by other members of the community both foster and are fostered by the person-to-person ties that link Miyamoto-chō's residents.

Personal ties not only enable these aspects of community life to flourish; they maintain the social fabric of local life without which other, more organized activities and formally constituted groups simply could not exist. These ties tend to lack some of the hierarchical structuring so characteristic of the chōkai and other groups, allowing the residents of Miyamoto-chō to relate to one another much more nearly as equals than they do within the confines of formal organizations. These generally horizontal ties form a backdrop—an egalitarian ethos—against which the chōkai can act in the name of community solidarity.

Interactions Among Neighboring Households

As we have seen, the chōkai and the women's auxiliary conduct their affairs at the most basic level through the kumi, or household clusters. But groups of neighboring households regularly interact with one another outside the chōkai framework, and these groups may or may not correspond to the kumi groupings.

Customarily when a new household moves into a neighborhood, its members pay courtesy calls on each of its immediate neighbors, bearing a small gift—a box of cakes or a *tenugui*, a small decorative hand towel—to introduce themselves; invariably, they request their neighbors' goodwill using the formal set phrases the Japanese language provides for such occasions. But though such customs are still a standard part of Japanese etiquette, this formality is not always followed in Miyamoto-chō. Most new residents moving into the neighborhood nowadays are young single people or young married couples, taking up residence in an apartment with little expectation of living there for any length of time. Self-consciously transient residents of this sort have little to gain from establishing close ties with their neighbors and are not much concerned with the niceties of neighborly etiquette.

Nevertheless, one family moving into the building where my wife and I lived did appear at our door one day. The Matsumuras were a trifle startled by the tall foreigner, but with calm composure they formally introduced themselves, presented me with a box of cakes, and asked my forbearance of any troubles they might cause as our new neighbors. As it turned out, the Matsumuras—husband and wife (both professionals employed outside the neighborhood), their nine-year-old son, Mr. Matsumura's eighty-year-old mother, and Tarō, their small dog—were moving into a "2DK" apartment only temporarily,[1] during the rebuilding of their permanent house on the far side of Miyamoto-chō. The Matsumuras' concern with formal introductions, therefore, may have been simply an extension of the careful neighborly ties they had already established elsewhere in Miyamoto-chō (or may have been to apologize in advance for Tarō's barking). The other people who moved into the building during our stay—a brother and sister attending college, and a childless couple in their fifties—apparently saw no need to go through the traditional observances of neighborly etiquette and never formally called on us, although they were perfectly friendly and conversational when we met in passing.

Mutual Aid

Formal self-introductions of this sort are the prelude to the new household's establishing neighborly ties with the several households immediately adjacent to it. In general these relationships underpin various forms of minor mutual aid. Neighbors keep an eye on each other's homes when household members are away, and accept deliveries for them. They borrow and lend small household items. A housewife who finds a special sale on some delicacy or a household member who brings back *meibutsu* ("famous local specialties") from a trip may present a portion of the item to a neighboring household. Housewives pass news about special sales, new shops, or the availability of seasonal specialties down one alley and up another. The ties some Miyamoto-chō households maintain with rural farmers provide an example of the minor aid and modest benefits neighbors may share. Two or three times a month, old farm women—their backs bent by the weight of the large wicker hampers of vegetables they carry—visit Miyamoto-chō from nearby prefectures to sell fresh produce. They do not hawk their vegetables on the streets but instead visit a regular round of households that have been their customers for years. Mrs. Tsunoda, for example, has "her" peddler, a woman who has been visiting the house since Mrs. Tsunoda was a child. Often Mrs. Tsunoda will make extra purchases of some special bargain and send one of her children running over to a neighbor's home to deliver the produce as a small gift in thanks for some favor the Tsunoda family received the week before.

Many neighboring households own property in common. The alleyways that lace through the blocks, and even some of the paved lanes wide enough for automobiles, are privately owned. In many cases, as the land was subdivided into house lots, the walkways were sold in tiny pieces to the adjacent households or to the entire group of householders abutting a given stretch of lane or alley. The households lining a walkway share responsibility for its upkeep and repair, and if it is jointly owned, for property taxes. Similarly, in those areas where old communal wells are still usable, the neighboring households share the minor costs of keeping up the hand pumps. Since all houses in Miyamoto-chō now draw water from municipal mains, no one uses well water for drinking, cooking, or bathing, but the wells remain a handy source of water for washing down the pavement or thinning the summer pesticide spray. More critically, residents, the fire department, and the ward government's disaster-preparedness office all regard the wells as important resources to be maintained for emergency use during fires or earthquakes.

The upkeep of the walkways—and paved streets and sidewalks, too, whether owned by the abutting households or not—requires occasional simple carpentry or stonework and a variety of daily chores that neighbors do for one another as a matter of course. When the garbage trucks arrive every other morning, housewives rush out to help the workmen lift trash barrels onto the truck and then tidy up the area as the truck moves on down the block. Housewives and shopkeepers sweep the sidewalks or streets in front of their property several times a day, and sprinkle the unpaved lanes and the asphalt streets with water to keep the dust down. From the windows of our apartment, it was hard to miss the sight of old Mrs. Makino, an octogenarian whose back was bent almost double, coming out several times each day to briskly sweep and sprinkle the street and sidewalk around her son's shop.

In the aftermath of a serious storm, such as the typhoon during the second autumn of my fieldwork (the first in over a decade to strike Tokyo directly), neighbors almost automatically turn to each other for help. Fortunately, this typhoon caused no extraordinary damage in Miyamoto-chō or elsewhere in the Tokyo region. As residents emerged from the shelter of their tightly shuttered homes under the suddenly blue skies that signaled the storm's passing, they hurriedly exchanged questions about the safety of each other's family and house. Assured that no one had suffered any injuries, neighbors throughout Miyamoto-chō pitched in to clear away downed branches, fallen roof tiles, and broken television aerials, to pick up overturned bicycles, trash barrels, and gates and fences, and to sweep up the mud, water, and other debris that clogged the back alleys. Next day, when I walked around the neighborhood, there was little indication that Miyamoto-chō had suffered through a major storm. Except for occasional patches of missing roof tiles, homeowners and their neighbors had put everything back to rights.

Immediate neighbors who have established close relationships may also exchange gifts on appropriate occasions. One such event is a *jichinsai*, a Shintō purification rite performed by the local priest when a building site is readied for new construction. Another is a *tatemae*, or roof-raising ceremony, held when a new house's frame is completed and its uppermost beams put in place. Throughout Miyamoto-chō in the late 1970's and early 1980's, homes were being rebuilt as the housing stock from before the war or the early postwar years reached the end of its normal life expectancy. Some households entirely rebuild their homes. Others rebuild in stages, adding a major new wing onto the existing structure and then replacing the older part five or ten years later. In either case, when the carpenters complete the house's frame, the homeowner holds a party for workmen, friends, relatives, and neighbors. It is indeed an event to celebrate, for the costs of building or rebuilding a home may require a generation's worth of savings: it is truly a once-in-a-lifetime event, of which household members are justifiably proud.

In rural areas in the past the guests at such an event would have been neighbors who had contributed their labor to the actual construction as part of reciprocal work exchanges within the community. The party and banquet partially repaid them for their work. Today in Miyamoto-chō professional craftsmen—who are in fact likely to be neighbors, since contractors and foremen are generally hired from within the neighborhood—do all the work. Friends and neighbors do not offer to provide labor, and homeowners would not think to expect them to. Guests at a tatemae other than the workmen, therefore, are few: several relatives, one or two close friends, and a few immediate neighbors, all of whose contributions to the project are more ceremonial than substantive. Each guest presents the homeowner with a gift, either of money (usually in multiples of 10,000 yen) or of elaborately wrapped bottles of *sake*. The recipient carefully records these gifts to ensure that he or she will be able to reciprocate properly at future tatemae, weddings, or funerals.

When the Yonedas added a new wing to the rear of their house and shop, replacing a picturesque but almost unlivable home that had been built in the 1920's, they sponsored a tatemae. They held the party in the midst of the construction, with workers and guests sitting on the exposed floor beams, and tables of food laid out on boards spanning the beams. Guests included several relatives from adjacent neighborhoods, half a dozen immediate neighbors (following the principle of *mukōsangen ryō-donari*, "the three across the street and the two next door," which I discuss below), a couple of close business associates, and the three local men in charge of the job: Mr. Iki, the general contractor, Mr. Yamamura, whose firm was doing the electrical work, and Mr. Ozawa, a *tobi*, a labor boss who hires and supervises the work crew.[2] A dozen or so laborers made up the rest of the party. As at most construction projects in Miyamoto-chō, the contractors and foremen were all from the neighborhood, straddling the divide between workers and neighbors, but the construction workers were from elsewhere. Mr. Takahashi, one of the Yonedas' immediate neighbors, helped out by recording the gifts of money and *sake* brought by guests or sent by relatives, friends, and business associates who could not attend the tatemae. Mrs. Takahashi and a couple of other neighboring housewives assisted with preparing and serving food.

As the guests and the construction foremen offered innumerable toasts, the head carpenter mounted a Shintō amulet near the top of the central pillar of the house frame. The workmen, at the intense urging of all the guests, sang a few old-fashioned craftsmen's songs. The construction trades still strongly identify themselves, and are identified by others, as heirs to many of the traditions of the old commoner classes of the Edo period. Even though many construction workers know barely more than snatches of these songs, several people at this and other such ceremonies commented to me that without the craftsmen's chants and songs one could not have a true tatemae.

After their singing the workmen left quickly. Old Mrs. Yoneda sent each off with a small bottle of *sake* and a packet of food, including *sekihan*, a dish of red beans and rice served on auspicious occasions. The other guests stayed on longer to eat and drink, and when eventually it was time to go home, they too had food and *sake* thrust into their hands to take back to their families.

Funerals and Incense Money

Neighbors' contributions and the careful observance of reciprocity are important not only on auspicious occasions such as tatemae, but also on the more common occasion of a resident's death. Through the posting of formal notices, the chōkai spreads the news of the deaths of all local people and informs residents of the time and place of the funeral. Though the chōkai helps the bereaved family with the logistics of the funeral, the family's chief source of assistance is not institutional, but the immediate neighbors and other neighborhood residents, either acting as individuals or representing their households, who rally around.

In Miyamoto-chō families usually hold funeral services in their homes, not in their ancestral temples, even if these are somewhere in Tokyo. But funerals are not simple, homespun affairs; they are invariably organized by a professional undertaker, who provides most of the equipment necessary to the rituals: altars, incense burners, funerary lanterns to be hung at the entrance to the house, the coffin, and other paraphernalia. At most Miyamoto-chō funerals the man called in to take care of these details, as well as the technical tasks of preparing the corpse, is Mr. Moriguchi, who lives near the elementary school. Both chōkai members and neighboring families pitch in to help as they can. In particular, during the tsuya (the wake) and the kokubetsushiki (the ceremony in which the corpse is taken from the home for cremation), they are on hand to attend to the many mourners who visit to pay their final respects.

Wakes are almost always held in the evening, and the koku-betsushiki the following day. The timing of both is determined on the old Buddhist six-day cycle of auspicious and inauspicious days; above all, care is taken to avoid the day known as Tomo-biki, which literally means "pulling along a friend."

Ordinarily during a wake family members hold a vigil before the coffin, which sits in front of a large altar erected in the main room of the home. A much smaller altar with incense stands in the house's entryway. The large altar, the coffin, and the circle of bereaved family members listening to the priest reading su-tras can be seen from the small altar in the entryway. Mourners coming to call give their name to a receptionist under an awning in the alleyway or street outside the home and present a mone-tary offering called *kōden* ("incense money"), then approach the small outer altar, where they bow, pray, add three pinches of in-cense to the burner, and offer their condolences to the head of the household, who sits closest to the entryway to bow to each mourner in turn.

Customarily the bereaved household offers refreshments to mourners, and the immediately neighboring housewives take care of preparing and serving the food. At a very small wake the mourners may be fed in another room of the home, but most wakes in Miyamoto-chō draw enough mourners to require the use of the chōkai hall. As neighboring housewives serve mourn-ers at the hall, chōkai officials make it their task to guide mourn-ers from outside the neighborhood to the hall from the wake. In a few cases wakes and funerals are held elsewhere. For example, the services for the wife of Mr. Hasegawa, the senior adviser on almost everything in Miyamoto-chō, were held at a large temple a half hour's drive from the neighborhood. But even in such in-stances neighbors not only attend as mourners but also come to help as ushers, receptionists, and servers. For Mrs. Hasegawa's wake a dozen neighborhood housewives were on hand to serve the several hundred mourners whom chōkai officials had ush-ered off into several banquet rooms. Each room held a different category of mourner: relatives, neighbors, business contacts, or other acquaintances of the deceased or the deceased's family.[3]

The kokubetsushiki is also an elaborate public event, but mourners generally do not play any role, nor does the bereaved family offer them any feast. By-and-large mourners stand in respectful silence in the street or alley before the home while the final sutras are read and the coffin is put into the hearse. As the hearse pulls away, followed by a small van carrying relatives and close friends who will accompany the corpse to the municipal crematorium, a truck is loaded with *hanawa*, large, elaborate, expensive paper wreaths, which have been sent by families, business associates, and friends. The wreaths are then taken to the crematorium to be added to the flames.

The most modest funerals in Miyamoto-chō may have only one or two hanawa, or perhaps none; others may have several dozen. On the death of the elder Mr. Kataoka, a well-respected local stateman and retired bureaucrat, the rows of hanawa stretched for almost a block on both sides of the street in front of his home, and several hundred mourners attended the kokubetsushiki. The funeral of old Mr. Wada, a retired contractor who had been a professional sumo wrestler before the war, had nowhere as many mourners or hanawa, but it caused a local stir when the ranking contemporary wrestlers from Mr. Wada's old sumo stable,[4] including a reigning *yokozuna* or grand champion, appeared to pay their respects.

At this funeral, as at all others large or small, the mourners received a small envelope containing a handkerchief, a printed note of appreciation for their condolences, and a tiny packet of salt for purification after their exposure to death. If there is no one at home to sprinkle salt on the mourner, or to put neat cones of salt on the doorsill, then the mourner can use the packet to sprinkle himself or herself before reentering the home. Mourners who are particularly fastidious about such things take a different route home from the funeral, a procedure variously explained to me as the way one avoids bringing home pollution, as the way one confuses the soul of the deceased, which might otherwise accompany the mourner home, or simply as the way things are done.

At all local wakes and kokubetsushiki neighbors and chōkai officials serve and escort mourners, but also fill the important roles of receptionists. Outside the home or outside the temple, an awning is erected, and two or three chōkai officials dressed in their best black suits man the receptionist's table, where all mourners enter their names into a register, perhaps leave callings cards, and present the mandatory kōden. Accurate records of kōden received are crucial if a household is to fulfill its future social obligations for reciprocity, so the chōkai officials who act as receptionists fill a critical role.

Kōden exchanges are not restricted to immediate neighbors who provide each other with reciprocal aid; kōden partners range across the spectrum of a household's social relationships. In Miyamoto-chō an individual payment may range from about 3,000 yen to upwards of 10,000 yen, depending on the interplay of several complicated factors. Amounts vary according to the deceased's age, sex, and status within the household, the status of the household itself, the relationship of the mourner (or the mourner's household) to the deceased (or the deceased's household), and the relative status between the mourner and the deceased (or between their two households).

In funerals, as in many other social relationships, the household may be a more important actor than the individual—deceased or mourner—and in most cases only one member of a household will attend the wake or the kokubetsushiki to pay respects, sometimes as an individual, sometimes to represent the entire household. Furthermore, mourners often attend not because of their personal relationship with the deceased, but because of their personal ties to some member of the dead person's household or because of some link between another member of their own household and the deceased. In short both mourners and the deceased represent households or other corporate bodies, which pay their respects to each other by the presence of one of their members regardless of any personal connection between the individuals involved. Thus, for example, if the mother of a company employee should die, his superior or his co-workers (or both) might attend the funeral services, not because they were personally acquainted with the dead woman, but because they wish to honor the relationship between themselves and a member of her family.

These indirect and frequently complicated relationships between mourners and the deceased make determining the proper amount of kōden a tricky business, and the many etiquette books the local bookseller stocks all have careful explanations of how to determine the proper amount and how to properly wrap and present it. Although there is general informal agreement among the neighborhood residents about the proper amounts to be offered for a given relationship between mourner and deceased (or between their households), much ambiguity remains. Even Mr. Takahashi, considered by many in Miyamoto-chō an expert on the nuances of local relationships, admitted to me that he kept in the back of his shop and consulted frequently an etiquette manual—an encyclopedic guide to the accepted behavior and proper gifts for all ceremonial occasions.

Presentations of kōden involve careful calculations. Since principles of noblesse oblige apply, people expect that in exchanges between individuals or households of unequal status, the superior will give more to the inferior, and never vice-versa. Too modest an amount would seem slighting to the deceased and the bereaved household, but too large an amount might be taken as an overelevation of one's status relative to that of the bereaved household. Moreover, mourners must take careful account of long-term relationships. The presentation of kōden is never a one-time transaction and is often part of a long-enduring web of obligations and counterobligations that may persist over generations.

My landlord once showed me the kōden register prepared after his mother's funeral half a dozen years before. Some 165 households (including many not resident in Miyamoto-chō) had presented kōden on that occasion, a large number by the standards of funerals I observed in Miyamoto-chō. Although Mr. Takahashi laughed when he told me that the register was the most important document he owned, he meant it. As soon as he heard of the death of an acquaintance, in Miyamoto-chō or elsewhere, he would immediately check the kōden register to find out if that household had made a presentation to his family, and if so how much; that figure became the basis for calculating the amount of his own obligation to reciprocate.

At the most fundamental level the elaborate system of kōden donations and record-keeping can be seen as simply a burial-insurance scheme that assures each household of large sums of ready cash to pay funeral expenses. Funerals can be staggeringly expensive—in the hundreds of thousands or even millions of yen. But a large share of the "funeral expenses" to be met involve repayments to mourners. Custom demands that the bereaved family make a return gift to each mourner, usually some months after the funeral. These *kōdengaeshi* ("return of kōden")—gifts of merchandise such as towels, blankets, or lacquered bowls and trays—generally equal half the value of the mourner's kōden.

Kōden and kōdengaeshi are not simply a form of insurance to meet unpredictable one-time massive expenses. These exchanges are a concrete expression of the networks of obligations and interdependence that link households with one another. In theory at least, these other households stand ready not only to help with funeral expenses but to provide various forms of social aid in other crises, large or small. In a very real sense, therefore, the kōden register Mr. Takahashi so highly values is a tangible record of the network of reciprocal obligations and social ties that his family has assiduously cultivated over the years—a veritable Domesday Book of his family's social capital. His concern with keeping an accurate accounting of the obligations his household has incurred (and must reciprocate) arises, therefore, not merely out of careful attention to the niceties of funerary etiquette, but out of recognition of the ties of obligation and the social relationships that kōden symbolizes.

Mr. Takahashi discussed the kōden system with me many times, overcoming his lurking suspicions that my interest in the intricacies of funeral customs was morbid if not downright perverted. He repeatedly stated his belief that the system was cumbersome and antiquated, and that it was foolish that funeral expenses were so high (and made all the more so by the obligatory kōdengaeshi). Occasionally he would mention neighborhoods he had heard about where residents had gotten together and abolished kōden payments and repayments (at least among neighborhood residents). He thought this was a fine idea, well worth emulating, but he believed that in Miyamoto-chō the system was too well established to end. Even if most residents felt as he did, that the kōden system was archaic and too expensive, who would want to be the first to opt out of it? To take that first step, a household would have to fail to keep up its own reciprocal obligations (and suffer the consequences to its social reputation) or it would have to decline to accept the kōden "due" it and meet all funeral expenses on its own (and also forfeit the hundreds of thousands of yen that the household may have "invested" over the years with the expectation of ultimate reciprocation).

Mr. Takahashi's explanation of why the system remains in place makes much sense, to be sure. But I suspect there may be other reasons why residents—even those who agree that kōden and the extravagant funerals the system spawns are wasteful and pointless—would be extremely reluctant to scrap kōden exchanges. The system endures not simply because of the short-term social and economic benefits, important as these are, but also because of its underlying significance. The ongoing exchanges provide continuing reassurance to the individual that there is a large body of people outside the immediate family who are under some obligation to him or her, and who can be counted on in a time of need.

The Sense of Neighborly Obligation

The sense of obligation that underlies kōden is reflected in many other social relationships among neighbors. But since these ties occur outside the framework of any established group or organization, there is considerable variation in the extent to which neighboring households interact. Households differ in how much effort they may wish to expend for immediate neighbors, and indeed in how many nearby households qualify for that extra effort.

In principle, by the customary guideline of mukōsangen ryōdonari ("three houses across the way, and the two next door"), each household has five immediate neighbors, and each household's set of immediate neighbors is unique (although households facing each other across the street would both be part of the same cluster of six immediate neighbors). However, the mukōsangen ryōdonari norm does not appear to be as strong in Miyamoto-chō as it seems to be in other communities (see, for example, Brown 1976). In fact no one ever volunteered the phrase to me in discussing relations among neighbors. Many residents of Miyamoto-chō, like many contemporary Japanese, seem to consider this notion a bit old-fashioned and too rigid a set of prescribed obligations among a too mechanically defined set of households. They prefer that their relations with neighbors be more respectful of individual *"puraibashii"* ("privacy") and carried out more in accord with individual circumstances on a *"keisu-bai-keisu"* ("case-by-case") basis. They want to preserve the freedom to pick and choose their neighborly ties and to judge for themselves their degree of involvement in their neighbors' affairs.

Even residents who carefully observe the proper reciprocal relations of mutual aid with their immediate neighbors tend to think of their relationships and their actions in terms somewhat different from the mukōsangen ryōdonari ideal. They may view these reciprocal neighborly relations as arising from a sense of obligation rather than from intimate friendship, but most see these ties as reflecting obligations incurred between specific households or individuals, *not* as general obligations toward neighbors based on nothing more than proximity.

Expectations of unspecified future benefits or returns that may accrue to households or individuals—because they have cultivated proper neighborly ties—also underpin these relationships. Residents characterize and perhaps justify these ties with the phrase *"tsukiai no tame ni"*—one does something (such as maintaining proper neighborly relations) "for the sake of *tsukiai.*" There is no good English single-word equivalent for tsukiai. Reiko Atsumi's (1979) gloss "obligatory personal relationships" certainly captures one important facet of the term. But as Miyamoto-chō residents use it, the term also implies a sense of calculating personal advantage (actual or merely potential) that may come from establishing or maintaining a particular relationship. What is crucial is not the interaction itself and the benefit that a particular transaction may bring, but the relationship and the potentialities it represents. In a loose sense, doing something "for the sake of *tsukiai*" means that one is keeping one's social options open.

Thus, as a foundation for ties among individuals or households, tsukiai differs significantly from friendship. Tsukiai is "cultivated as a result of social necessity or feeling of obligation, . . . a means to attain an instrumental goal," whereas friendship is "developed out of mutual likings, interests, attractions, and likemindedness . . . for its own sake, i.e., for enjoyment" (Atsumi 1979: 65). This sense of obligation or *giri* (first analyzed as a crucial factor in Japanese social relationships by Ruth Benedict 1946) is considered the foundation for all manner of reciprocating relationships, including the kōden and kōden-gaeshi exchanges mentioned previously. As Harumi Befu (1968) has pointed out, however, the increasing individualization of social ties accompanying Japan's modernization has undermined (though not eliminated) giri as a basic motivating force in social relationships. It is commonly noted (and sometimes deplored) that in contemporary urban Japanese life people have greater flexibility in observing social obligations and greater freedom in maintaining or downplaying social ties, especially with neighbors. In Miyamoto-chō many established residents who maintain elaborate ties with their neighbors nevertheless cast the relationships as a matter of free choice based on individual, one-to-one obligations rather than on neighborliness for its own sake. This individual determination of neighborly obligation, rather than adherence to any community norm governing such ties, means that there is great variability in relations among nearby neighbors. As is true with most forms of neighborhood participation, recent arrivals are less likely than longer-term residents to interact with their immediate neighbors in any significant fashion, and apartment dwellers less so than homeowners. Conversely, young apartment dwellers' lack of interest in relations of mutual obligation provides a rationale for established residents to exclude them from systems of neighborly reciprocity.

Even with this apparent flexibility, the relationships of neighbor to neighbor are based in a sense of obligation (still considered a matter of giri by many residents), and however physically close people's homes may be and however frequently they may interact with one another, relations among neighbors need not be, and often are not, intimate. The relationship generally contains an element of reserve, leading at times to a formal correctness seemingly devoid of real friendship.

Informal Social Control

At least potentially neighbors represent agents of social pressures for conformity, the control of deviance, and the sanctioning of offenders (Salamon 1975), and this element of social control can take many forms. As Robert J. Smith's research on village ostracism (1961) makes clear, social control over the lives of residents was a central characteristic of the rural Japanese community. But in the urban setting most of the conditions of mutual economic dependence that make this control so effective in a rural hamlet are lacking, and norms are not "clearly stated and closely sanctioned" (R. J. Smith 1961: 522).

In Miyamoto-chō there are no formal mechanisms for controlling the actions of residents. The chōkai and other groups shy away from any suggestion that they can coerce residents or apply pressure on individuals. In part local groups are reticent for fear of reviving memories of the authoritarian role that chōkai played throughout Japan before and during the Second World War. Indeed, through policies of political and social reform in the immediate postwar period, the Occupation authorities intended to limit the coercive powers of neighborhood groups. As a result—local leaders point out (and at times bemoan)—the chōkai and its leaders lack the authority or the legitimacy to enforce community decisions. They must rely on the willingness of residents to go along with informal social pressures exerted by their neighbors. Nevertheless, some forms of neighborly social control exist and function effectively.

The most outstanding case I ran into occurred a couple of years before my fieldwork, when a household put up a magazine vending machine outside its home, which doubled as a small factory. Now, there was nothing unusual in this: automatic vending machines are a commonplace of Japanese life, and many households that engage in no other entrepreneurial pursuits may put one or two of them on a corner of their property. The range of machine-dispensed merchandise in Japan is awesome. Batteries, bags of rice, instant hot noodles, hamburgers, ice cream, candy, cosmetics, cigarettes, soft drinks, milk, cans of beer, small bottles of whiskey, and tumblers of *sake* are sold by machine. So are condoms, "girly" magazines, and violent, sexually explicit comics. For several years the ward's Board of Education, PTAs, and other citizens' groups have been trying with some success to put limits on the hours of operation of some types of machines (such as those selling alcoholic beverages) and to eliminate others (such as those dispensing sexually oriented magazines).

In this case, which I heard about from residents other than the principals, a salesman from a magazine distributor apparently approached Mr. Oda with an offer to install, service, and stock a vending machine for a split of the profits. The Oda home stands along a major street in the neighborhood, a road the elementary school designates as an "approved" route for children going to and from school. When Mr. Oda agreed to the proposal and the machine was installed, local residents were shocked to discover the graphically sexual nature of the magazines sold. They immediately lodged complaints with Mr. Oda as well as with local leaders, who said they were powerless to do anything. Protracted arguing went on, with neighbors urging that the machine be removed and Mr. Oda protesting that it was within his rights to keep the machine, and that indeed he was contractually obligated to do so. (Reportedly, Mr. Oda maintained he had been given no idea of the nature of the magazines when he agreed to the scheme, and that had he known he would not have gone ahead.) In the end Mr. Oda bowed to the informal sanctions applied by neighbors and local leaders. The machine disappeared.

None of my informants provided exact details of the subtle and then more insistent sanctions applied here, but they are not difficult to imagine: snubs by neighbors suddenly too busy to stop and chat; complaints by someone who lost patience with a bicycle that had routinely blocked a communal pathway; an abrupt halt of neighborly aid in taking out the Odas' trash and sweeping up afterward, or in picking up an extra item on sale to share with Mrs. Oda. All these and similar sanctions may be only minor irritants, but cumulatively they signal an end to the accommodation that is almost essential for life in a neighbor-hood as densely packed as Miyamoto-chō.

The case of the vending machine revolved around a concern that is often the focus of local social control: protecting chil-dren. Since the same comics and magazines are sold in the Kishis' pharmacy, the Umezus' bookshop, and the Araharis' li-quor store, as well as at shops and newsstands near all the rail-way stations, it was not a matter of their content, but a concern with their unsupervised sale and pernicious influence on young children who could buy them from the machine unnoticed. This attempt to maintain a healthy environment for children is en-tirely consistent with a general effort on the part of adults in Miyamoto-chō to supervise and control the actions of children and adolescents. Most residents routinely keep an eye on young-sters and admonish misbehavior. And throughout the summer vacation members of the junior high school PTA patrol the neighborhood after dusk—carrying lanterns similar to those used by chōkai officials during the winter fire watch—on the lookout for children who should be home; the PTA patrols pay particular attention to dark, secluded patches of shrubbery, back alleys, and the far corners of the shrine precincts, where adoles-cents might hope to hang out unnoticed.

Similarly, residents keep a wary eye on the entertainment dis-trict near the Otani station for the potentially harmful influ-ences it may exert on children. Many Miyamoto-chō residents consider the area dangerous even for adults and try to avoid wan-dering at night through the several square blocks of small bars, cabarets, strip joints, Turkish baths, and "love hotels." Ordinar-ily, however, the denizens of the district's demimonde and the solid citizens of the mostly residential neighborhoods that ring it maintain a peaceful coexistence. The hoodlums make no overt attempts to control territories or enterprises beyond the station area, and local neighborhoods resist encroachments of what they see as undesirable enterprises into otherwise respect-able neighborhood shopping areas. An adult bookstore that opened in a neighborhood adjacent to Miyamoto-chō, a few blocks beyond the generally recognized limits of the entertain-ment district, went out of business within a few months. None of my informants in Miyamoto-chō could (or would) say with any certainty what sorts of pressure local residents and their chōkai and shōtenkai might have applied to either the bookseller or the man who leased him the space. But most people agreed that the bookstore should not have been opened along an ordinary shopping street, and that the immediately affected neighbors were justified in whatever actions they might have taken. My sources speculated that the store's quick demise was the result of more than simple market forces (though the location, in the informed opinion of Miyamoto-chō shopkeepers, was probably ill-suited for that kind of high-traffic-volume business); they were firmly convinced that local pressure of some sort had been successfully applied.

Neighborly social control exists in less dramatic forms as well, and is more frequently aimed at inhibiting people's actions than at squelching them after the fact. Residents depend in many ways on each other's goodwill and on maintaining a good reputation in the eyes of their neighbors. Often, for example, the opinions of neighbors are solicited about a candidate for employment by a prestigious company or for an arranged marriage. Thomas P. Rohlen, in his study of the white-collar world of a Japanese bank, describes how the bank seeks out an applicant's neighbors to ask about an array of personal matters: the nature of family relationships; the character and health of family members; the family's reputation, including its religious and political activities, attitudes, and affiliations; the prospective employee's relations with members of the opposite sex; and even the cleanliness and upkeep of the house itself as a clue to the candidate's upbringing (Rohlen 1974: 70–73). Similar questions come up in the investigations that precede formal agreements over an arranged marriage: these inquiries are normally carried out by the go-between and occasionally by private detectives hired for the purpose (Vogel 1961). A person's immediate neighbors are of course ideally situated to provide information on these matters, and most households therefore have a strong interest both in remaining on good terms with neighbors and in presenting the best possible image of themselves. This goal necessarily carries with it fears about becoming too intimate and letting private secrets slip out.

Gossip is one expression of neighborly social control. Lapses in behavior or judgment are noted—and remembered for years. The subject of criticism can be almost anything. To cite just some of the tidbits confided to me: a husband's gambling, a wife's infidelity, a shopkeeper's stingy business dealings, a family so strapped that the wife had to take a part-time job, a household's lack of appropriate concern for the comfort of an elderly grandparent, the drinking problems of a leader in a nearby neighborhood, a henpecked husband's demeanor, a mother's ambitions for her children, a household's lack of reciprocity in its dealings with its neighbors, and the personal rivalries and ambitions of local leaders. The possibilities are almost endless; any of a thousand other complaints, more trivial or more serious, may be passed on from neighbor to neighbor.

Gossip as a pastime is considered primarily a feminine pursuit, visibly and audibly carried out in local vegetable shops or in front of the butcher's during each afternoon's peak shopping period. But gossip as a means of communicating information, both pro and con, about local residents knows no gendered bounds. Information about the personal problems and peccadillos of many residents is therefore common knowledge throughout the neighborhood in that peculiar category of information that consists of "public" secrets. As a means of passing time, gossip as an activity may be an end in itself, but gossip as communication is an important vehicle for passing information that ultimately makes or breaks local reputations, and is the basis on which residents make decisions—sometimes unconsciously—about who to do business with, who to trust as a leader, who to turn to for aid or advice, and who to avoid.

Gossip also reflects competition among neighbors. Keeping-up-with-the-Joneses is hardly a uniquely American phenomenon. Neighbors constantly vie with one another in Miyamoto-chō, although they do not carry this to the extremes found in suburban Tokyo's large *danchi* (apartment complexes). There, or so the popular press often reports, housewives allegedly spend large sums on fancy new futon so as not to be humiliated by invidious comparisons when the bedding is hung out to air each day on apartment balconies. Such overt examples of conspicuous consumption are rare in Miyamoto-chō, and residents generally disapprove of flaunting displays of wealth or success. To be sure, Mr. Kitayama has an enormous karaoke machine in his living room that is the envy of his friends, and many women prize the gorgeous kimono that they may only have one or two opportunities a year to wear. However open displays of wealth are frequently targets of criticism: Mr. Ukawa, heir to a now-successful machine shop, drives a Mercedes, but neighbors bitingly remind one another of the days after the war when Mr. Ukawa's parents went door-to-door soliciting loans from other residents to keep the family business going.

Even behavior that only suggests one is putting on airs can bring criticism. Mrs. Minami, a college-educated housewife whose husband is a moderately successful manufacturer, only rarely is needed in the factory and so she spends her time supervising her children's education, pursuing her own studies, and working part-time in a day-care center. Other merchant wives comment negatively on Mrs. Minami's not working in the family business. Some think she is a woman who flaunts her "leisure," and who (by encouraging her children to advance themselves through education) sets herself above the other wives.

Many families invest heavily in their children's education, and this can become a focus for competition and for gossip. Families apply strong pressures on children to study long and hard for the entrance examinations that mark all advancements to educational levels beyond junior high school (and to lower levels, too, for those who opt for private schooling). Though the drive for educational success taps motives much more deeply rooted than simple neighborly rivalries, the attainments of one's children are a source of much pride, to be communicated subtly or otherwise to one's neighbors. By the same token a child's failure to live up to expectations is something to hide or disguise—if possible.

The Nomura family agonized through the examination season, suffering repeated disappointments as their son, in his final year of junior high school, was rejected by one prestigious private high school after another. Finally he was accepted at a prominent public high school, but only after being placed on the alternates' list. During the long, bleak wait the entire family retreated into a shell, and the subject of children and of education in general became noticeable by its sudden absence from conversations with the Nomuras.

Education may be pursued quietly, to ward off criticisms that one is pretentious or over-ambitious for one's child, and to avoid embarrassment should the child fail. In almost total secrecy the Sakumas' elementary school daughter studied evenings and weekends in central Tokyo at an extremely famous *juku*, a type of cram school that prepares students for entrance examinations. This juku was in fact so elite that it had its own entrance examination (and it was rumored that some children attended other cram schools to prepare for this juku's entrance examination). Mr. Sakuma told me about his daughter's studies in the strictest confidence and cautioned me not to mention it to anyone else in the neighborhood; he was concerned both with looking too eager and with the possible repercussions of failure. (In the end, his daughter performed brilliantly and was admitted to a prestigious private girls' junior high school, an "escalator school" where she can study through college with no further entrance examinations.)

Friendship

The foregoing descriptions of relationships among neighbors—reciprocity born of a sense of obligation—may suggest that neighborhood social life is so greatly overburdened by formality and excessive attention to obligations that it stunts the development of close friendships. Although some Miyamoto-chō residents who interact constantly with their neighbors informally and through various local organizations might choose other associates if they felt free to do so, others develop close friendships based on their shared experiences, interests, and tastes.

Active involvement, as opposed to mere membership, in local groups is a matter of choice, and friendships may easily grow out of these voluntary interactions. Every local organization has several cliques of friends who interact with one another far more than the demands of tsukiai might dictate. Indeed some of these groups spend much of their free time together: sipping tea and chatting to pass the time during a free moment in a busy day, joining in a common hobby, going out drinking together,[5] planning impromptu trips to a hot spring or to a famous festival in Tokyo's shitamachi.

Joint excursions like these are much favored by friends, and my wife and I were invited to join many such jaunts: to the Tori no Ichi, a late autumn fair held halfway across the city near Asakusa, where the Kitayamas and their friends went to purchase elaborate good-luck charms, called *kumade*, bamboo rakes (to "rake in good fortune"); to the celebration of Oeshiki, the birthday of the medieval Buddhist priest Nichiren, at the great temple of Ikegami Honmon-ji not far from Miyamoto-chō, where our group of friends encountered some members of the Nakajima family who belong to a group of festival buffs that roams the city lending a shoulder and a strong set of lungs wherever there is a float to be hoisted; on a hot summer night to see the fireworks over the Sumida River that runs through the heart of old shitamachi; and others. The calendar of Tokyo's festivals and customary events provides ample opportunities for friendly outings, and on the way home people vie to show off their knowledge of some out-of-the-way restaurant that specializes in an exotic seasonal delicacy available nowhere else in Tokyo.

These local friendships show none of the formality and reserve that so often characterize relations among neighbors. Friends are much more likely to entertain each other informally in their homes and to know and interact with each other's families than are neighbors or others whose interactions are based largely on reciprocal obligations, however homey those obligations may be.

At New Year's many Japanese are busy carrying out the duties attendant upon ties of obligation: paying formal calls on kin, employers, or patrons, and receiving similar calls in turn. Such visits are fraught with formality; they can be enjoyable, but they are not occasions that put their participants at ease. But some residents of Miyamoto-chō also hold informal gatherings for their friends, typically parties for couples (in marked contrast to ordinary sexually segregated public events), where the formality is dropped and the major motive is relaxed fellowship. My wife and I were invited to several such parties. The easy give-and-take, the relaxation of etiquette, the dropping of formal greetings and salutations, and the general spontaneous hilarity of the conversations on these occasions made for an atmosphere dramatically different from the stiffness at other small gatherings we attended. Indeed our hosts and hostesses set these occasions apart from other sorts of entertaining by describing them with the English loanword *paatii* ("party"). To our friends no Japanese term did justice to the feeling of spontaneity these gatherings are meant to convey; ordinarily there is little established custom in Japan for informal group entertainment in the home.

Many local friendships, at least between long-term residents, grow out of school ties. Mrs. Tsunoda, for example, keeps in close touch with her friends from elementary school and visits with one or another (or a group) of them several times a week. In places like Miyamoto-chō, where many local elementary school graduates continue to live in the vicinity as adults, childhood friendship creates a particularly intimate base that is overlaid by the interactions of their contemporary daily lives. Other, more distant friends may see each other only once a year or so, when someone organizes a class party, either as a formal reunion to which old teachers may be invited or simply as an informal evening out at a restaurant.

Other local friendships develop out of (or are encouraged by) the enjoyment of common hobbies or recreational activities. Although the Wakamono Shinbokukai, the Young Men's Friendship Association, is now something of a political organization, it originated as a travel club and has depended on the camaraderie of its members to sustain it for almost a generation. The dozen or so members of the club are all good friends who share quite closely in one another's personal lives, interacting far more often and more intimately than the dictates of tsukiai or the demands of political maneuvering would suggest. Also in this category are the several groups of women who enjoy traditional folk dancing and who study together with one or another of the local dance teachers. These women do not meet simply to rehearse for their performances at various local events—the annual festival, the midsummer Bon Odori, the farewell party the neighborhood held for my wife and me—but get together several times a month to practice, to talk, and to enjoy each other's company. The friendships that grow out of, or underlie, these activities are not totally divorced from considerations of mutual obligation, and they may well serve instrumental ends. However, people enter into them not out of calculations of possible benefit, but simply out of the enjoyment of another's company.

School Ties

So far I have made only passing mention of the public elementary and junior high schools, two institutions that play a major role in creating a basis for innumerable social ties among neighborhood residents that crosscut and underlie the many other formal and informal links between them.

Both schools are important community institutions (and both happen to be located within the boundaries of Miyamoto-chō), but the elementary school is more closely connected to local social life for several reasons. First, it serves a much smaller area, drawing students from Miyamoto-chō, three adjacent neighborhoods and parts of two more. The junior high school brings together students from five elementary schools and encompasses an area that includes parts of almost a dozen distinct neighborhoods. Furthermore, the junior high school students come from neighborhoods in the old ward of Ebara and from neighborhoods that were—over a generation ago—in another ward; some residents of Miyamoto-chō mention that the mingling of students and parents from two such "different" backgrounds leads to a dilution of the old "Ebara spirit" of communal solidarity.

Second, the elementary school is much the older one. It was established at about the same time the area around Miyamoto-chō first became urbanized, whereas the junior high school was not founded until a few years after the Second World War. The history of the elementary school, therefore, parallels the history of the neighborhood, and many of the present local leaders graduated from it. Few of them attended the local junior high school.

Third, in the Japanese educational system in general elementary schools tend to be much more closely linked to local communities than junior highs. This is probably true of other urbanized, industrialized societies for some of the same reasons: children of elementary school age require far more parental attention than older children and are less independent, and parents (particularly mothers, in Japan) spend much more time with their younger children. Since Japanese children attend elementary school for six years, compared with three in junior high school, length of contact alone suggests that families would become more significantly involved in the elementary school community.

Finally, there are structural factors in the Japanese educational system that remove older children from community life. In recent years, as the pressures of school entrance examinations have increased, more and more students have opted out of public education at the junior high school level in favor of private schools that presumably prepare them more effectively for the next level of examinations.[6] At the same time, whether they attend a public or a private junior high school, the intense pressures to prepare for the all-important high school entrance examinations have led to an almost total curtailment of their extracurricular nonacademic activities. With the attention of parents of junior high school students so narrowly focused on the issue of exam preparation, a family may now be in closer contact with teachers to monitor a child's progress. But at this point education has become a serious, and competitive, business. A mother for whom involvement in the elementary school's PTA was at least partially a social outlet may be less inclined toward socializing and school-centered community involvement at this stage in her child's career. Just as young adolescents withdraw from many aspects of social life because of educational pressures, so too do their mothers.

Whether because of the schools' differing historical associations with the neighborhood or the structural features of the contemporary educational system, the elementary school far overshadows the junior high school in neighborhood life. Along with its PTA and alumni club, it is an extremely prominent institution, providing an important framework for local social relations and local community identity apart from that promoted by the institutions of Miyamoto-chō and other communities in the school district. School activities attract the participation and interest not only of pupils and their parents, but also of almost all residents in the district, particularly the many alumni who still live in the area.

Ties established through the school are important not only for the children themselves, but for their parents, too. Children provide an important stimulus for the development of ties of neighborliness and friendship among adults who might otherwise have no reason to interact. One leader in Miyamoto-chō commented that newly arrived households most frequently become involved in neighborhood affairs, and accepted by other residents, if they have children in the elementary school. He added that participating in school affairs ultimately transfers over into acceptance in other neighborhood groups—such as the chōkai—because the relationships thus established continue after the children have graduated.

Classmates may remain intimate friends all their lives, even when their statuses diverge sharply. Dr. Nishino, a physician who now lives elsewhere in the ward, stays in close touch with his elementary school friend, Mr. Arakawa, a baker who with his son runs a tiny shop near the railroad tracks. The two talk on the phone several times a week, visit each other's very different homes often, exchange gifts and favors, and speak to each other using childhood forms of address and with none of the formal status markers that would normally be part of a conversation between a doctor and a shopkeeper. To be sure, there may be good instrumental reasons for each to keep up the connection; still, childhood ties enable them to maintain an intimate relationship that transcends the differences in their adult social and economic statuses. Even if such ties do not always develop into warm bonds of adult friendship, the childhood relationship can remain strong enough to be called upon in certain circumstances, particularly among classmates who continue to live in the area, as many graduates of the elementary school do.

Even less intimate ties endure, and for many residents school ties form a significant frame of social reference that extends throughout Miyamoto-chō and the surrounding areas. For example, residents often casually identify adult acquaintances as their younger brother's classmate, or the mother of their daughter's former classmate, or someone two years behind their wife's sister at school. This ability to so classify innumerable other residents and thus identify some connection to oneself is an important social resource, useful in many ways. It can be the basis for creating a new relationship or reclaiming an old one, for example. Residents often explained to me their patronage of a given shop or business (or others' patronage of their own) as due in part to old school ties. Tsurumi-sensei the politician, who is not a native of the area himself, uses his connections to the school—his wife and children graduated from it, and he is a past president of the PTA—to garner support through these networks of tsukiai and to bolster his status as the candidate of the local community. Even in matters of social control, old school ties have force.

Relationships between *kōhai* and *senpai*—between a subordinate and a superior, based on seniority within an educational institution or a bureaucratic organization—characterize Japanese social life in many domains: higher education, companies, government bureaucracies, political parties, and artistic groups, among others. Typically a kōhai may rely on his or her senpai for advice and aid; in turn a senpai should be able to count on the kōhai's loyalty and respect. Such ties—based on elementary school classes—function at the level of neighborhood social relationships, too, and even well into adult life senpai retain some degree of moral authority over their kōhai, as one incident during my fieldwork illustrated.

One evening, as my wife and I entertained some foreign friends in our apartment, an acquaintance from the other side of Miyamoto-chō appeared at our door—very drunk—and invited himself in. He stayed for an hour or more and made a great racket both entering and leaving. This did not go unnoticed by the Takahashi family next door, and the next morning Mr. Takahashi offered to give our uninvited guest a severe tongue-lashing. Although both men were in their fifties, the discomfited Mr. Takahashi, in denouncing the offender to me, repeatedly returned to the point that the man was his elementary school kōhai. Mr. Takahashi therefore felt he had every right to reprimand the man, not only for his unseemly behavior in public and his rudeness to me, but for his rudeness by extension to Mr. Takahashi, the owner of the apartment building and in a sense my host.

The social networks resulting from school ties are analytically separable from ties created through local associations and other institutions, but of course in actuality the two overlay and interpenetrate one another, strengthening the fabric of local social relationships generally. Where a whole neighborhood falls inside a single school district, as Miyamoto-chō does, the social ties that result from school affairs may parallel and intensify ties created through other neighborhood organizations. Moreover, the extension of school-based social ties across neighborhood boundaries within the district provides an important means of integrating the various neighborhoods with one another (Embree 1939: 190; Befu 1963: 33). Chie Nakane (1970: 66) argues that primary school districts create the most likely arena within which local community organization may emerge in contemporary society. In the case of Miyamoto-chō strong organizations exist at the level of the immediate neighborhood as well, but the school and its related organizations lay considerable claim on the identification and loyalty of local residents.[7]

An event like the school's annual athletic field day is attended by alumni of all ages, who compete in special races and contests and are given special seats as guests of honor. The event attracts far more interest and participation than a similar one sponsored by the ward government's branch office for the ten neighborhoods in its burokku (block). Graduation and school entrance ceremonies, too, are well attended by alumni and local notables, including chōkai leaders from the several neighborhoods in the district, each of whom delivers a brief speech to praise the children for their successes thus far (and admonish them to continue to study hard in the future)—all in the name of their neighbors. In the annual celebration commemorating the school's anniversary, students carry a secularized version of a mikoshi throughout the school district; the event closely resembles a central feature of the annual festival for the Shintō tutelary deity held in each neighborhood and suggests analogies to the festival's ritual marking of community boundaries to promote social solidarity within them. In the school's case the anniversary celebration—as well as the many other events that bring the school together with the surrounding communities—serves to define the school district itself as a communal unit and to integrate residents into this broader unit of local social life, regardless of their personal stake in the school's educational functions.

Since the elementary school is one of the oldest local institutions, its history—echoing as it does the neighborhood's history and the life histories of many residents—offers a powerful rallying point for local community sentiment and identification, particularly among the current generation of local leaders. Dr. Nishino, the physician who now lives some distance away, Mr. Kobayashi, the member of the chōkai inner circle who coordinates the travel club, Ku-chan the carpenter, and several other participants told me of the elementary school's fiftieth anniversary celebration in 1978. For these residents and several dozen others, the high point was a long-delayed and highly emotional graduation for the classes of 1944 and 1945. The children in these classes had been evacuated en masse to the countryside in Toyama prefecture on the Japan Sea coast, leaving their parents and siblings behind to face the increasingly devastating American bombing raids. For all who witnessed the "graduation" it was a cathartic event, and those who told me of it later reflected that it had offered them a chance to reclaim something of the normal childhoods shattered by the war.

For these people, as for many others whose experiences with the school have been far less dramatic, the school remains a central focus for local communal identification. It offers, too, an ongoing basis for social relationships alternative to, yet not in competition with, those that the chōkai and other neighborhood institutions provide.

The personal relationships that link individuals and households to one another in Miyamoto-chō exist largely, though not totally, apart from the activities and structures of formal organizations and groups. Many of these interpersonal ties seem mundane, undramatic, and at times even trivial, only occasionally highlighted in crises such as funerals or even more rarely by catastrophes such as typhoons or the encroachments of pornography. But in their absence Miyamoto-chō would lack much that makes it a community in the eyes of its residents. Taken together, the passing, incidental interactions among residents and those of lifelong significance form the fundamental social bases of community life upon which other, more institutionalized activities and functions may be built, and without which formally constituted groups such as the chōkai would be unable to function.

The informal ties linking residents together on a roughly equal footing extend among a far wider range of people than the ties created through the activities of formal neighborhood organizations. These informal ties lend credibility to the neighborhood's ideology of egalitarianism, an important foundation for the sense of communal solidarity that the chōkai and other formal groups strive to promote. Yet at the same time this egalitarian ethos seems to stand in contradiction to the hierarchical structure of local organizations. Nowhere is this contradiction more striking than in Miyamoto-chō's annual festival—the neighborhood's premier event promoting community identity—in which principles of egalitarianism strike a careful balance with those of hierarchical structure.

CHAPTER SEVEN

The Festival and the Local Social Order

STACCATO WHISTLES, hoarse shouts of "*Washoi! Washoi!*," and the rhythmic counterpoint of wooden clappers shatter the late summer afternoon as a seething mass of sweaty men lurches down the shopping street under a float the size and weight of a small automobile.[1] Brass ornaments glitter and tinkle in the frenzy. The tassels of the float's purple lashings spin wildly above the men's shoulders. Bystanders rush to remove bicycles and other obstructions from the mob's path. Tiny children peer out from behind their mothers' aprons, enchantment and fear in turn playing across their faces. Strong men push float and mob back, steering them away from a plate-glass window. Chortling grandmothers gleefully toss buckets of water from second-floor windows onto the steaming backs of the churning mass of men below. Bus and taxi drivers watch—some with amusement, others with impatience—as they sit stranded in the midst of the thronging celebrants who clog the streets and stop the flow of traffic for a few minutes. The mob of men— some clad like old-fashioned craftsmen in matching blue and brown *hanten* (workmen's jackets), *hachimaki* (headbands), and *haragake* (tight-fitting black vests and leggings), others stripped to the waist—spin and whirl their way through all corners of the neighborhood during two or more hours of ecstatic exhaustion, almost hypnotized by the incessant, deafening, pounding rhythms of the cadence, of the clappers, of the whistles.

Miyamoto-chō's festival is under way, and the O-mikoshi[2]—the palanquin of the tutelary deity of the local Shintō shrine, the Kami-sama of Tenso Jinja—has taken over the neighborhood's streets during the deity's annual round of inspection.

Each year for one weekend in the middle of September the normal pace of daily life alters as local residents pause to take part in the festival. For some the festival, or O-matsuri, is no more than an excuse for a brief outing with the kids to munch on cotton candy sold by peddlers at the shrine. For others, however, the matsuri looms large in the annual calendar and is one of the central reference points of community life. For weeks ahead of time preparations for the festival occupy all their free time. "*O-matsuri wa mō jiki desu ne*" ("The festival is coming soon, isn't it!") replaces the conventional greetings, "*Ohayō go-zaimasu*" ("Good morning") or "*Konnichi wa*" ("Good day"). During the four days of the matsuri itself, these residents find themselves caught up in an almost constant round of activity. And with exhausted pleasure that the festival went well but sorrow that it ended so soon, they part from one another after the final banquet with a farewell that suggests lonely year-long anticipation—"*Ja, mata rainen . . .*" ("Well, until next year . . .").

Although it is a momentary punctuation in the year's activities, the festival illustrates many of the themes that suffuse Miyamoto-chō's mundane social life throughout the year: the hierarchical structure of neighborhood groups and the egalitarian ethos that permeates many residents' conceptions of the neighborhood; tensions between internal and external definitions of the community; Miyamoto-chō's assertion of its identity and autonomy through local events and activities that are self-consciously seen as parts of the neighborhood's evolving body of "tradition." These themes manifest themselves in one form or another in all aspects of neighborhood life. But they are perhaps nowhere more clearly and coherently evident than in the annual festival for the Shintō tutelary deity.

The festival—examined here less as a religious event than as a social occurrence, a secular ritual—is a particularly good example, since it is vivid, compact, and discrete. As a secular rite, the festival has many of the overtones of such other events as the midsummer Bon Odori folk dance, the New Year Eve fire patrols, and the ceremony to celebrate the new streetlight system, which equally (although less dramatically) express the same interconnected social themes that run throughout much of neighborhood life. Themes that stress the solidarity of the community run parallel to sharp distinctions between insiders and outsiders; themes of communal harmony and egalitarianism are juxtaposed against rankings of status and differential prestige within the neighborhood; themes that emphasize the importance of tradition are subtly but firmly underscored even as events are pragmatically and flexibly adapted to changing circumstances.

In this chapter I first discuss the local Shintō shrine and its position in local life. Then I describe Miyamoto-chō's autumn festival and examine its organizational framework, as well as the ways in which it has become an arena for conflicts over the leadership of the neighborhood. Finally, I analyze the interaction and integration of the diverse social themes expressed through the festival. These illuminate not just the ritual side of neighborhood life, but also the social dynamics and cultural values that undergird Miyamoto-chō's social life more generally.

The Shrine

Miyamoto-chō's shrine, Tenso Jinja—dedicated to the local tutelary deity, the *ujigami,* familiarly called the Kami-sama, without whom there would be no festival—takes as its parish borders the boundaries of the premodern hamlet. Miyamoto-chō and six adjacent neighborhoods constitute the shrine's parish and share equal responsibility for administering its affairs. The parish borders, based in history and corresponding to the outer boundaries of the seven neighborhoods as a whole, lend support to the insistence of the several neighborhoods on the legitimacy of their own boundaries. These borders go far to bolster the neighborhoods' self-definitions, even though none of them corresponds to any local unit or community that existed within the hamlet. Miyamoto-chō's chōkai takes pride that Tenso Jinja is located in the neighborhood and therefore considers itself somewhat first among equals, at least in those activities that revolve around the shrine.

Tenso Jinja claims a history dating back to at least 1624. During the Meiji period—until the merger of the hamlet of Kumodani into the larger village of Hiratsuka-mura—it was the hamlet's official tutelary shrine, designated by higher levels of government to serve as the religious and ideological bulwark of local administration. Throughout the prewar years, when State Shintō was not only integral to the national government's official ideology, but also important to local government (Fridell 1973), shrines like this played a critical role in the politics and ideology of community life; documents, monuments, and old photographs suggest that Tenso Jinja was then much more a center of local political, economic, and social life than it is today. In recent years the shrine—like most Shintō institutions in the postwar period—has been a quiet place, with few daily worshippers and only occasional events that draw more than a handful of parishioners. Yet it remains historically and symbolically the center of local communal life.

Tenso Jinja's precincts stand in silent testimony to the generosity of generations of parishioners. Beside the main shrine stands the tiny, weathered wooden shrine for O-Inari-sama, the agricultural deity always accompanied and symbolized by foxes. This tiny structure stands at the end of a narrow avenue of wooden torii and vermilion pennants that colorfully screen off the approach to the Inari shrine from the rest of Tenso Jinja's precincts. Both the pennants and the torii are emblazoned with the names of the parishioners who donate them each February, just before the annual winter festival for the O-Inari-sama. Throughout the year all events and observances at Tenso Jinja, whether large or small, offer opportunities for people to publicize their donations on banners, posters, pennants, and signboards.

Other displays of pious generosity persist throughout the years. The several hundred names inscribed on the stone posts that line the walkway to the main shrine record the names of all who donated to the shrine's reconstruction in the early 1970's. The shrine precincts are dotted with monuments from earlier days, each listing dozens of names of people who had somehow aided Tenso Jinja: a pair of stone *komainu* (guardian dogs) donated in the 1930's by the village fire brigade, a large stele commemorating the work of the land-rationalization committee, which consolidated farm plots and redrew field boundaries in the early twentieth century just before the village was engulfed by Tokyo's growth, a stone water basin commemorating the reconstruction committee of the 1970's, to name just a few. Even a single electric light pole has a mounted plaque noting the name of the donor. An observer may wonder whether the donors' motives are solely pious; these prominent plaques are lasting advertisements, reflecting compliance with the standards of noblesse oblige expected of leading citizens or competition for social standing and public recognition among the community's nouveaux riches.

The shrine is the focal point for the activities of several local organizations with which it has long had ties. The seven chōkai of the parish are of course the most important of these, since it is they who control the board of governors; five of them have storehouses behind the main shrine hall where they keep festival paraphernalia. The volunteer fire brigade also has close ties to the shrine; it is the only local institution besides the shrine parish to take the old hamlet's borders as its own, and at least in this sense the two share histories. Many of the monuments around the precincts bear testimony to the activities of these groups and to the prominence of their leaders in various generations throughout the twentieth century. The oldest surviving records documenting the existence of Miyamoto-chō's chōkai are a pair of photographs taken in the early 1930's showing chōkai officials stiffly posed before the main shrine hall, some in formal kimono, others in Western suits and winged collars. Mr. Takahashi, the photographs' owner, can point out in the pictures a few still-living residents of Miyamoto-chō, including his father (now in his mid-eighties); most of the neighborhood leaders captured on the prints are long dead, and some cannot now be identified.

A 14-member board of ujiko sōdai (parish delegates) governs the shrine, employs its priest, oversees its property, and manages its financial affairs. All seven chōkai presidents serve as ex officio members of the board, and each chōkai appoints another ujiko sōdai. The middle-aged greengrocer Mr. Asakawa has been Miyamoto-chō's delegate for many years.

The shrine is self-supporting. Its income comes from offerings made by its few daily worshippers, from larger donations by local patrons, from contributions made by each chōkai during the annual festival, from collections and the sale of amulets at festivities during the year, and from the rental of parking spaces inside the precincts. When the ujiko sōdai plan a particularly large project—such as reconstructing a building or making other major improvements—they solicit special contributions from parishioners and from the seven chōkai; the names of all who contribute are duly inscribed on a plaque or monument. The shrine once owned land elsewhere in Miyamoto-chō and surrounding neighborhoods, donated by parishioners long before the area became urban. During the 1920's, as farm land became prime residential and commercial real estate, these plots were leased for home and business sites. When the main shrine building was rebuilt in the early 1970's, the ujiko sōdai sold the land to the tenants, to help finance the project.

Unlike many shrines in contemporary Japan, Tenso Jinja has a resident priest, or *kannushi*. The post is hereditary, and the current priest, Mr. Kuroda, succeeded his father. Mr. Kuroda, now in his late fifties, is an unassuming man who could pass unnoticed except on festival days and when he is presiding over a Shintō rite for a parishioner. At those times, resplendent in his priestly robes, he projects a quiet, dignified authority. But most days Mr. Kuroda is not in evidence. The shrine's board of governors is able to give him only a small stipend, and even with the honoraria he receives for performing individual rites for parishioners, his priestly duties do not pay a living wage. He therefore supplements his income with a part-time office job outside the neighborhood.

Other members of his family assist Mr. Kuroda from time to time. His son—a handsome young man in his early thirties—has trained for the priesthood. He does not live in Miyamoto-chō at the moment, but returns at particularly busy times—such as New Year's and the autumn festival—to help his father, and local residents expect him to succeed his father. Mrs. Kuroda can often be seen cleaning and sweeping the shrine precincts, and she and her daughter-in-law occasionally don the robes of shrine maidens to help Mr. Kuroda serve ritual cups of *sake* during festivals or sell amulets at the New Year's holidays.

Mr. Kuroda and his family are little involved in the day-to-day social life of Miyamoto-chō, perhaps because their ritual position sets them apart from other residents, perhaps because the postwar segregation of religion from community institutions prevents their taking more active roles, or perhaps simply because of personal preference. They are ritual specialists who assume center stage only when a festival is in the offing or when a parishioner requires some rite, such as the jichinsai to purify a building site before construction begins. Even the rites of the individual life cycle do not keep Mr. Kuroda terribly busy. Buddhism is the religion of Japanese funerals, and in Tokyo weddings—traditionally a Shintō observance—are now performed almost exclusively at the great wedding halls of famous shrines or at fancy hotels. It has been many years since a wedding banquet was held in Tenso Jinja's meeting hall.

The shrine's major buildings are modern ferro-concrete versions of traditional Shintō architecture, built in the early 1970's to replace weathered wooden structures dating from the late nineteenth century. Rebuilding the shrine was a matter of great pride—and great expense—for its parishioners, but only occasionally is this monument to devotion a place of worship. Normally, those few parishioners, typically old people, who come to worship on an ordinary day cannot enter the main hall. Instead they offer their prayers at the railing barring the entry, their faces floating above the inner altar, reflected back by the circular mirror that symbolizes Amaterasu Ōmikami (the Sun Goddess). As they pray they signal the deity of their presence by ringing the bell that hangs above the railing; they clap twice, bowing deeply, silently invoking the deity and offering prayers; and they toss a few coins into the large offering box. Beside the offering box a small, coin-operated vending machine dispenses printed fortunes. Customarily after people read a fortune they tie the slip of paper to a tree or some other object, to share a favorable fortune with the world or to let the winds disperse an inauspicious one; shrubs near the steps to the outer hall are always festooned with dozens of these small slips, carefully knotted around the twigs and branches, looking like flocks of white butterflies momentarily at rest.

The shrine precincts, though not especially large, provide the only public open space in the neighborhood, and residents use the grounds constantly—as a children's playground, as a place for quiet strolls and walking the dog, and as a parking lot.[3] On any given day no more than a handful of parishioners visit the shrine to offer their private prayers; several old people visit daily, and once or twice a week a new mother comes to present her infant to the Kami-sama 30 days after birth, a custom known as *miyamairi*. Only a few times each year do religious events at the shrine attract much attention. Most dates on the religious calendar pass almost unnoticed, observed only by the priest—a mostly unwatched technician of the sacred—in rites that, during my fieldwork, were often attended by no one but me.

Occasionally a popular Shintō holiday—days more like Halloween or St. Valentine's Day than Rosh Hashanah or Ash Wednesday—punctuates the shrine's calendar. For a day or two residents flock to the shrine precincts, to be attended by the priest and his family; and some of the ujiko sōdai may come along, to help out by selling seasonal charms. Apart from the autumn festival, the shrine's busiest time is New Year's Eve, when hundreds of residents converge to offer prayers at the stroke of midnight, purchase amulets ensuring health, prosperity, educational success, and traffic safety, and cast last year's charms and talismans into the bonfire to the tolling of distant temple bells. But from time to time throughout the year, other, smaller festivities briefly enliven Tenso Jinja.

Twice a year, in February and July, the small shrine for the O-Inari-sama holds a small festival. The governance of the Inari shrine is left to the elders; its separate ujiko sōdai are drawn from the seven neighborhoods' old people's clubs. The February festival is a cold and solemn event, attended only by a few old men and a handful of the main shrine's ujiko sōdai. July is more cheerful. Trees are hung with colorful lanterns prepared by the neighborhood children, who decorate them with scenes from classical literature and popular comic strips, and with simple invocations of peace and prosperity, health and safety. The daytime observances before the Inari shrine's altar are as quiet and solemn as those in February, but in the evening, under the twinkling lanterns, the shrine holds a small folk dance around a large taiko drum. Presiding are the lay officers of the shrine organization, like Mr. Asakawa, the quiet, dignified ujiko sōdai from Miyamoto-chō, and Mr. Honma, a perpetually cheerful glazier who represents a nearby neighborhood. Also in attendance are uniformed officers and members of the volunteer fire brigade. The shrine and fire brigade officials freely offer visitors O-miki, sanctified *sake*, in ritual sips or in healthy slugs. As young men take turns beating complicated folk rhythms on the taiko, a dozen or more men and women, children, and grandparents dance in a ragged circle. The dancing is unrehearsed and obviously so, but unlike the large Bon Odori of the summer, this is not a flashy event, showing off the skills and organizational abilities of the sponsoring neighborhoods; it is just a comfortably low-key affair in keeping with the scale and spirit of the Inari shrine.

Other events at the shrine throughout the year correspond to the annual cycle of popular religious holidays. The Setsubun holiday in February (at the end of winter, according to the old calendar) is a time for assuring good luck for the coming year by scattering dried beans to the chant of *"Oni ga soto, fuku ga uchi!"* ("Out with the devils, and in with good fortune!"). Members of the ujiko sōdai and other prominent local leaders (especially those born in the current year of the 12-year zodiacal cycle) toss dried beans—loose and in packets—from the shrine veranda as children, housewives, and grandmothers clamber to catch the scattered beans in hands, purses, or shopping bags; beans caught at the shrine are taken home for household exorcisms.

At midsummer and midwinter the shrine sponsors purification rituals for parishioners; paper talismans are distributed to local households, to be returned to the shrine marked with the names and any particular afflictions of people who wish to cleanse themselves.[4] At midsummer some of the ujiko sōdai take the talismans out into the middle of Tokyo Bay to cast them into the water; at midwinter the talismans are added to the bonfire that marks the stroke of the New Year.

The shrine comes briefly alive in November for Shichigosan, when children aged three, five, and seven, dressed in their finest clothing, are presented to the deity. Accompanied by mothers and grandmothers dressed in their best kimono, and by proud fathers carrying cameras or video recorders, the children receive blessings from the priest and a bag of candy from the ujiko sōdai who collects the parents' donations.

But these are momentary events that only briefly disturb the quiet of the shrine, and that never attract more than a few dozen people at a time. The annual autumn festival is a far different story. For the several days of the festival and the weeks of preparation leading up to it, the shrine precincts become a busy place indeed.

The Festival

The shrine comes into its own in the late summer as preparations begin for the matsuri. It is officially called the autumn festival, or *aki-matsuri*, but so dominant is its place on the ritual calendar of both the shrine and the parish neighborhoods that it is simply *the* festival.[5] In principle, the festival day is September 15, but nowadays the date is adjusted so that the two-day observance falls on the third weekend of September.

For several weeks before the festival the shrine precincts are a beehive of activity. Representatives from the five chōkai that store their festival paraphernalia in the sheds behind the main shrine buildings come to reassemble the equipment, polish the brass fittings, and check to see if anything needs to be repaired or replaced before the festival begins. The priest and his wife carefully clean the shrine grounds and instruct the renters of parking spaces to find other spots during the festival. A few weeks before the festival, the boss (*oyabun*) of the *tekiya*—the peddlers who run the many food stalls, game booths, and fortune tellers' stands that crowd the shrine precincts during the matsuri—calls on the priest to make a donation to the shrine and to prepare for the *ennichi* (festival day) fair, the most conspicuous activity at the shrine during the matsuri.

One might expect the shrine to be the focus of religious attention during the festival, but things do not work that way in practice. The focus of activity for many people, perhaps most, is the separate observance held in their own neighborhood. According to the religious beliefs at the root of the matsuri, this is the occasion when the tutelary deity leaves its normal abode in the shrine's inner sanctum to visit its parishioners and to survey the territory under its protection. Accordingly, the priest installs the deity into the mikoshi of each of the seven neighborhoods, which are then carried to every corner of their respective neighborhoods to bestow the blessings of the Kami-sama and to ensure that all is well.[6] Whether for these religious reasons or for social ones, the neighborhood observances are largely separate from, and more important than, those at the shrine.

The matsuri is a vivid symbol of communal identification, and all the neighborhood celebrations draw wide participation. Although the festival is a Shintō rite, for most participants it is in practice an almost secular ritual of obscure religious significance but of great social meaning. Since it is a religious event, one would expect that those whose beliefs are incompatible with Shintō would be excluded or would exclude themselves. The New Religion Sōka Gakkai, for example, is ideologically opposed to Shintō, and to participation in the matsuri (and by extension in chōkai, which are considered intimately linked to Shintō shrines through their support of local festivals.) Thus its local adherents stoutly refuse to contribute to the festival (although their children are sometimes seen hanging around the mikoshi, and dodging in and out of the shrine's fairgrounds). Most residents, however, do not see the festival as a religious issue. As Mr. Chiyoda, a prosperous merchant and chōkai leader from a nearby neighborhood, explained to me, he felt no compunctions against playing a leading role in the festival despite his personal faith as a Christian, since he considered it a community event, not a religious observance.[7]

The matsuri and the month or so of preparations leading up to it express several important, though sometimes seemingly antithetical, social themes. Social stratification and ranking in Miyamoto-chō are expressed and enforced through the assignment of positions on the festival committee and through public postings of residents' contributions. Strong distinctions are underscored between newcomers and longer-term residents in the selection and duties of committee members. Stratified authority governs decision-making for the festival. Tasks in managing and running the festival, and even the spatial and temporal distribution of activities during it, reflect rigid divisions of labor by age and gender. Yet despite the social differentiation that plays so visible a role, sentiments of solidarity and egalitarianism prevail, and when residents talk of the festival's meaning, they speak of this spirit of communal unity as the matsuri's dominant motif.

Running the Festival

The chōkai does not directly organize Miyamoto-chō's festival. Each summer it assembles a festival committee (*saireiiin*), which convenes solely for that purpose and disbands after the festival is over. Although the saireiiin includes many of the chōkai leaders, other people play important roles: not only leaders of other local organizations—such as the rōjinkai, the shōtenkai, and the volunteer fire brigade, but also residents who otherwise do not take any active part in neighborhood affairs. A person's standing in the chōkai and his position in the festival organization are not explicitly linked, and there is no formally recognized progression of secular and ritual offices to be passed through in the climb to the top of local leadership.[8]

Each August leaders of the saireiiin draw up an elaborate organizational table of assignments for some 150 households (see Appendix C). Two or three weeks before the festival, a delegation of committee leaders—dressed in the neighborhood's special festival yukata—delivers a printed copy of the list, along with a pair of straw sandals of the sort worn during the festival, to each household on the list, and formally requests its continued cooperation and support of the festival. Residents are assigned tasks on subcommittees—for example, serving on groups charged with overseeing the cart on which musicians sit, or arranging the dancing troupe organized by the women's auxiliary, or supervising the children's mikoshi. Both the subcommittees and the positions on them are implicitly ranked in prestige by the degree of seniority (or other attributes, such as gender) required of the position-holders. The records of the saireiiin over a number of years show that people will generally serve on the same subcommittee for several festivals, gradually working their way up in status and rank in that group before being promoted to a more prestigious subcommittee appropriate to their gender, age, and growing standing within the community.

In part these positions and people's status in general determine the financial contributions they make. Usually no more than one-third of Miyamoto-chō's households choose to contribute, and those who do not hold any special position on the festival committee generally give around 3,000 yen; leaders are expected to contribute at least 10,000 and perhaps as much as 30,000 yen. However, there is no direct cause-and-effect relationship between contribution and position—no buying one's way into a position of authority. Residents seem more concerned with making a contribution commensurate with their status than with getting a position that corresponds to their contribution. As with the calculations of kōden funerary payments, festival contributions can be tricky. Determining the proper amount requires a careful assessment both of one's standing in the community and one's standing in the festival organization. It is easy to err in either direction in making a donation; too small an amount, of course, marks a person as stingy, but too large a contribution betrays arrogance and overweening ambition, not open-hearted generosity.

The O-tabisho

During the festival Miyamoto-chō's hall is the nerve center, staging area, and rest spot for leaders and participants alike; it is simultaneously stage center and backstage. During the matsuri the hall is called the O-tabisho, a temporary shrine, a resting place for the deity, or the O-mikisho, the place where the sanctified *sake* (O-miki) for the gods is kept.

A day or so before the festival begins, leaders erect a flimsy framework of wooden slats that covers the entire front of the hall except the windows, which are removed to leave the interior open and easily accessible to the street. Throughout the matsuri older leaders of the festival committee sit at the windows, accepting donations from local residents. From midday Friday, when most preparations are well under way, through late Saturday, steady streams of residents drop by to present their donations, carefully placed in the red-and-white ceremonial envelopes customarily used by Japanese for presenting money on auspicious occasions.

Not all donations are cash. Local *sake* dealers (there are three in Miyamoto-chō and at least four others nearby who count large numbers of Miyamoto-chō residents among their regular patrons) shuttle back and forth between their shops and the hall, making deliveries of *sake*, beer, and other beverages donated by parishioners. *Sake* is particularly appropriate, because of its ancient connections to Shintō and its use in purification rituals, and the ever-increasing array of bottles, wrapped in the customary red-and-white paper, stacked beside the altar in the O-tabisho forms an impressive backdrop to the carefully arranged fruits, vegetables, and dried seafood displayed thereon.

As donations of cash, *sake*, or crates of oranges and other produce are received, Mr. Ikeda and two or three older leaders carefully record the donations in a ledger. Mr. Nakane, an old shopkeeper noted for his elegant calligraphy, prepares a small paper banner for each donation, announcing the amount and the donor's name. These banners are carefully posted on the wooden slats that cover the front of the chōkai hall and are just as carefully studied by leaders and ordinary residents alike throughout the festival. People compare their own donations with those of their neighbors and spice their comments with mildly disparaging remarks about leaders who contribute too little or too much for their position. As the donations are posted, everyone comments with delight at the large contributions from the several local branch banks in the area and from the companies that maintain dormitories in Miyamoto-chō. Narita-sensei and young Mr. Watsuji, who paid formal calls on the local managers of those firms to request donations, are complimented for their skill in extracting so much.

The assembling of the altar is left in the hands of the most elderly festival leaders. It is assumed that only they really understand what should go on the altar and in what form. Old Mr. Hasegawa—the omnipresent senior adviser—is at his liveliest, directing this person to tie up a bundle of seaweed just so, or calling for that one to add additional pinches to the several saucers of salt and rice that grace the altar. Younger leaders fear that when the current elders are no longer on the scene no one will know how to set up the altar, so Narita-sensei asks hangers-on (including the anthropologist) to take lots of photographs as the altar takes shape. Mr. Watsuji, the mukoyōshi or adopted son-in-law of a local shopowner who has emerged as one of the most dedicated and methodical of the younger leaders, sits quietly beside the altar making sketches of each step, and carefully noting the composition and construction of each bundle of vegetables. In his notebook he jots down the number of pieces of fruit to be put on each offering plate, the way in which strands of *kanpyō* (a fibrous dried gourd) and *konbu* (dried kelp) should be twisted around bundles of vegetables, and the placement of dried fish in relation to other elements. Earlier Mr. Watsuji had carefully sketched each of the complicated knots that bind the pieces of the mikoshi together, so that these too can be re-created again and again in the future, when the elders no longer are there to direct the festival preparations. Along with the donation ledgers and the other records of the festival, these sketches and photographs will be carefully stored away for future reference.

During the matsuri of 1979 and 1980, an empty lot just down the shopping street from the O-tabisho was reserved for the use of a troupe of talented amateur musicians from a nearby neighborhood (outside the shrine parish), who specialized in *matsuri-bayashi*, the genre of music for flute, drums, and gongs that typifies festival music. For a nominal honorarium of 20,000 yen, the four musicians played for the better part of two days, seated on Miyamoto-chō's *hayashi*, a cart for musicians, part of the festival paraphernalia the chōkai stores throughout the year in the shed behind the shrine. By 1983 Miyamoto-chō had ceased hiring outside musicians, and matsuribayashi came on cassette tapes. Mr. Shigemori, who was in charge of music for that year's matsuri, explained that the festival commmittee had decided against hiring live musicians for two reasons: they were outsiders rather than Miyamoto-chō residents, and in the wake of an expensive drive to purchase a new mikoshi, they were trying to keep expenses down. Other residents hoped that the loss of live music would only be temporary, and pointed to the recent revitalization of a taiko drumming group in a nearby neighborhood that included several participants from Miyamoto-chō.

Among them were young Mr. Matsushita, the heir to a prosperous retail shop in Miyamoto-chō, who in his mid-twenties was already emerging as one of the most active participants in neighborhood affairs of his generation, and the Nakajimas' youngest son, also in his mid-twenties. In the future, many festival leaders confidently told me, the drum troupe could be called on to provide live music for the festival, performed by insiders.[9]

The Mikoshi

On several levels the mikoshi, or palanquins for the tutelary deity, are central to the religious and social symbolism of the festival, and for many residents the processions that carry them around the neighborhood represent the essence of the matsuri. Mikoshi are replicas of shrine buildings mounted on a framework of horizontal beams. The miniature shrines may be as small as half a meter or as large as two meters in height, depth, and width, and of course the size of the framework of supports varies accordingly. A large mikoshi—with a one-meter shrine—will rest on eight or ten poles. The entire structure, with five-meter shafts stretching front to back and three-meter supports from side to side, may weigh 200 or 300 kilograms and is carried on the shoulders of 30 or 40 people. In Miyamoto-chō the mikoshi begin and end their circumnavigations at the O-tabisho, where the neighborhood's two small mikoshi are kept on display in between processions.[10]

Once the priest sanctifies a mikoshi and installs the deity in it, the mikoshi is said to be under the deity's control, not the bearers'. And indeed the mikoshi appears to take on a life of its own and becomes a bucking, pitching, careening force beyond the control or influence of any single bearer (who may be more than a little influenced by *sake*). The mikoshi is steered, if that is the correct term, by two or three men, who clear away bystanders and try (not always successfully) to prevent damage to property. They must continually shove against the bearers to try to turn the direction of the mikoshi, to slow its speed, or to calm its gyrations.

In Miyamoto-chō the mikoshi normally make four or five circuits of the neighborhood during the two days of the festival, depending on the weather and the number of people available to carry them. At least two of the circuits are made by processions of children carrying the small mikoshi, but the processions that really count are the adults' seething, grinding, exhausting circuits in the afternoon and evening.[11]

In part the religious rationale for the mikoshi processions is that they enable the tutelary deity to inspect and bestow blessings on its territory. Thus they serve as compelling markers of a community's boundaries and identity. In Miyamoto-chō all mikoshi circuits follow the same route, a figure eight that starts and ends at the O-tabisho on the shopping street. In each circuit, the mikoshi is carried (or perhaps directs itself) to the borders of the neighborhood—and no farther. Sandwiched between the elementary school and the railway tracks, completely cut off from the rest of the neighborhood by the school yard, is a tiny sliver of land on which half a dozen houses stand; the mikoshi never fails to visit that corner. At some points along the old river the mikoshi goes out into the middle of the bypass, stopping traffic on this busy road for a few moments; at other points it does not even travel all the way to the bypass, because the neighborhood's old boundary ran a few meters to this side of the road, reflecting a long-ago bend in the river that was straightened out even before it was channeled underground.

Where Miyamoto-chō and the ward government disagree over local boundaries, the mikoshi observes the neighborhood's definition. The mikoshi carefully visits all corners of the neighborhood and follows the neighborhood's boundaries as closely as possible; it is more important that the mikoshi trace all the perimeters than that it traverse all the internal streets of the neighborhood. When a mikoshi's route unavoidably takes it through the territory of an adjacent neighborhood—when roads or alleys linking parts of one neighborhood run through another, or when a mikoshi is brought from another neighborhood to the shrine in Miyamoto-chō for the priest's blessing—the festival committees from the neighborhoods involved negotiate the route beforehand. When a mikoshi (or a women's dance troupe) takes a sudden, unannounced detour through another neighborhood, leaders of the invaded neighborhood grumble and expect a formal apology from the offenders' festival committee.

In short the tutelary diety's annual inspection tour offers

powerful symbolic support for the discreteness of the neighborhood. Through the mikoshi processions the festival reaffirms the legitimacy of Miyamoto-chō's borders and the solidarity of those who live within them. In this fashion the mikoshi and the matsuri provide a rationale for maintaining the integrity of those boundaries and the community they surround in the face of pressures from the ward to reconstitute the neighborhood.[12]

Whether residents help carry the palanquins or merely watch, most consider the mikoshi processions the highlight of the festival. Each year's processions differ slightly, sometimes by conscious design, sometimes because of external circumstance, sometimes through inertial drift. The following account of the mikoshi procession blends descriptions of the festivals of 1979, 1980, 1983, and 1984.

Before the procession begins, the mikoshi is brought out from the O-tabisho and set up on lacquered sawhorses in the street. When the priest arrives, he performs a ten-minute service before the altar inside the O-tabisho, and then he and his son—both garbed in their most resplendent silk robes—stride out to the street to bless the mikoshi and to install the temporarily visiting deity in it. With a deep and dignified intoning of prayers and a crisp waving of boughs of *sakaki* (a leafy green shrub used in Shintō rituals), the priest bows low and puts a tiny slip of folded paper into the mikoshi to confirm the presence of the kami, the deity. This done, the priest accepts the leaders' thanks and rushes off in his waiting car to the next neighborhood in the parish.

As the priest leaves, Miyamoto-chō prepares to launch the mikoshi on its rounds. Each adult is given a teacup of O-miki, the sanctified *sake* from the altar, and at the command of the chairman of the festival committee, all drain their cups in a ceremonial toast. Mr. Ozawa, a rough-and-tumble construction foreman (a *tobi*), who is one of the four *wakagashira*, or "young chiefs," in charge of the mikoshi, grabs the bottle of *sake* that has rested on the crossbeams of the mikoshi as it was being blessed. He takes a large swig and then dramatically sprays a mouthful on each of the lashings that hold the framework together. O-miki is a crucial element in Shintō purification, but the men assure me that this is done for practical reasons as well:

as the *sake* dries on the ropes, they contract enough to tighten the knots.

1984 was the 360th anniversary of the founding of the shrine, and in commemoration of this (and perhaps to accentuate the neighborhood's status as the *miyamoto*, the seat of the shrine), that year's festival included a number of special activities. Chief among these were an extraordinarily sedate intitial mikoshi procession that circumnavigated the neighborhood and ended up at the shrine. The mikoshi was carried quietly, preceded by a procession of local leaders (including leaders of several adjacent neighborhoods, who were specially invited to participate), all dressed in robes reminiscent of the 1600's. Following the mikoshi was a procession of several dozen children, each dressed in costumes (rented for the occasion at 5,000 yen apiece) loosely based on the court dress of the tenth or eleventh century.[13] A crier marched solemnly ahead of the entire parade, calling in deep, measured, and highly formal tones "This is the procession of the *mikoshi* of the Yanagi Miyamoto-chō, honoring the 360th anniversary of the local shrine."

At the shrine the priest came out to offer special prayers for the mikoshi and then presided over a small ceremony to bless the costumed children. The children stood patiently lined up on the shrine steps while phalanxes of fathers took photographs, movies, and videos of them, and then in a flash of colored silk, they were off, running hither and thither among the stalls of the festival's arcade. The dignified elders from the procession, still wearing their medieval robes, retired to the shrine's hall to sip *sake* and chat about local affairs. But Mr. Ozawa, one of the four wakagashira, ripped off his formal garb, leaped into the air, and screamed, "Let's get this *mikoshi* MOVING!" The young men who had patiently, sedately carried the mikoshi to the shrine responded with a roar, and within seconds the mikoshi was hurtling out the gate at a full, frenzied tilt.

On average a mikoshi procession makes a circuit in two hours. Only the hardiest bearers keep to their task for more than a few minutes at a time, but several dozen other men and women straggling on behind stand ready to take their places. Everyone wears some version of festival garb, adapted from the clothing of the carpenters of Edo, and everyone who carries the mikoshi must be wearing one of the neighborhood's *hanten,* a loose long coat emblazoned with Miyamoto-chō's name. This requirement is in part intended to keep outsiders from crashing the festival; there are a few hanten at the O-tabisho that can be rented ahead of time, but most residents who are interested in the festival purchased hanten when the neighborhood ordered a new batch in the early 1980's.

As the mikoshi processions continue, more and more people shed their festival clothing, especially the hanten. It is too hot, and part of the bravado of the old-fashioned festival is to strip down. Although the elders mildly disapprove, by the end of the processions at least a couple of the more rambunctious men will be wearing little more than loincloths (fundoshi) and headbands (hachimaki).

The routes and the hours of the festivals require advance police approval, but as the afternoon fades into evening, the adults show no signs of stopping. In one innovation the leaders of the mikoshi committee have mounted spotlights on the four corners of the mikoshi's roof, powered by two 12-volt car batteries anchored on the underside of the structure. The mikoshi—the first in the area to have electricity—makes a fine sight as it lunges through the dusk, its metal fittings glittering in the light that plays as well across the glistening shoulders of the sweating, hoarsely shouting, exhausted men who take it one more time up and down the shopping street. To the dismay of the police and the delight of onlookers, someone gets the idea to extinguish the shōtenkai's streetlights, and the street is plunged into semidarkness. On and on the mikoshi goes, until finally an older leader, with bullhorn raised, steps in front of the frenzied horde, and in his politest, most formal phrases asks everyone to return the mikoshi to its resting place and to gather under a canopy for beer and *sake,* fried chicken and sushi.

The mikoshi circuits for children, though much more sedate and held in the late morning or early afternoon, follow roughly the same pattern. Beginning bright and early Saturday morning, swarms of elementary school children—both boys and girls— excitedly clamber around the smaller of the two mikoshi in the O-tabisho, awaiting the chance to carry it through the streets. Most hurry to mark their chosen spots by tying the towel that will cushion their shoulders to the framework. All wear *happi* (a jacket modeled on old-fashioned workman's apparel). The neighborhood owns about 150 children's happi, which parents may rent for a nominal charge. But they must take care to sign up ahead of time to reserve one, for all are always spoken for by the first day of the festival. Without a happi a child is not allowed to help carry the mikoshi.

As the procession gets going, cries of *"Washoi! Washoi!"* mingle with occasional shouts of *"Genki ga nai zo!"* (roughly "You weaklings!" or "You guys aren't trying!"). Sometimes the taunts come from adults trying to spur the children on using their best drill-sargeant barks; most often they come from macho youngsters trying to get the mikoshi bouncing and whirling at a frenzied pace.

Every two or three blocks the children take a rest stop in an alleyway, in a parking lot, or at a wide spot in the road. As they approach, housewives rush out with trays of cold drinks— juices, colas, or *mugicha*, a chilled barley tea—or with boxes of frozen ice candies. The accompanying adults pause for cigarettes and keep a watchful eye out for traffic. In front of the several local liquor stores, the children stage mock attacks on the shops, shouting, *"Sakaya wa kechinbō, shio o dase!"* ("The *sake* dealer is a skinflint, toss us some salt!").[14] At Yokokawa-ya, the oldest shop in the neighborhood, the old grandmother douses the kids with a bucket of water tossed out of a second-story window, but at all the other shops someone scurries out with soft drinks or ice cream bars, which the adults distribute at the next rest stop.

Throughout the year but especially in the months before the festival, the women's auxiliary holds regular folk-dance practice under the watchful eye of Mrs. Hara, a professional dance teacher who lives in the lower part of Miyamoto-chō. During the festival the fujinbu women—mostly middle-aged—dance with precision in single file around the same route that the mikoshi follow, to music from a large tape recorder that Mr. Shigemori, the festival's music master, pulls on a handcart at the head of the parade. The mikoshi and dance processions take place simultaneously, but only rarely do the two groups meet.

The women's auxiliary is also largely responsible for Miyamoto-chō's contribution to the entertainment presented at the shrine. Each of the seven parish neighborhoods is allotted about 20 minutes both evenings, and the shrine's open-air stage becomes the setting for shamisen soloists, koto ensembles, comic mimes loosely derived from classical kyōgen farces, and some dreadfully serious folk-dancing. The audiences are appreciative, applauding enthusiastically and laughing uproariously at the stale jokes that each neighborhood's master of ceremonies interjects. The attention of the crowd is short-lived, however, for most are parents or grandparents with children in tow, who have eyes only for the magic of the fair: the toy peddlers and fortune-tellers and games of chance.

On festival nights the shrine precincts do take on a magical glow, as sputtering generators power flickering lights strung among the several dozen stalls. Many of the young girls are dressed in brightly colored yukata of gauze, with sashes that almost drag on the ground. Babes in arms, blinking wildly at the clamor around them, are dressed in little festival happi coats. Children with a few hundred yen run back and forth among the peddlers, all of whom are professional carnies who appear at similar events throughout the ward. Some sell masks of comic-book heroes or offer chances to win a prize by tugging free a snarl of three dozen ropes. An old man fashions strands of molten candy into dogs and cats and birds and fish. A cotton-candy vendor stands next to a woman selling roasted corn on the cob; a fried noodle stall adjoins a stand offering pancakes laced with chopped ginger and octopus. A fortune-teller will sell you an amulet based on your sign of the East Asian zodiac, and for 200 yen you can try to scoop up goldfish with a rice-paper strainer that dissolves almost immediately. It is garish and tacky and fun. If the shrine has any appeal to match the parish neighborhoods' during the festival, this is it.

Interneighborhood Competition and the New Mikoshi

In some ways the festival suggests or nominally encourages cooperation among the parish neighborhoods: common celebration in honor of a common tutelary deity; logistical coordination to ensure that seven simultaneous neighborhood observances do not tangle each other up; even the adoption of common patterns for the women dancers' yukata by some of the neighborhoods. At the same time, however, the festival—and particularly the mikoshi and their processions—provide ample opportunities for competition.

Four of the seven neighborhoods in the parish, including Miyamoto-chō, represent sections of Yanagi, the administrative name for the area that parallels the now paved-over river. These neighborhoods lie adjacent to one another along the shopping street and have to coordinate their festivals the most closely for both practical and social reasons. Because they contain two major cross-ward arterials on which traffic is certain to be disrupted and must each get formal police approval for the mikoshi processions, some coordination is inevitably necessary. Additionally, among the seven neighborhoods, these four form the most geographically compact set and are linked to one another by the greatest number of institutional ties, through school districts, shopping areas, and so forth (see Table 7).

The festival is an opportunity to demonstrate the closeness of ties among residents of these four strongly linked neighborhoods. On the other hand it is also an opportunity for exquisite one-upmanship. In recent years the neighborhood next to Miyamoto-chō triumphed with an impressive new mikoshi, hand-built by local young men over a period of three or four years. This neighborhood, Yanagi 4-chōme, took great pride in parading its large, ornate palanquin through the streets of Miyamoto-chō uninvited, and the neighborhood was as pleased by the mikoshi as it was by the resurgence of interest among young men in neighborhood life that accompanied and followed the completion of the new palanquin.

In 1979 Yanagi 4-chōme took the lead in suggesting that the four Yanagi neighborhoods stage a joint mikoshi procession in which the children from each chōkai would carry their mikoshi on a grand circuit throughout the four neighborhoods. The plan was agreed upon, and the mikoshi of the four Yanagi chōkai gathered at the shrine on Saturday morning for a blessing before starting out on the circuit. From Miyamoto-chō's perspective the event turned out to be a disaster. Instead of the expected small mikoshi, Yanagi 4-chōme sent its elaborate new one, and instead of a group of elementary school children, Yanagi 4-chōme's contingent was made up of husky high school students and shop apprentices. Miyamoto-chō had simply sent its standard small mikoshi—generally considered to be appropriate only for children, though in the absence of another larger one Miyamoto-chō's adults used it too. The third neighborhood followed suit with Miyamoto-chō, while the fourth showed up with a lightweight mikoshi the children had especially constructed out of a straw-covered *sake* keg festooned with paper flowers.

As the procession wound its way through the streets of all four neighborhoods under the hot September sun, the young men of Yanagi 4-chōme and the children with the *sake* keg carried on with great gusto, while the children from Miyamoto-chō and the remaining neighborhood struggled on, more and more exhausted with each block. Cries of *"Genki ga nai, zo!"* were not sufficient that day to rouse their spirits. By the time the procession had reached one end of the shopping street, where local leaders were to make speeches to close the day, frustrated children were slipping away and angry mothers were looking for festival leaders to whom they could complain. To add insult to injury, suddenly a truck arrived from the most distant neighborhood to transport its youngsters and mikoshi back home; Miyamoto-chō's festival leaders had made no such plan, and the children had to carry their mikoshi back to the neighborhood.

Miyamoto-chō had lost every round; its mikoshi was outclassed and it had failed its children by neither creating a special lightweight mikoshi nor arranging transportation home. Miyamoto-chō's leaders were visibly furious at the public relations fiasco that confronted them in the neighborhood—and in inter-neighborhood competition. The following year there was no talk of cooperative mikoshi processions.

But Miyamoto-chō did have a card up its sleeve in 1980. It countered Yanagi 4-chōme by prominently featuring in its processions the unsurpassed spectacle of a foreign anthropologist and his exotic, red-haired, folk-dancing wife. The redhead was a particular coup. Throughout the year my wife had been practicing folk-dance steps with the women of the fujinbu and had joined with them in sewing the yukata made every other year for the festival. As the dance troupe planned its routines for its performances at the festival in 1980, someone suddenly came up with the idea of putting my wife on display in their processions. With some difficulty slightly larger *geta* and *tabi* (sandals and two-toed socks) that matched the troupe's were obtained. Carefully the women coached and recoached my wife in all the steps. They checked and rechecked the hang of her yukata and giggled over the difficulty of fitting a Western female shape into the yukata's idealized cylindrical contours.

Finally everything was ready and off they went. As expected my wife received an inordinate amount of attention, both from encouraging neighbors and from incredulous spectators from other neighborhoods. After making a standard circuit of Miyamoto-chō, the troupe suddenly made a right turn where it should have gone straight. The detour around a single block took it directly in front of Yanagi 4-chōme's festival headquarters, where the reaction was shock, followed by strained cordiality. The next day Yanagi 4-chōme's women's troupe similarly broke interneighborhood etiquette by dancing unannounced up the shopping street through Miyamoto-chō. But in the eyes of the Miyamoto-chō women there was no question that they had come out ahead in the competition. As one delightedly told me, "It was much, much better than the time we put Mr. Oda in a panda costume and had him dance with us."

But of course as temporary residents we provided no long-term solution to the problem of keeping ahead of the other neighborhoods. When we left in 1981, the debate was beginning in earnest about whether Miyamoto-chō should commission a new mikoshi that would match or surpass Yanagi 4-chōme's and attract additional participants to Miyamoto-chō's festival.

The following year the neighborhood's younger leaders finally agreed to take the initiative on a project they had talked about for years. In the spring of 1982, about a year after they lost power in the chōkai with the selection of an older man to succeed one of their own as president, they launched a drive to raise funds for a new mikoshi. They successfully enlisted several prominent older leaders of the neighborhood as patrons of their venture's campaign, created a new organization—formally quite separate from the chōkai, the festival committee, and the ujiko sōdai—set themselves on having the new mikoshi in time for the September festival, and went out in search of funds.[15]

In the early fall I received letters with photographs of the neighborhood's magnificent new mikoshi. The fund-raising drive had been a smashing success. In less than three months the self-styled Action Committee for the Presentation of a Mikoshi (Mikoshi Hōken Jikkō Iinkai) had raised (in cash or pledges) slightly more than 10.6 million yen from 408 households, an average contribution of over 26,000 yen from more than half of Miyamoto-chō's households. Indeed, left with a surplus of about two million yen, the younger leadership faction in its guise as the Mikoshi Action Committee had scored another, unexpected coup by providing its new organization with a hefty endowment.

The Mikoshi Action Committee itself was a successful stratagem by younger leaders to reassert their role in neighborhood affairs. The committee had deliberately been formed separately from the chōkai, with its own membership, officers, and finances. It sought and received official recognition by the ward authorities as a charitable group authorized to solicit funds from the public. This authorization was valid for two years, until the summer of 1984, at which time the committee was required to dissolve itself, and its leaders were forced to rethink the group's future existence as a separate organization. Following much discussion during and after the 1984 festival, the committee agreed to present the mikoshi (and the group's balance of almost two million yen) to the *neighborhood* of Miyamoto-chō (not directly to the chōkai) through the organizational device of becoming a standing committee under the umbrella of the chōkai, but retaining autonomous control of both the mikoshi and the money.

In essence the committee's leaders—the chōkai's young leadership faction out of power since 1981—negotiated their reconciliation with the chōkai's older leaders on their own terms. Their bargaining position was bolstered not only by the surplus cash the committee held but also by the evidence the campaign provided of their ability to motivate residents' participation; the 408 households that had contributed represented a larger percentage of local residents than had supported any neighborhood activity in recent memory. Successfully using traditionalistic symbols of community life—the mikoshi and the festival—the young leaders had been spectacularly more successful than the older, more "pragmatic" chōkai leaders in raising funds and increasing residents' interest in community affairs.

At its debut for the 1982 festival, Miyamoto-chō's new mikoshi met all expectations. It was clearly the largest, most expensive, and most ornate in the area. In public statements leaders of the fund-raising campaign focused on the benefits the mikoshi would give the community: attracting more participation in the festival—and hence in neighborhood affairs generally— by making the matsuri more impressive and exciting. Privately, they pointed out with pride that Miyamoto-chō's new mikoshi eclipsed the homemade one next door, and they talked with unconcealed glee about another adjoining neighborhood that considered trying to match it and then withdrew from the competition.

In many ways, some unanticipated, the new mikoshi subtly changed the character of the matsuri. As leaders in the campaign had hoped, the excitement generated by the new mikoshi and by the stylish new festival garb the committee had purchased brought out unprecedented numbers of young men (and women). Indeed the size and weight of the new mikoshi required larger numbers of participants simply to carry it through the neighborhood. To their mild chagrin the committee's young leaders found that they were no longer young enough, and that the new mikoshi was simply too heavy for them. Their success in getting the new mikoshi put them on the sidelines as a younger generation shouldered the burden.[16] The great expense of the mikoshi meant greater concern to protect it, and no longer were men allowed to clamber up to dance on top of the whirling palanquin. In the new mikoshi's second year, spotlights powered by two car batteries were added to display the mikoshi to best advantage in the twilight—and to enable the processions to continue well after dark—and there is no denying that the new mikoshi glowing in the dusk as it hurtled down darkened alleys was a stunning sight.

But new prominence brought with it new problems. Never before had Miyamoto-chō had to worry about outsiders crashing their festival. Now, suddenly, people from surrounding areas (as well as some total strangers from farther afield) flocked to join in.[17] During the 1984 festival the Mikoshi Action Committee was faced with an ugly brawl between tough young laborers and a leader of the festival who had argued with them as they sought to take over the mikoshi's itinerary for the day. The laborers had come to the festival at the invitation of one of their bosses who lived in Miyamoto-chō, but as their insistence on running the show grew and their drunken boisterousness increased, sharp words led to blows. Committee leaders had to step in physically to separate the brawlers and prevent serious damage to person and property. Some residents stayed away from the matsuri that year, grumbling that things like this never happened in the good old days.

Nevertheless, most residents (and especially the younger leaders who had formed the Mikoshi Action Committee) feel that even if the impressive new mikoshi has led to changes in the festival, it was well worth it; the neighborhood had gained prestige and, indirectly and almost in spite of itself, the chōkai had gained the participation of some younger men who were initially attracted by the new mikoshi.

Ritual and the Local Social Order

The festival is the most colorful and widely supported celebration of community life, but it is only one of many events sponsored by local groups throughout the year that help define Miyamoto-chō more sharply as a community. The themes expressed through the festival—ranked stratification and hierarchy, communal solidarity and egalitarianism, and neighborhood identity and autonomy—are not unique to this event; they interweave all aspects of neighborhood-centered social activity. In the festival and in other activities, the neighborhood's partisans manipulate social and symbolic meanings to cloak themselves with prestige and legitimacy, and to invest Miyamoto-chō with an aura of communal identity and autonomy. By accentuating seemingly traditional customs of community life, local events imbue Miyamoto-chō with the legitimacy that tradition so amply bestows. This mantle of legitimacy in turn can become a tool in local power struggles, and can help to overcome—to dampen or defuse—the potential divisiveness that might arise from the open expression of the various competing, contradictory social themes implicit in many of the neighborhood's communal events.

In putting on the matsuri Miyamoto-chō's residents seek to highlight those aspects of *their* festival that distinguish it from the festivals in the other parish neighborhoods. Many of the distinctions they draw seem mundane and devoid of great symbolic content. For example, they point to their method of gathering festival contributions, eschewing what they see as the coercive direct door-to-door technique used in adjoining neighborhoods in favor of a "voluntary" system in which households that wish to contribute bring their donations publicly to the chōkai hall. By the same token, even as leaders moan about inadequate participation in the festival, they steadfastly refuse to let matsuri aficionados (of whom there are many in Tokyo) from outside the neighborhood join in the activities, and look with scorn on those nearby neighborhoods that have sacrificed their local character by welcoming outsiders. In these and dozens of other seemingly minor elements, residents of Miyamoto-chō point to their festival as being *theirs*, carried out in accord with what they see as *their* distinctive ways of doing things, ways that are best suited—almost by definition—to Miyamoto-chō's circumstances.

One way in which residents judge that their festival is distinctively theirs, of course, is by perceiving it as unchanging, carried out year after year within the bounds of precedent. The festival committee is slow to allow changes in the content and the performance of the mikoshi processions and other elements of the festival, for adherence to established ways of doing things is, leaders argue, an essential component of the stable continuity of neighborhood life. At the same time the committee's concern with faithfulness to principles and past practice, and residents' perception of unvarying ritual, often ignore or overlook almost random, sometimes opportunistic alterations. Some changes are by their nature temporary, such as flaunting my wife in the streets of other neighborhoods. Other changes, perhaps equally casual in their origins, may become permanent—may establish a tradition—if they can be interpreted as serving the purposes tradition is locally presumed to serve: enhancing the sense of the neighborhood as distinctive and as unified.

Thus, even as the stability of tradition is lauded as great virtue, innovation and flexibility are highly regarded. In the local view it is the ability to adapt local institutions and practices to changing needs, circumstances, and demands of residents that demonstrates that community life in Miyamoto-chō is far from moribund. The vitality of the community is the raison d'être for preserving (or creating) tradition, not the other way around.

Some innovations are successful and endure, such as the decision in the early 1980's to let women help carry the mikoshi (cf. Littleton 1986). Others flop and are quickly forgotten. An outstanding example was the decision in 1980 that the post-festival banquet (called the *hachiarai*, lit., "washing the bowls") for roughly 60 matsuri leaders and other active festival participants be held outside the neighborhood, and most radical of all, in a formal Western-style banquet hall, where waiters in dinner jackets served filet mignon to a stiffly ill-at-ease crowd that had been expecting the loose give-and-take of sushi, *sake*, and song on tatami mats.

Certainly the most successful innovation represented the most old-fashioned of motifs. The purchase of the new mikoshi in 1982 introduced major changes and altered the pool of matsuri participants in ways not to everyone's liking. The campaign to obtain the mikoshi mirrored or exacerbated tensions between younger and older leaders of Miyamoto-chō and led for a time to the existence of two separate institutions concerned with the management of the festival: the old-line saireiiin and the upstart Mikoshi Action Committee. Nevertheless, few leaders now dispute the success of the project. It was successful in part because of its very traditionality, which promoted a sense of vigorous local custom and identity. This traditionality also was an unassailable tool in the hands of younger progressive leaders (paradoxically the promoters of tradition, in this case) in their successful power struggle against older conservative neighborhood leaders.

Many scholars have noted the Japanese penchant for "instant tradition"—the ability to cloak new circumstances and institutions with a mantle of traditionalism, imparting depth and resiliency to what might otherwise have shaky foundations.[18] In Miyamoto-chō symbols are appropriated from various sources—from the customs of the shitamachi districts, from the ethos of the prototypical rural hamlet, and from the general inventory of Japanese cultural symbols, both contemporary and past—to create and embellish the neighborhood's own tradition and identity. In the festival the "distinctiveness" of local tradition is most obviously emphasized and utilized to distinguish Miyamoto-chō from its peers—the other neighborhoods of the parish. In a more general sense, however, what local activities enable Miyamoto-chō to assert is more properly its discreteness, the actual uniqueness of local tradition being less important than the simple perception of it as being local. The assertion of discreteness, made in the name of unique local tradition, is in part a response to the policies and claims of external agencies, such as the ward government's branch office, which Miyamoto-chō's leaders interpret as threats to undermine or replace the neighborhood as the primary unit of local society.

Octavio Paz describes the Mexican fiesta as anarchic: "During a fiesta the ranks and stations of life are violated. We poke fun at the army, the state, and [the] church. We flagrantly violate the hierarchies of life" (quoted in Turkle 1975: 97). Hiroshi Soeda (1973) uses the term "anarchitecture," combining anarchy and architecture, to describe the urban Japanese festival, which he sees as a liberation of residents and their neighborhoods from the control of the civil authorities. But in Miyamoto-chō autonomy from external control is not the only issue, and if anything Miyamoto-chō's festival validates many of the social arrangements of the mundane secular world as it exists within the neighborhood.

While the festival and similar events resolve, to the neighborhood's satisfaction at least, questions of community identity, they also point up the internal tension between the neighborhood's ethos of egalitarianism and its hierarchical stratification. Leaders maintain that the community is clearly set off from the wider society, and that such events, with their emphasis on communal solidarity and equality, demonstrate that the status systems of Japanese society at large do not apply to neighborhood matters. Obviously in the status system of contemporary Japanese society all are not equal; but *within* Miyamoto-chō, according to the local view, the bureaucrat, the symphony musician, and the teacher are no more and no less than the butcher, the baker, and the tofu maker.

By setting the neighborhood's social life apart from the status systems of society as a whole, events and activities that emphasize Miyamoto-chō's communal solidarity and nominal egalitarianism also help mark off the neighborhood as an alternative social world. Within this closely held social arena, those who find the neighborhood most meaningful and who are most active in it can find the status and prestige not usually accorded them elsewhere. In a sense the vitality and internal complexity of neighborhoods like Miyamoto-chō can be seen as a consequence or reflection of Japanese class dynamics. Members of the "old middle class" who lack recognition in a society where status and prestige are generally granted on the basis of education and employment can cordon off a corner of the world in which recognition is based on other criteria—their own criteria.

By developing (or legitimating, or sanctifying) hierarchies of status within this separate though limited world of the neighborhood, merchants, petty industrialists, and artisans excluded from recognition in wider arenas of society can in turn exclude others (and justify that exclusion on the grounds of lack of participation in neighborhood activities). Because the events and activities—in this instance the festival—are so avowedly "traditional," so self-consciously heir to the cultural heritage of all Japanese, the events themselves, as well as the institutions and the systems of ranking and exclusion that derive from them, are immune from all but the most radical challenge or critique. Thus Miyamoto-chō's localized hierarchy of status could not exist without events such as the festival, which by stressing communal solidarity and egalitarianism gloss over and momentarily hush the competing (and much stronger) status rankings of society as a whole.

Conclusion

IN THE SUMMER OF 1984, a year and a half after I finished writing my dissertation and a little over three years after my wife and I left Miyamoto-chō, I returned to the neighborhood for two months of follow-up research. With me I brought copies of a short, nonscholarly article in which I had discussed Miyamoto-chō: a brief account of arts and crafts in daily life. Eager to demonstrate that I had been doing something productive with my time, I distributed copies of it to a few chōkai leaders and several of my closest friends.

The Takahashis, the Tsunodas, Tsurumi-sensei, and others received the article with pleasure and looked at the photographs with mock outrage: why had I caught only the corner of their storefront? Why did only the back of grandfather's head appear next to the mikoshi? As I summarized the article's content, they nodded and asked why I had not published a book yet. I assured them that it was on the way and reassured them that I did not intend to reveal any secrets. We joked about what I would do with all the money the book was certain to make once it was published.

One night, as I sat drinking with a group of the younger leaders discussing the new mikoshi and the formation of the Mikoshi Action Committee, Mr. Noda—the prosperous owner of a local factory—began to talk about my article. Mr. Noda graduated from one of Tokyo's best private universities; he has been to the United States several times; he drives a Buick. He said that he had read my piece carefully (although laboriously), and that he was upset. Pouring me another scotch-and-water, he asked, "Do you really think we are so old-fashioned?"

His objection was a simple and honest one: my article had indeed stressed "traditional" aspects of Miyamoto-chō. Written for an audience in the United States not terribly familiar with Japan, it concentrated on the "Japaneseness" of daily life.[1] Did I honestly feel, he asked, that he and the others in Miyamoto-chō about whom I had written were somehow exotic, somehow less "Western" than other people in contemporary Japan?

No, I replied, I did not think of Miyamoto-chō as a quaint place, full of people engaging in traditional lifeways out of sync with modern life. In writing for an American audience, I had necessarily stressed those details of life that Americans would find different from their own, hence my discussion of traditional arts and crafts as hobbies, of the matsuri's significance, and of the superb dexterity of sushi chefs as they carve scenes of Mount Fuji out of folded bamboo leaves. I had wanted to show how what many Americans see as quaint, old-fashioned customs and habits are seamlessly woven through the lives of modern Japanese, to show that for most Japanese these things are not extraordinary but commonplace, not things that suspend them schizophrenically between two worlds but things that are simply part of a smoothly integrated way of life made up of social and cultural elements from diverse but rarely contemplated sources.

Mr. Noda was eventually satisfied, and as we continued drinking, the conversation passed on to other things. His remarks have stayed with me, however, and as I have written about Miyamoto-chō since, his questions have always lingered in the back of my mind. My answers have evolved, I hope, since that bleary evening, and here I will attempt to explain, for him and for others, what the significance of my study of Miyamoto-chō seems to me to be.

Past and Present and Japanese Social Organization

Certainly this book is about traditionalistic forms of social organization in contemporary Japan. To many readers this may seem an unremarkable admission, for tradition is what anthropologists are supposed to look for. Tradition in this sense is simply another name for culture, conceived of as the fundamental and somehow ahistorical patterns underlying social life. In the words of Sydel Silverman (1979: 414): "The expansion of the anthropology of complex societies took place during a period when modernization theory dominated the social sciences. Anthropologists became specialists in the remnants of 'traditional' society and in the transition to 'modernity,' . . . documenting the bipolarity of tradition and modernity."

My intent, however, has not been to try to document a bipolarity, to try to tease apart those aspects of Miyamoto-chō's social life that can be ascribed to the persistence of past forms and to juxtapose them with features of the neighborhood's social organization that are the product of modernization, however construed. My interest in the relationship between the past and the present lies in other directions.

On the one hand I examined the history of Miyamoto-chō's development to understand how that history has shaped today's patterns of social organization. But my goal was not to demonstrate processes of direct cultural continuity on which so many conventional accounts of Japanese social change rely. Instead, I hoped to show how social change itself created many of the features now labeled "traditional" and now thought to represent the survival of the past.

On the other hand, in discussing present-day Miyamoto-chō, I have focused on "traditionalism," the use of social idioms or metaphors that seek to clothe the present in a mantle of venerable antiquity. I am interested in how residents construct and manipulate ideas about what are supposed (both by most observers and by most participants) to be ahistorical patterns of community organization so as to shape the present to their own advantage. Both these perspectives on the past and the present provide useful vantage points not only for understanding urban neighborhoods, but also for examining much broader domains of Japanese social organization.

I have tried to outline the history of Miyamoto-chō's development to demonstrate that historical antecedent is an insufficient explanation for contemporary social organization. But history is not bunk, and to properly understand contemporary Miyamoto-chō and how it came to be the neighborhood it is today, one must understand the growth of Tokyo's population and the city's outward expansion since the turn of the century. Further, one must look within the social turmoil accompanying the city's demographic and physical growth at the solutions then proposed: the configurations of social institutions and ideologies that metaphorically called upon the "traditional" rural village as a model for urban life. From this chaotic urban growth (and from the ideological responses it called forth) resulted the development of neighborhood associations and related patterns of community life in Miyamoto-chō and in urban Japanese society generally. Contemporary patterns of neighborhood life, therefore, were and are created through the general processes of urban growth, combined with the particular historical circumstances of the community and of Japanese society during the twentieth century.

The historical explanations with which I take issue are those that see contemporary neighborhoods as a residual survival of a preindustrial or rural past. As I noted at the start, studies of urban neighborhoods in the older shitamachi districts of Tokyo consistently link contemporary social patterns to the social structure of the preindustrial city, just as those of newer neighborhoods on the fringes of old Tokyo tend to portray them as embodying patterns of rural social organization. Whichever perspective one chooses, the implicit thesis remains the same: in those communities that today manifest strong communal institutions and identity, the explanation is historical. The past accounts for the present (and additionally the countryside accounts for the city) through assertions of direct (but not clearly specified) links of historical continuity.

Many of Miyamoto-chō's residents join the scholars of Japanese urbanism in this view. But neither the institutions nor the traditionalism of the neighborhood can be taken as historical givens. They are not the products of social stasis; they developed during periods of great social change. Miyamoto-chō was created during Tokyo's urban growth; it is successor to neither a rural hamlet nor a preindustrial merchant quarter. In the contemporary as well as the historical perspective, Miyamoto-chō as an organized community emerges as a response, both by individual residents and by governmental bodies, to a variety of social, political, and demographic features of the urban environment that require collective action, action necessitated by both internal community needs and external demands. Although idioms of traditionalism and elements of traditional social patterns are invoked in the symbolic creation and maintenance of the neighborhood as a community, this should not blind analysts from examining these ideas for what they are: metaphors for the organization of social life, which may be manipulated either consciously or unconsciously. Observers should not take them at face value as evidence of historical continuity or cultural stagnation of the individuals and social groups involved.

The failure to recognize these points distorts our understanding not only of urban neighborhoods, but of social patterns throughout all realms of Japanese society and the processes of social change that have shaped them. Analyses that place the locus of Japanese social structure firmly in the social patterns of the past or argue that similarities between the rural past and the urban present result from static continuity explain little. They perpetuate a view of social change as involving simple movement along a continuum between rural and urban, traditional and modern. They relegate those aspects of society and culture deemed traditional to a limbo in which no further explanation or analysis is required, and they fail to examine the dynamic manipulation, reinterpretation, and creation of "tradition" that takes place during the process of social change. As I have noted, they rely on "invented history," those explanations of contemporary life that imply an imagined past from which change is believed to have occurred (R. J. Smith 1973: 164).

That residents of Miyamoto-chō themselves readily indulge in "invented history" brings me to my second interest in the relationship between past and present: the ways in which people refer or allude to the past—to "tradition"—to explain, or to make sense of, or to manipulate contemporary social arrangements for contemporary ends. As Sylvia Yanagisako has argued, "Tradition [is] a cultural construct whose meaning must be discovered in present words no less than past acts" (1985: 18).

But not all Japanese engage in the same cultural constructions. Many Japanese do not give a whit for festivals and neigh-borly social ties, and indeed in many communities—the upper-class suburbs on the western fringes of Tokyo come immedi-ately to mind—residents strive to create other understandings of the relationship of neighbor to neighbor, of community to government, of citizen to state. Why, then, in neighborhoods like Miyamoto-chō are these particular constructions of com-munal tradition so readily called upon to forge—in both senses of the word—links between a past and a present? Why this tra-ditionalism and not some other? The answer lies, I believe, not so much in Miyamoto-chō itself as in the larger society of which it is a part.

Traditionalism, Community, and the Old Middle Class

The members of the old middle class, the petty bourgeoisie, are typically the mainstays of local community life throughout urban Japan, and Miyamoto-chō is no exception. The common explanations for this phenomenon are neither difficult to re-hearse nor terribly informative. On the one hand merchants have both the motive and the opportunity. They typically have more of a stake in local life than sarariiman since it provides their bread and butter. Because their occupations tend to keep them around their home, they spend more time in the com-munity, so the chances for community involvement are greater. On the other hand it is widely assumed that the old middle class is inherently conservative, prone to embrace feudal values and culturally stagnant;[2] the merchants' involvement in local affairs therefore simply reflects an outmoded social and cultural ori-entation that keeps them apart from the mainstream of Japanese society.

The first set of explanations is certainly true—small mer-chants do have motive and opportunity, time and access—but this begs the question of why their involvement in community life should necessarily have a traditionalistic cast. The second set of explanations provides an answer to this question, but an unsatisfying one. In proposing that the old middle class is iso-lated from Japanese society and unaffected by the currents of social, cultural, economic, and political change that have so drastically altered the face of Japan over the past century, it relies on "uncritical assumptions about the mechanical transmission of culture from one generation to the next" (Yanagisako 1985: 18) and maintains that traditionalism is an index of isolation.

To the contrary, I argue that traditionalism—as an active agent creating and re-creating images and meanings that attach to the social forms around which people organize their lives— is an index not of *isolation from* but of *interaction with* the broader society. I turn on its head Howard Wimberley's view of cultural style as something maintained through the internal dynamics of a group or class,[3] and argue instead that style—here consisting of traditionalism—comes into play and is impelled through the interactions of members of different groups.

In my view neighborhood institutions and the values that support them—as features of an old middle-class lifestyle—far from being internal to a static and isolated social class, are dynamically related to the contemporary forms of identity and meaning that members of the old middle class attach to their lives. The content of this identity—in this instance its emphasis on localism and active participation in neighborhood affairs— draws its significance from the dynamics of interclass relations. The maintenance or development of subculturally distinctive lifestyles stems not from the stability of intraclass subcultures, but from the changing nature of interclass relations through a process that Bennett Berger refers to as symbolic stratification:

In a prosperous society there occurs not only individual mobility between strata in a relatively stable hierarchy; the entire hierarchy is pushed upwards by prolonged, widespread prosperity, and is rearranged by changes in occupational or income distribution. At the same time, the function of stratification symbols is to maintain viable distinctions among different categories of people, and when criteria which formerly distinguished rank no longer do so because they have become widely available, it is not too much to expect a restructuring of the symbolic aspects of stratification—if that is, their distinction-making function is to remain viable (Berger 1960: 93).

Berger's point, made in a study of a working-class suburb in the United States, applies as well to the Japanese case. The particular content of the subculturally different lifestyles of various classes—the symbolic aspects of stratification—are not the inheritances of static traditions that survive within the vacuum of a single group's (or class's) existence. Instead, the content of different subcultures and the symbols that convey or imply these subcultures' differences are created and reformulated through the interaction of one group or class with others, and through the shifting positions or rankings of one group vis-à-vis others.

The past several decades have brought great prosperity to many members of the old middle class: they have profited as the retail and service sectors have kept pace with the growth of Japanese consumer demand; the inflationary spiral in real estate values, especially in Tokyo, has benefited established shopowners who have frequently also become apartment owners and petty landlords; and inequities in the tax laws have enabled the self-employed to shelter far more of their income than salaried employees can.[4] Indeed in purely economic terms the old middle class may be in many respects better off than the new. In the status game of contemporary Japanese society, however, the old middle class loses out to the sarariiman.

Although self-employed merchants and artisans were never a highly regarded social class, they long held a commanding position in establishing the character of Japanese urban life. But in the postwar decades members of the old middle class have been steadily losing even this social high ground to the new middle class of sarariiman. As the sarariiman way of life has gained ascendancy—if not as a statistical norm at least as the normative ideal against which all Japanese lifestyles are now measured and compared[5]—the individual and collective social status of the old middle class has declined. Given that the major avenues to social advancement are now elite education and employment in large, prestigious bureaucratic organizations—not the self-sufficiency of individualism or simply the accumulation of personal wealth—the old middle class necessarily falls behind. Self-employment, small-scale entrepreneurship, and the not terribly prestigious educational credentials required in many lines of family-run businesses all set the old middle class apart from the mainstreams of contemporary social advancement.[6] As the homogenized lifestyle of the "new middle mass" becomes ever more hegemonic,[7] members of the old middle class lose even more ground.

I have argued that by stressing participation in local institutions and adherence to values of neighborhood solidarity as the prime determinants of local social standing and worth, merchants and small factory owners are able to create an alternative social world in which rank, prestige, power, and status are assigned according to criteria they can define and control. They can do so by setting up and playing a game that pretty much excludes the new middle-class sarariiman from the start—by the nature of *his* occupation he has neither the time nor the local resources to participate—and that assigns worth independently of status determinants that apply in society as a whole.[8] Status that accrues from neighborhood leadership may be derived solely from interactions within Miyamoto-chō, and the prestige may be expressed (or be recognized) only within the confines of the neighborhood. But in some cases leadership, status, and prestige gained within the neighborhood may be both augmented by and contribute to the success of one's dealings outside the neighborhood, representing Miyamoto-chō to politicians, officials, and others from the wider world.[9] In either case these local sources of status are the prerogatives of the old middle class.

The traditionalism of the old middle class, including the emphasis placed on sustaining neighborhood life, can be seen as a symbolic aspect of stratification, subject to change, modification, and elaboration as the positions of various groups and classes change in relationship to one another. But the specific symbols of traditionalism—those cultural elements whose content or meaning can be implied, managed, or rearranged to lend a patina of comfortable habit or unassailable antiquity to a present-day institution or social pattern—are not arbitrary. The lustre of venerable legitimacy is in the eye of the beholder, as much as anywhere. To have proper effect the images of traditionality one presents must be as recognizable and as valued by the audience as by the actor.

Images of community are appropriate and effective symbols with which to associate oneself, for notions of communal life strike an immediate chord with the audience. Whether local residents (or local government officials) *like* the chōkai or its leaders or its policies is not the question. Like them or not, residents and officials are presented with a community structure and an ideology of community as faits accomplis—social structures and their supporting values that because of their traditionality, their very Japaneseness, are unassailable. Residents can simply ignore the neighborhood if they wish. Or they can choose not to participate, basing their refusal on a principled radical critique that challenges the very basis of Japanese "tradition" (as in very different ways members of the Sōka Gakkai and the Communist Party do). Or they can fight fire with fire (as local government officials do when they try to outshine neighborhood communities by creating similar structures on a larger scale). But in its own terms the legitimacy of the cultural symbolism of community invoked in support of the existing neighborhood is unquestionable.

Traditionalistic trappings of community are an effective device for the old middle class in other ways as well. Evoking associations with shitamachi, now widely portrayed on television, in the press, and in other media with nostalgic romanticism, and by extension evoking some distant link to the glories of Edo and its *chōnin* (townspeople), the old middle class can situate itself in the heartland of Japanese urbanism as a way of life (Bestor n.d.). Through matsuri, through "preservation" of neighborliness, through support for localism against centralism, its members link themselves to a great tradition (not Japan's Great Tradition but a great tradition nonetheless), again in ways that are both recognizable to themselves and to members of society as a whole and unassailably legitimate because they invent and then represent a history of cultural continuity with the preindustrial past, the cultural legitimacy of which no one could or would dispute.

The involvement of the old middle class in sustaining the viability of local communities raises other issues revolving around the political significance of chōkai and other neighborhood institutions. For many observers it matters little whether chōkai are cynical creations of a government that seeks to cloak its apparatus in the trappings of community or are remnants of some primordial spirit of "natural" community sustained into the present by an old middle class that clings to outmoded social roles and values. Either way neighborhood institutions themselves are inherently conservative and dominated by local governments.

In presenting something of the complexity and richness of the social life that local institutions and networks sustain, I have tried to demonstrate that chōkai and neighborhoods cannot be characterized in black and white terms. Clearly, many aspects of Miyamoto-chō's formal and informal structure are administrative in character, and the entire ethos of the local community lends itself to potentially political forms of mobilization. But Miyamoto-chō is more than just a political or administrative entity. The community is created and maintained by a variety of social, economic, and political ties, and to conceive of it exclusively in political or administrative terms would seriously misrepresent the motivations and perceptions of many of those who are most active in neighborhood affairs.

Furthermore, the local government's political and administrative relationships with the neighborhood are complex and bilateral, not unilateral. To be sure, the chōkai leaders and active members are generally conservative and usually cooperative in their dealings with the government. Nonetheless, by drawing on particular features of the neighborhood's history and by emphasizing communal solidarity through various putatively traditional activities, Miyamoto-chō defines itself in terms different from and independent of the definitions the local government attempts to impose. This sense of community is the basis, in principle and occasionally in practice, for opposing or defying the ward government.

The ward government, on the other hand, continues to rely on chōkai to carry out many tasks, but at the same time pursues policies that seek to lessen community identification and solidarity at the neighborhood level and to redirect those sentiments toward an institutional level directly under its control. To this end, the government competes with chōkai on neighborhoods' own terms because many of the activities and organizational forms promoted by the ward are modeled after those of chōkai and draw on some of the same idioms of traditionalism that chōkai draw on. The effect appears to be not a weakening of the chōkai's position, but a further legitimation of traditionalistic activities and organizational patterns, and the chōkai respond to government challenges with an intensification of traditionalism.

The traditionalism that sanctifies and invests the local community with meaning cannot be understood apart from the contemporary situation in which local residents find themselves. According to Abner Cohen, the creation and maintenance of lifestyles and social identities such as these "involves a dynamic rearrangement of relations and of customs, and is not the outcome of cultural continuity or conservatism." Further: "To the casual observer it will look as if there is here stagnation, conservatism, or a return to the past, when in fact we are confronted with a new social system in which men articulate their new roles in terms of traditional . . . idioms" (1969: 194, 199).

Winston Davis's study of a Japanese religious cult (1980) situates the movement within the class dynamics of contemporary Japanese society. He finds that the cult provides a "world of meaning" for its adherents, a world that lends order to their lives and a sense of their own significance in a highly competitive society where social rewards are unequally distributed. Neighborhoods are not cults and residents are not true believers; but in roughly analogous fashion, for some residents of Miyamoto-chō the alternative social world created by the chōkai and other local organizations provides a meaningful, intrinsically interesting, and socially satisfying arena in which to act out significant aspects of their lives, and in which to achieve forms of recognition they are unlikely to command in the wider world.

Like hundreds of similar neighborhoods, Miyamoto-chō contains complex configurations of ties and institutions that bind neighbors to one another. These develop out of administrative exigency, out of informal patterns of neighborliness, and out of the dozens of instrumental and expressive activities sponsored by various organizations at each level in the institutional framework that surrounds local social life. The juxtaposition of these tangible social relations with the sense of identity and distinctiveness engendered through these ties and activities (and particularly through events like the matsuri) gives life and resiliency to Miyamoto-chō not as a unit of the government's crea tion or as some primordial "natural community" somehow isolated from the currents of urban social life around it, but as a response by local residents to the conditions of contemporary urban life as they find it.

Writing about American urban society, Albert Hunter notes (1974: 179): "An individual's local orientation, his 'sense of community,' is likely to vary with particular statuses he occupies, within both the local social structure and the wider society." Writing in a similar vein, Gerald Suttles concludes (1972: 40–41): "To evaluate the viability and vigor of a neighborhood, then, it is not enough to find out the proportion of all residents who are appreciably involved in 'neighboring' or local voluntary organizations. A far more pressing problem is the extent to which [members of] select groups, no matter how few in number, are able to keep intact neighborhood boundaries, to provide a general knowledge of its internal structure, and to keep alive their myth of unity and cohesion." Here the burden falls squarely on the willing shoulders of the merchants of Miyamoto-chō.

APPENDIXES

Miyamoto-chō's Population

Because local perceptions of the significant units of community life have so often been at odds with the government's definitions of neighborhoods, and because neighborhood boundaries have shifted so many times, Miyamoto-chō has not often corresponded to the divisions the government uses to calculate and report census data. Consequently, it is impossible to precisely track changes in Miyamoto-chō's population.

By my best estimate, the population of the territory now occupied by Miyamoto-chō increased from perhaps as many as a couple of hundred residents to somewhere slightly above 3,000 between the Kantō earthquake of 1923 and 1940, then fell sharply to stand at well under 1,500 when the Second World War ended. As was generally true throughout Shinagawa-ku and much of central Tokyo, the neighborhood gradually recovered to the level of its prewar population by the early 1960's, then steadily lost residents.

Data collected for the national census show that Miyamoto-chō had 3,296 residents in 984 households in 1960; 2,475 residents in 829 households in 1975; and 2,115 residents in 899 households in 1980 (SKNT 1961; Shinagawa-ku 1976, 1981).[1] Over these 20 years, Miyamoto-chō's population declined almost 36%. Despite this decrease, the neighborhood remains thickly populated, with some 2,100 people living in an area of

TABLE A.I

Household Size in Miyamoto-chō, Shinagawa-ku, and Tokyo, 1980

Household size (members)	Miyamoto-chō households				Shina-gawa-ku (pct.)	Tokyo (pct.)
	N = 744	Pct.	Residents			
			N = 1,916	Pct.		
1	283	38.0%	283	14.8%	35.6%	31.3%
2	119	16.0	238	12.4	19.4	18.9
3	115	15.5	345	18.0	16.3	17.0
4	137	18.4	548	28.6	19.0	21.5
5	54	7.3	270	14.1	6.5	7.5
6	25	3.4	150	7.8	2.3	2.6
7	8	1.1	56	2.9	0.7	0.8
8	1	0.1	8	0.4	0.2	0.2
9	2	0.2	18	0.9	0.1	0.1

SOURCES: *Miyamoto-chō.* Household-residence registers as of April 1, 1980. *Shinagawa-ku and Tokyo.* Sōrifu Tōkei-kyoku 1980: 452–53.

NOTE: In this and the following tables, percentages may not total 100 because of rounding. Tokyo, here and in the following tables, refers to the 23 wards of Tokyo, unless otherwise noted. Workers living in the two company dormitories are excluded in all tables.

only 0.071 square kilometer. This works out to almost 30,000 people per square kilometer, about twice the density of the 23 wards of Tokyo as a whole.

Because official statistics on Miyamoto-chō's population are published only at infrequent intervals and then in aggregated form, in 1980 I began to record and analyze household-residence registers (*jūmin tōrokuhyō*) for the neighborhood. I found 2,094 residents in 922 households on April 1, 1980, a figure slightly different from the results of the 1980 census conducted on October 1, 1980. (The functions and characteristics of household-residence registers, which in part account for differences between my figures and those obtained by the census, are discussed at the end of the appendix.) However, unless otherwise noted, I have excluded from consideration in this appendix the workers residing in the two company dormitories in Miyamoto-chō. Without them, Miyamoto-chō had a registered population of 1,916 residents in 744 households as of April 1, 1980.

Almost 40% of these households consist of a single person (see Table A.1). The average household in Miyamoto-chō had 2.58 members, compared with 2.53 in Shinagawa-ku and 2.68 in Tokyo (Sōrifu Tōkei-kyoku 1980: 453). Using the national cen-

TABLE A.2
Household Composition in Miyamoto-chō, Shinagawa-ku,
and Tokyo, 1980–1981

National-census category	Miyamoto-chō N = 759	Miyamoto-chō Pct.	Shina-gawa-ku (pct.)	Tokyo (pct.)
Family nuclei				
1. Married couple	78	10.3%	13.5%	12.9%
2. Couple with child(ren)	244	32.1	33.8	38.1
3. Father with child(ren)	8	1.1	0.9	0.9
4. Mother with child(ren)	50	6.6	5.5	5.5
Other relatives				
5. Couple with parents	0		0.2	0.2
6. Couple with parent	2	0.3	0.7	0.6
7. Couple with child(ren) and parents	14	1.8	1.3	1.5
8. Couple with child(ren) and parent	35	4.6	4.0	4.1
9. Couple with relatives other than child(ren) or parent(s)	0	—	0.3	0.3
10. Couple with child(ren) and relatives other than parent(s)	3	0.4	0.6	0.7
11. Couple with parent(s) and relatives other than child(ren)	2	0.3	0.2	0.2
12. Couple with parent(s), child(ren), and other relatives	10	1.3	0.8	0.8
13. Other relatives	21	2.8	2.6	2.6
14. Non-relative households	0	—	0.1	0.4
15. Single-person households	292	38.5	35.6	31.3

SOURCES: *Miyamoto-chō.* Household-residence registers as of April 1, 1981. *Shinagawa-ku* and *Tokyo.* Sōrifu Tōkei-kyoku 1980: 514–19.

NOTE: In classifying the composition of households, the Japanese census uses the youngest married couple in the household as the central figures in the domestic group. Thus a young married couple living with the husband's father would be considered "couple with parent," not "father with children." (See Sōrifu Tōkei-kyoku 1980: ix, xviii–xix, for a fuller explanation of the classification system.) I have used the census's system to classify Miyamoto-chō's households.

sus's classification system, just over half of Miyamoto-chō's households were family nuclei, a slightly smaller proportion than for the ward or for Tokyo (see Table A.2).

As indicated in Table A.3, there is not much residential continuity in Miyamoto-chō. In 1980 fully 43% of all households had been in the neighborhood for less than 10 years, and 38%

TABLE A.3
Date of Households' Entry into Miyamoto-chō

Date of entry	Households (N = 744)		Pct. of total	
Prior to urban growth				
Pre-1901	1		0.1%	
1901–10	1		0.1	
1911–20	8		1.1	
SUBTOTAL		10		1.3%
During prewar urban growth				
1921–25	27		3.6%	
1926–30	31		4.2	
1931–35	44		5.9	
1936–40	31		4.2	
SUBTOTAL		133		17.9%
During war and postwar recovery				
1941–45	44		5.9%	
1946–50	59		7.9	
1951–55	31		4.2	
1956–60	40		5.4	
1961–65	37		5.0	
SUBTOTAL		211		28.4%
During current population decline				
1966–70	70		9.4%	
1971–75	123		16.5	
1975–80	197		26.5	
SUBTOTAL		390		52.4%

SOURCE: Household-residence registers as of April 1, 1980.

NOTE: Figures are based on the earliest dates that households residing in the neighborhood on April 1, 1980, are recorded as having established a residence in the neighborhood. The establishment of residence need not have been by a household member who was still living or who was part of the household on that date.

had arrived in the neighborhood in the 30 years between 1941 and 1970; only 18% dated from the two decades of intense urban growth between 1921 and 1940, and fewer than 2% could be traced to the period before 1920 and the beginnings of urban development. Among households residing in the neighborhood in 1980, the mean length of residence was 20.2 years. Not only does Miyamoto-chō lack the historical depth of other, more central areas of Tokyo, but even within its more limited time span, it has had an almost continuous turnover of population.

In recent years at least, direct rural-to-urban migration has had little impact on Miyamoto-chō's population. Most of the movement into and out of the neighborhood has been quite local, often from or to places no farther than nearby neighborhoods. An analysis of the household registers for 1,290 residents living in six of Miyamoto-chō's nine blocks in 1981 found that 325 residents (about 25%)—206 under the age of 24, and 119 aged 25 and older—had been born in the neighborhood and had lived there continuously since birth. For in-migrants, the data do not identify place of birth, nor do they trace a person's entire history of residential moves. They only identify one or two previous addresses, and so can only be used to analyze recent mobility. Among the 960 in-migrants, 428 (44.6%) moved to Miyamoto-chō from within Shinagawa-ku. At least 290 (30.2%) came from elsewhere in the Tokyo metropolitan region (including Tōkyō-to, and four neighboring prefectures: Chiba, Ibaragi, Kanagawa, and Saitama). And no more than 25% of in-migrants moved to the neighborhood from outside the metropolitan region.[2]

By the same token, analysis of the destinations of 176 former residents of the same six blocks of Miyamoto-chō found that 52 (almost 30%) moved within the ward. Ninety-four (53%) moved elsewhere in the metropolitan region, split almost evenly between the ward area of Tokyo and the suburbs (46 vs. 48). Only 30 (17%) moved outside the metropolitan region.

Since the early 1960's, a major demographic trend in the Tokyo metropolis has been the decline of the central city's population paralleled by the growth of the suburbs (Kuroda 1979). Shinagawa-ku reached its postwar peak population of 415,728 in 1964, almost the level of the prewar peak population (in 1940) of 419,403 for old Ebara-ku and old Shinagawa-ku together (Shinagawa-ku 1972: 87–88). The population of the ward fell by 76,000 (a decrease of 18%) between 1964 and 1980, before leveling off in the early 1980's at around 340,000 (SKNT 1984: 13–14). Over roughly the same period (1960–80), as noted above, Miyamoto-chō lost twice as much (36%) of its population.

Out-migration to the suburbs has certainly played a part in this population decline, but it does not appear to be the sole, or even the major, cause. Well over half of those who have left Miyamoto-chō have moved within the 23 wards that make up

TABLE A.4

Previous and Subsequent Residences of Sojourners

Subsequent residence	Previous residence				Total	Pct.
	Shina-gawa-ku	Other wards	Metro-politan region[a]	Outside metropol-itan region		
Shinagawa-ku	9	4	4	3	20	25.3%
Other wards	9	10	3	8	30	38.0
Metropolitan region	1	10	6	4	21	26.6
Outside metropolitan region	0	3	1	4	8	10.1
Total	19	27	14	19	79	100.0%
Percent	24.1%	34.2%	17.7%	24.1%	100.0%	

SOURCE: Sample of household-residence registers for households that moved away from Miyamoto-chō between April 1, 1980, and April 1, 1981.

[a] The metropolitan region includes the suburban areas of Tōkyō-to as well as Chiba, Ibaragi, Kanagawa, and Saitama prefectures.

central Tokyo, not to the suburbs of Tōkyō-to or to neighboring prefectures. Examination of a small sample of former Miyamoto-chō households that had moved there from elsewhere— that is, sojourners, or households that were first in-migrants and then out-migrants—confirms that mobility is highly localized, and that much of it represents circulation within the metropolitan core rather than rural-to-urban or urban-to-suburban movements (see Table A.4). Not only did the majority of sojourning households go on to live elsewhere in the same ward or the other central wards of Tokyo, but a slightly larger percentage moved to those areas than came from them (63% vs. 58%). That is, the patterns of population flow through Miyamoto-chō tend to take people toward more central places rather than toward the suburbs.

Another factor that has contributed to Miyamoto-chō's declining population is the simple destruction of housing stock. The expansion of the shutchōjo and the public schools during the past couple of decades has taken a toll on the neighborhood's housing. More significantly, the land market and the legal framework of tenant rights have in some cases encouraged landlords to replace dilapidated housing with parking lots (see Bestor 1984c).

But the most substantial influence on Miyamoto-chō's population size has been the general trend throughout urban Japan toward smaller households. The decrease in household size over the last 20 years—3.35 people per household in 1960 vs. 2.35 in 1980, according to the previously cited national census figures—simply mirrors a much longer decline in the wider area: old Ebara-ku in 1940 had 40,865 households with an average size of 4.60 residents, but in 1983 the same district's 62,642 households averaged only 2.33 residents (Tōkyō-fu 1940; SKNT 1983).

In part shrinking average household size reflects Japan's declining marital fertility rate. It also stems from changes in the cycles of household formation and dissolution of urban Japanese families. The household residence registers do not permit historical comparisons, but today Miyamoto-chō has large numbers of households made up of young single people and newly married couples, presumably accounting for a greater proportion of local households than in the past. Tracing the residence records of long-established multigenerational families, one sees them splintering into smaller households for increasingly long stretches in the cycle of domestic life. The fissioning of households as children grow up and marry has always been a natural part of the domestic cycle, but reconsolidations of households (where married adult children take in their parents) now appear to occur less frequently, and often today all the adult children eventually depart, leaving aged parents alone in one- or two-person households.

Household-residence registers (*jūmin tōrokuhyō*) are maintained by the Shinagawa-ku government for all citizens of the ward, to establish legal residence for such things as voting, school registration, application for national pension benefits, and the like. These registers are distinct from the better-known household genealogies (*koseki*) maintained by the Ministry of Justice, which are now legally sealed from public inspection. Koseki provide fairly complete retrospective data on kinship relations over time; jūmin tōrokuhyō generally offer only a snapshot of current household composition.

Household-residence registers yield population figures somewhat different from the results of the national census because the registers are based on self-reporting. Consequently, they are perhaps demographically less precise but sociologically more relevant. Thus, an old couple and their married son living next door may register as a single household though the census might count them as two. Similarly, someone temporarily absent for work or education but nevertheless considered to be a household member will be registered as such, even if the census would not count the person that way.

The jūmin tōrokuhyō list basic data for each household and for each current member of the household. For the household, the register lists the name of the household head, the household's address, and the date at which the household was established at the present address. For individual members, the registers provide name, date of birth, sex, relationship to the household head, registered address for koseki purposes, name of the registered head of the koseki household (who need not be the same person as the head of the household of residence), previous residence, and date of first residence within the jurisdiction of the local registry office (the ward government's branch office— the shutchōjo). Other data—primarily technicalities involving the record-keeping system itself—are also recorded.

For both entries into and departures from households, the date of the move, the point of origin or destination, and the reason for the change are noted. Besides births, deaths, and actual relocations from one place to another, all affiliational changes are recorded—adoptions, marriages, divorces, household consolidations (as when elderly parents enter the household of a son), or household divisions (as when a married son establishes his own household)—whether or not they involve changes in residence or living arrangements. The personal name changes that can result from affiliational changes are important clues for tracing links among households.

Whenever a member officially leaves a household, the data on that person are crossed out (though in most cases they remain legible). When a household's record has become cluttered with changes and deletions, the shutchōjo will remake the register, eliminating all information now obsolete, so one cannot rely on a register for historical perspective on any given household farther back than about a decade at best.

The Yanagi Miyamoto Chōkai

Constitution

This translation of the constitution (kiyaku) is based on the form printed in the association's 1972 and 1975 membership directories.

Chapter One: General Provisions

ARTICLE ONE: This association shall be known as the Yanagi Miyamoto *Chōkai*.

ARTICLE TWO: This association shall be made up of the several households within Yanagi Miyamoto-chō.

ARTICLE THREE: The offices of this association shall be located in the Yanagi Hall (the Yanagi Miyamoto *Chōkai* office).

Chapter Two: Aims and Activities

ARTICLE FOUR: This association shall be dedicated to contributing to the advancement of the public good through neighborly cooperation for mutual aid, self-government, crime prevention, and fire prevention.

ARTICLE FIVE: To fulfill the goals set forth in the preceding article, the association shall act upon the following matters:

1. Fire and crime prevention
2. Traffic safety

3. Public health and sanitation
4. Festivals and support for the local tutelary deity
5. Activities for women and youth
6. Expressions of condolence
7. Other issues that may become important

Chapter Three: The Organization of Leadership

ARTICLE SIX: This association shall have the following officials:

Kaichō [president]—one person
Fukukaichō [vice-presidents]—five persons
Kōtsūbuchō [chief of the traffic-safety section]—one person
Fukubuchō [assistant chief]—[no number specified]
Jōninriji [permanent representatives]—a number of persons, including one person from each of the thirteen *bu* [geographical sections] into which the neighborhood is divided (*bu* may be further divided into A and B subsections); and three persons from the *fujinbu* [women's auxiliary]
Riji [representatives]—a number of persons (a number of persons from each *bu* mentioned above)
Kaikei [treasurers]—two persons
Kaikei kansa [auditors]—two persons
Ujiko sōdai [representatives of the *chōkai* to the governing board of the local shrine]—two persons

ARTICLE SEVEN: As the representative of the association, the president shall preside over the association's affairs. The vice-president shall assist the president, and shall stand in for him when he is ill or otherwise unable to perform his duties. The vice-president, the chief of the traffic-safety section, the permanent representatives, and the representatives shall conduct the association's affairs under the direction of the president. The treasurers shall manage the finances and property, and the auditors shall supervise this and make a report at the *sōkai* [general meeting].

ARTICLE EIGHT: The president and the auditors shall be elected by the general meeting; the vice-presidents, the treasurers, the chief of the traffic-safety section, the assistant chief, and the permanent representatives shall be appointed by the president; and the representatives shall be elected by the several *kumi* [household clusters].

ARTICLE NINE: The term of office of the president shall be two years, and the terms of office of the other officers shall be one year. However, re-election shall not be prohibited.

ARTICLE TEN: The association may designate *komon* [advisers] and *sōdanyaku* [counselors]. The president shall commission *komon* and *sōdanyaku* on the resolution of the general meeting or the *yakuinkai* [officers' meeting]. *Sōdanyaku* may express their opinions at the officers' meetings.

Chapter Four: Meetings

ARTICLE ELEVEN: The meetings of this association shall consist of three types: the general meeting, the officers' meeting, and the *jōninrijikai* [permanent representatives' meeting]. The general meeting shall be held annually in April. Matters to be discussed shall include reports of the association's activities, discussion of the proposed budget, and the settling of accounts for the previous year. The president shall have the power to call special general meetings when deemed necessary in consultation with two-thirds of the officers. If the officers and permanent representatives deem it necessary, the president shall call a meeting.

ARTICLE TWELVE: The president shall preside at the general meeting, the meetings of officers, and the meetings of the permanent representatives.

ARTICLE THIRTEEN: Matters shall be decided at meetings by a majority of those in attendance. In the case of a tie the president may cast the deciding vote.

Chapter Five: Accounting and Auditing

ARTICLE FOURTEEN: The expenses of this association shall be met by means of membership fees, contributions, donations, and other miscellaneous income.

ARTICLE FIFTEEN: The fiscal year of this association shall be from April 1 through March 31 of the following year.

ARTICLE SIXTEEN: The membership fees of this association shall be determined in accordance with that year's budget.

ARTICLE SEVENTEEN: To the extent that it does not interfere with the conduct of business, the following sets of account books to be kept by the treasurers shall be available for examination by members: (1) Register of income and expenses, and (2) register of property.

Bylaws

ARTICLE EIGHTEEN: The provisions of this constitution shall be enforced by decisions of the officers.

ARTICLE NINETEEN: Amendments to this constitution may not be made without the agreement of two-thirds of those in attendance at the general meeting.

ARTICLE TWENTY: This constitution shall come into effect as of April 15, 1966.

Financial Statements, 1979–80 (in yen)

General Chōkai *Budget*

Item	Projected budget	Actual budget
INCOME		
Balance forward	72,600	72,600
Membership fees	1,400,000	1,364,200
Miscellaneous income	150,000	142,941
Subsidies	248,100	248,100
TOTAL	1,870,700	1,827,841
EXPENDITURES		
Expenses for meetings	100,000	88,107
Maintenance	250,000	291,081
Street lighting	190,000	172,742
Sanitation activities	120,000	95,157
Contributions	100,000	118,800
Liaison	110,000	139,370

Item	Projected budget	Actual budget
Youth group expenses	160,000	138,123
Shrine expenses	120,000	112,600
Congratulatory and condolence payments	40,000	16,000
Clerical and office expenses	50,000	54,460
Expenses for events [*gyōjihi*]	300,000	272,604
Traffic-policy expenses	20,000	21,190
Equipment	20,000	16,750
Fire-watch expenses	10,000	14,860
Miscellaneous expenses	20,000	7,690
Transportation expenses	15,000	1,380
Subsidy to fujinbu	50,000	50,000
Subsidy to rōjinkai	30,000	30,000
Festival expenses	100,000	100,000
Emergency expenses	15,700	—
Auditing expenses	20,000	20,000
Special reserve fund[1]	30,000	30,000
TOTAL	1,870,700	1,790,914
BALANCE FORWARD	—	36,927

Recycling Campaign Fund

Item	Actual budget
INCOME	
Balance forward	302,796
Earnings from recycling	252,463
Interest	4,629
TOTAL	559,888
EXPENDITURES	
Gift to fujinbu	62,000
Miscellaneous expenses	1,000
TOTAL	63,000
BALANCE FORWARD	496,888

Roster of Upper-Level Chōkai Offices, 1980

Honorary advisers (*komon*): 4 men
Honorary counselors (*sōdanyaku*): 3 men
Parish delegates (*ujiko sōdai*): 2 men [2]
Social welfare representatives (*minseiiin*): 2 women[3]
President (*chōkaicho*): 1 man
Vice-presidents (*fukukaichō*): 4 men, 1 woman[4]
Treasurers (*kaikei*): 2 men
Auditors (*kaikei kansa*): 2 men
Women's auxiliary (*fujinbu*): chief (*fujinbuchō*); 4 assistant chiefs (*fukubuchō*)

Chiefs (*buchō*) and assistant chiefs (*fukubuchō*) of the five functional divisions: 10 men. The divisions are the Beautification and Sanitation Division (*bikaeiseibu*); the Youth Division (*seishōnenbu*); the Traffic-Safety Division (*kōtsūbu*); the Crime Prevention Division (*bōhanbu*); and the Fire Prevention Division (*bōkabu*).

Roster of Festival Committee Offices, 1980

This roster is based on the printed list of officers distributed throughout Miyamoto-chō a few weeks before the 1980 matsuri by the saireiiin (the committee).

Honorary advisers (*komon*): 5 men
Honorary counselors (*sōdanyaku*): 16 men
Festival chairman (*iinchō*): 1 man
Vice-chairpersons (*fukuiinchō*): 4 men, 1 woman
Treasurers (*kaikei*): 3 men
Auditors (*kaikei kansa*): 2 men
Parish delegates (*ujiko sōdai*): 2 men
Shrine liaison officer (*jinja-zume*): 1 man
Patrons (*sewanin*): 99 people[1]
Chōkai representatives (*chōkai riji*), 30 people[2]
General affairs committee (*shomu kakari*): 5 men (1 chief, 3 assistants, 1 additional member)[3]
Festival headquarters (O-mikisho) committee: 5 men (1 chief, 3 assistants, 1 additional member)[4]
Traffic committee (*kōtsū kakari*): 3 men (1 chief, 1 assistant, 1 additional member)
First *mikoshi* committee (*mikoshi dai-ichi kakari*): 6 men (1 chief, 3 assistants, 2 additional members)
Second *mikoshi* committee (*mikoshi dai-ni kakari*): 8 men (1 chief, 2 assistants, 5 additional members)

Band float committee (*dashi* [*hayashi*]): 5 men (1 chief, 2 assistants, 2 additional members)

Drum float committee (*dashi* [*taiko*]): 6 men (1 chief, 2 assistants, 3 additional members)

Entertainment committee (*engei kakari*): 5 women (1 chief, 4 additional members)

Reception committee (*settai kakari*): 18 women and officers of the women's auxiliary[5]

NOTES

Notes

CHAPTER ONE

1. In this study "Tokyo" refers to the 23 wards, or *ku*, commonly thought of as the city of Tokyo. In fact, not since 1943 has Tokyo existed as a single municipal entity. Rather, the core of the metropolitan region is divided among these 23 wards under the jurisdiction of the Tokyo Metropolitan Prefecture (Tōkyō-to), which also includes over two dozen suburban cities, towns, and villages. This administrative superstructure will be discussed in more detail in Chaps. 2 and 3.

2. The terms *chōkai* and *chōnaikai* (lit., "town association" and "within town association") are used almost interchangeably in contemporary Japanese. These institutions are also known as *jichikai* ("self-governing association") and by a wide variety of local names. There is no scholarly consensus on a preferred usage or any standard translations of these and other terms referring to the units of local government and community structure. What I call neighborhood associations (chōkai) others have glossed as ward associations or block associations. In particular I differ from Dore (1958); he refers to *chō* as wards and to *ku* as boroughs. I follow the current Japanese practice of translating chō as neighborhood and ku as ward. Therefore throughout this study I translate chōkai, chōnaikai, and jichikai as "neighborhood association."

I use the term chōkai in preference to chōnaikai simply because this more closely reflects usage in Miyamoto-chō. But where I use the phrase "the Miyamoto-chō chōkai," to refer to the "neighborhood association of Miyamoto-chō," residents would consider this redundant; they would simply call it *the* chōkai or, if they wish to distinguish it from the associations of other neighborhoods, the "Miyamoto-chōkai" (the association, *kai*, of Miyamoto-chō).

The character used to write chō 町 can also be read *machi*, and chō and machi are similar in meaning if not usage. Chō is rarely used as a freestanding word; it appears most often either as part of a compound (as in chōkai) or as a suffix for a place name (as in Miyamoto-chō). Although machi does appear in compounds (*machi-zukuri*, "community-building") and as a place-name suffix (e.g. Ōtemachi, a business district in central Tokyo), it can be used as a freestanding word, meaning either neighborhood or town (in the sense of a small municipality). People in Miyamoto-chō rarely use the term machi to refer to the neighborhood, preferring *chōnai* ("within the chō") when they want to specify something in or of the particular neighborhood. When simply talking loosely about something in the vicinity, the terms *kinjo, kinpen*, or *kono hen* are used, all of which in their adjectival forms mean something like "hereabouts" or "around here."

3. Some sense of the number and scale of organized neighborhoods in Tokyo can be gleaned from the accompanying table, based on data on all such organizations compiled for disaster-preparedness planning by the Tokyo Fire Department.

4. Fridell (1973) discusses the significance of official tutelary shrines at the hamlet and village levels as elements in State Shintō during the late 19th and early 20th centuries.

5. The name Miyamoto-chō itself is a pseudonym, meaning "the neighborhood where the shrine is located." The neighborhood is indeed the *miyamoto*—"the seat of the shrine"—and as such it assumes (at least in the eyes of its own residents) some slight edge in prestige over the other 6 neighborhoods that jointly make up the parish and contribute to the shrine's upkeep. The neighborhood I studied uses the shrine's name in the titles of most local organizations, and this shrine-derived name is known and used by residents throughout the area. Yanagi, the name attached to the area by the government in the 1940's, bears no relationship to the local customary name. In the 1960's the government introduced a new system of *chōme* (block) numbering that made Miyamoto-chō part of a larger administrative entity, officially known as Yanagi 4-chōme. This official name is generally not used by local residents (or even by government officials) except in official contexts (such as postal addresses and voter registrations) or in talking with outsiders unfamiliar with local terminology.

6. Yokokawa-ya is a *yagō*, an old-fashioned kind of shop name. The

TABLE TO NOTE 3
Neighborhood Associations in Tokyo's 23 Wards, 1978

Ward	Number of associations	Households per association	Average area per association (sq. km)
Chiyoda[a]	107	246	.108
Chūō[a]	154	253	.065
Minato[a]	229	382	.085
Shinjuku[a]	191	812	.094
Bunkyō[a]	155	554	.074
Taitō[a]	202	368	.049
Sumida[a]	150	567	.092
Kōtō[a]	215	604	.147
Shinagawa	178	812	.091
Meguro	91	1,254	.158
Ōta	209	1,263	.221
Setagaya	192	1,613	.306
Shibuya	107	1,062	.141
Nakano	109	1,361	.144
Suginami	173	1,308	.194
Toshima[a]	132	973	.098
Kita	168	924	.122
Arakawa	112	638	.092
Itabashi	223	823	.143
Nerima	200	1,015	.235
Adachi	359	564	.148
Katsushika	216	675	.157
Edogawa	195	849	.231
TOTAL/AVERAGE	4,067	801	.143

SOURCES: Tōkyō Shōbōchō 1978 (col. 1); SKNT 1978 (cols. 2–3).
[a]Ward falls at least partly within the boundaries of the pre-1932 city of Tokyo.

suffix -ya simply means shop, and is often added to a noun—a family name, a historical or literary term, the name of a bird, flower, or animal, or a geographical place-name—to create a yago. In the case of Yokokawa-ya, the yago (lit., "along the river") refers to its location, not the name of the owners, the Maedas. In Miyamoto-chō members of merchant families are often known and identified more commonly by their yago or by their occupation than by their family names. Thus, Mrs. Maeda is sometimes called "Yokokawa-ya no okusan" ("the wife of Yokokawa-ya"), or "Sakaya no okusan" ("Mrs. Sake Shop"). Old Mr. Umezu, whose bookstore does not have a yago, is sometimes addressed as "honya-san" ("Mr. Bookshop") or "honya no ojiisan" ("the granddad of the bookstore").

7. Industrial subcontracting, known as *shitauke*, is a prominent feature of the Japanese economy. See Broadbridge (1966) and Caldarola (1965) for economic and sociological discussions, respectively.

8. As shown in Appendix Table A.3, less than 2% of Miyamoto-chō's households can be traced back as resident in the area before 1920.

9. The Sōka Gakkai's intolerance toward other religions, including Shintō, is well known, and some members of the sect do not participate much in the activities of chōkai, which are tainted by their association with Shintō shrines and festivals. The slightly scornful term gakkai-dōri generally implies a criticism of the Sōka Gakkai's intolerance and the presumed lack of neighborliness of its members, rather than a conscious effort at sociological description.

One practice that earned the Sōka Gakkai popular disfavor in the past was its allegedly coercive proselytizing—called *shakubuku*—in which members attempted to gain new converts among their family, friends, co-workers, and neighbors by relentless argument and group pressure. Since the late 1960's the organization has curtailed recruitment by shakubuku, but in Miyamoto-chō, as elsewhere, it has colored the image of the sect's members and their relations with nonmember neighbors.

The success of past shakubuku campaigns directed against immediate neighbors is suggested by the fact that the street known as gakkai-dōri in Miyamoto-chō stretches through several adjacent neighborhoods and is similarly known in each of them. One evening I sat chatting with leaders from local chōkai about efforts to raise funds for the annual Shintō festival. One Miyamoto-chō leader groaned about his difficulty in collecting donations around his home on gakkai-dōri, and an official from a neighborhood some distance away (whose home is also near the old river, an area very similar to Miyamoto-chō's shimo) looked startled. "You have one, too?" he asked, and suddenly the group of local leaders began to compare notes, apparently realizing for the first time that there was a trans-neighborhood pattern of Sōka Gakkai membership. See White (1970) for a detailed analysis of the organization and its sociological characteristics.

10. A ken is an old linear measurement equal to 1.8 meters, the standard length of a tatami mat.

11. The hourly breakdown was as follows: cars and taxis, 140; small delivery vans, 125; small trucks, 90; large trucks, 18; and buses, 15.

12. Turkish baths, called *toruko*, are universally known to be houses of prostitution. In the early 1980's Turkish residents of Japan protested this slur. A trade organization sponsored a nationwide cam-

paign to select an appropriate alternative name, which turned out to be "Soapland."

13. For years there have been abortive plans to redevelop the commercial district around Otani station, but—according to local rumor—they have been blocked by shady real estate speculators. When I returned to Miyamoto-chō in the summer of 1986, I discovered that the ward government had finally begun to act, and was publicizing a series of new public works projects and joint public-private developments centering on rebuilding the station as part of a major shopping arcade.

14. Karaoke (lit., "empty orchestra") is a popular attraction in many bars. Karaoke tape decks play instrumental versions of popular and traditional songs to which patrons sing the vocals using a microphone that electronically enhances the singer's voice by adding a vibrato effect.

15. "Chan" is a diminutive form of san, most frequently used with the names of children and women, or in terms of address (i.e., *ojiisan*, grandfather, becomes *ojiichan*, granddad). When used with a man's personal name, chan implies an intimate relationship, and often the man's name is abbreviated to the first one or two syllables. In settings like those that abound in Miyamoto-chō, some men are on such good terms with everyone and so totally lacking in pretension that they are known universally by a diminutive of their personal names. Thus, throughout Miyamoto-chō the middle-aged carpenter Kunosuke Tanami is known not as Mr. Tanami (Tanami-san), but as Ku-chan.

CHAPTER TWO

1. The name Kumodani is a pseudonym. I use the term hamlet to refer to the settlement of Kumodani before its amalgamation with other, similar settlements in 1889; today these would be called buraku. I reserve the term village for the *mura*, the administrative entity created in 1889 by the amalgamation of several hamlets.

2. Masai's map of land use (1975) in and around Edo at the end of the Tokugawa period shows the agricultural nature of the entire area surrounding Kumodani (and its proximity to the highway and the city).

3. One koku equals 180 liters dry measure (a little more than 5 U.S. bushels). During the Tokugawa period this was the amount of rice assumed necessary to sustain one adult for one year.

4. Seidensticker (1983: 26) and H. D. Smith (1986) discuss the renaming of Edo.

5. The Tokugawa Shogunate established the system of sankin kō-tai, or alternate attendance, in 1653. It required each daimyo to spend

alternating periods of time in Edo and his own fief; when not in Edo, daimyo were required to leave their wives and families in Edo as hostages. Guards at the barriers erected on the post roads leading out of Edo had instructions to watch for "guns coming in and women going out," sure signs that a rebellion was being planned. The sankin kōtai system impoverished daimyo by obliging them to maintain two expensive households and to travel back and forth between them in suitable style at frequent intervals. The system enriched Edo and the post towns along the Tōkaidō and other highways. H. D. Smith (1986) describes the devastating economic impact the abolition of the sankin kōtai system had on the city.

6. As the name goningumi (lit., "5-person groups") suggests, these units were extremely small, incorporating only 5 to 10 households. Membership was compulsory, and members were held collectively responsible for tax payments, for properly obeying laws, and for one another's good behavior. Forerunners of the goningumi system developed in Japan as far back as the Nara period (710–94), but the system was moribund for centuries thereafter. It was resurrected in the early Tokugawa period in part to register households and enforce the ban on Christian worship and belief. Fukawa (1963) provides a detailed history of goningumi.

7. A roster of local place-names identifies half a dozen names inside Kumodani that dated back to the Tokugawa period (SKKI 1973: 83–84). It is unclear, however, whether these were the names of kumi or other social subdivisions of the hamlet, or whether they simply identified geographically distinctive features and places. Except for one name now taken by the local public elementary school, none of the names are currently used by residents.

8. One rough measure of the continuing dominance of agriculture can be gleaned from a 1908 directory identifying the people in Tokyo prefecture who were eligible to vote for members of the lower house of the Diet. From the promulgation of the Meiji Constitution (1889) until 1910, only adult males who paid direct national taxes of more than 15 yen could vote in Diet elections. The voting rolls in 1908 therefore indicate the richest (and presumably most influential) strata of society: 1.26% of the population representing roughly 6% of the nation's families (Reischauer 1981: 144). The directory lists voters in each village and ō-aza, along with their tax payments, and classifies them by occupation into 2 categories, agricultural and commercial. All but 10 of the 126 eligible voters in Hiratsuka-mura listed agriculture as their occupation (Teikoku Dōshinkai 1908: 43–45).

9. The City of Tokyo (Tōkyō-shi) and Tokyo Prefecture (Tōkyō-fu)

existed as separate entities until 1943, when the national government merged them into Tōkyō-to (Tokyo Metropolitan Prefecture).

10. Because of shifting neighborhood boundaries and the lack of clear correspondence between census reporting units and locally recognized neighborhoods, as well as a general lack of disaggregated data, it is impossible to find consistent population figures for the neighborhood itself. My best estimate of Miyamoto-chō's prewar growth is that between the Kantō earthquake of 1923 and 1940 the population increased from several hundred to something over 3,000, well above its present population.

11. The figures exclude those not born in Japan proper (i.e., those born in the colonial areas of the then Japanese Empire, including Taiwan and Korea, as well as the dependent state of Manchuria).

12. Unfortunately there are no established indexes that display the effects of inflation on the cost of living or the price of land throughout the entire period being discussed here. A wholesale price index for the early decades of this century indicates a level of 231 in 1901, 285 in 1911, 708 in 1921, and 522 in 1928 (based on an index of 100 in 1868); a retail price index (where 1 equals 1934–36 levels) shows 1.54 for 1922 prices, 0.885 for 1931, 1.716 for 1941, and 309.5 for 1951. Data on changing land values is also discontinuous. The price of dry fields in the Kantō region increased from 163 yen per *tan* in 1916, to 456 in 1926, 300 in 1936, 1,143 in 1946, and 17,061 in 1950. An index of residential land values in all Japanese cities (with a 1936 baseline of 100) shows an increase to 120 in 1941, 443 in 1946, and 9,745 in 1950. Figures are from Ohsato (1966: 76–77, 80, 87–89).

13. Data on landholding patterns in Miyamoto-chō from the 1920's onward were derived from the official land registration records for the neighborhood maintained by the Ministry of Justice and held in its Shinagawa registration office.

14. The only ward with an average population density below this level was Akasaka-ku, which contained many Imperial palaces and government office buildings.

15. Hitoshi Takeuchi, writing in the *Kodansha Encyclopedia of Japan* (1983, 2: 140), explains: "Measurements on the earthquake scale of the Meteorological Agency of Japan, in use since 1949, vary only slightly (±0.3–±0.4) from measurements on the well-known Richter scale. . . . The Meteorological Agency scale differs from the Richter scale in that the former is based on measurements of horizontal movement, while the latter is based on measurements of vertical movement."

16. Seidensticker (1983) traces many of the historical, social, and

cultural consequences of the earthquake. Kurabayashi (1983) presents a demographic analysis.

17. Lee and DeVos (1981: 21–26) gives a detailed account of the anti-Korean hysteria and rioting.

18. Hiratsuka simply means flat hill or mound, whereas Ebara (the etymology of which is unclear) was once the name of the entire sub-province of the Kantō plain, and hence was a much more historically evocative name for the new town to adopt.

19. Sanseidō (1974) provides a convenient overview of amalgamations and boundary changes of ward and lower-level units throughout Tokyo during the past century. To summarize the complicated history of amalgamations relevant to Ebara and Shinagawa, the present-day ward, Shinagawa-ku, was created in 1947 during the Tokyo-wide revision of local administration. The new Shinagawa-ku was created out of the merger of 2 older wards, Ebara-ku and Shinagawa-ku, both of which had been created in 1932 during the extension of the boundaries of the City of Tokyo.

The old Shinagawa-ku was created in 1932 out of the amalgamation of 3 towns: Ōi-machi, Ōsaki-machi, and Shinagawa-machi. Together these 3 towns included areas that had been, prior to the creation of the modern ward system in 1889, parts of 7 hamlets, 1 town (*machi*), 4 *juku* (post stations on the Tōkaidō highway), and a section of a ward (ku) within the old city of Edo.

On the other hand Ebara-ku was the direct successor to a series of municipal entities—Ebara-machi (1927), Hiratsuka-machi (1926), and Hiratsuka-mura (1889)—whose boundaries had remained unchanged since 1889, when the municipality was formed out of the amalgamation of 5 hamlets and fragments of a 6th.

Thus Hiratsuka/Ebara existed as a single administrative unit throughout the entire period of urban growth and local institutional development, an unusual accomplishment given the whirl of administrative reshufflings and amalgamations that have characterized Japanese local administration since the late 19th century. This persistence of a single municipal framework may be a clue to the stability of local institutions and the existence even today of what some residents of Miyamoto-chō call the "Ebara spirit," a strongly particularistic sense of local consciousness often expressed by residents who grew up in Ebara before the war. This relationship between particularistic identity and the structure of newly created administrative systems suggests one way in which a traditionalistic ethos of community may be created and sustained.

20. The national system of hōmeniin was established in 1936 to

"guide" the poor; in 1946 these volunteers were renamed *minseiiin*. Hastings (1984) provides detailed information on the prewar system in Tokyo.

21. The fee was 30 sen (¹⁄₁₀₀ of a yen) for each service. The regulations allowed the ku to reduce the fees to 10 sen or to waive them entirely for the very poor; residents could also make voluntary contributions to pay the fees of the destitute.

22. This map and membership directory was the oldest written document about neighborhood affairs I could locate *in* Miyamoto-chō. Generally no one there thinks to preserve records and documents of contemporary neighborhood institutions in any systematic fashion— the chōkai maintains no archives—and so rosters of officials, membership directories, or old listings of festival contributions usually are not kept for more than a few years. Records tend to get dispersed with each rotation of officers, and eventually forgotten (and probably discarded). Prewar records exist not at all, in part because of similar sorts of attrition suffered by more recent records, but also of course because of the war and the dispersion of the population during and after it.

The compilers of Shinagawa-ku's official history were similarly handicapped by the lack of documents about neighborhood-level events, and comment specifically on the rarity of documents from and about prewar Ebara (SKS, 2: 1072). Officials of the Shinagawa-ku Iinkai and the Shinagawa Kuritsu Toshokan Chiiki Shiryō Shitsu confirmed to me that nearly all official records of Ebara in the 1920's and 1930's were destroyed, most in a fire that gutted the Ebara Ward Office in the late 1930's, and the others during the war.

23. Old photographs are a more common source of information about the prewar neighborhood than written documents. Two photographs of chōkai officials formally arrayed in front of the local shrine, one dated 1936 and the other taken a few years earlier, are in the possession of Mr. Takahashi, and in both photographs his father is one of the local leaders. Going over these photographs together, Mr. Takahashi and his father were able to identify about three-quarters of the faces, and almost all of them were, like the elder Takahashi, newcomers to the neighborhood in the 1920's. Some were still alive: Motofuji-sensei, a now-retired local politician; Mr. Tsurumi, the father-in-law of the present representative of Miyamoto-chō in the ward assembly; and of course Mr. Takahashi's father. Others, now dead, included the father of Mr. Arakawa, a baker with a shop near the tracks; the father-in-law of Mr. Asanuma, who with his wife runs a tiny snack bar near the river; and Mr. Sakuma, the recently deceased grandfather of a family still living in the neighborhood. Only a couple of the men were members of

TABLE TO NOTE 24
Establishment of Chōkai by Period, 1887–1932

Period	No. of chōkai established in original 15 wards of Tōkyō-shi (N = 986)	No. of chōkai established in 20 wards added in 1932 (N = 1,274)	No. of chōkai established in the 35 wards	
			Total (N = 2,260)	Percent of total
Pre-1887	8	6	14	0.6%
1887–1892	12	3	15	0.7
1893–1897	19	4	23	1.0
1898–1902	38	4	42	1.9
1903–1907	60	11	71	3.1
1908–1912	26	12	38	1.7
1913–1917	77	37	114	5.0
1918–1922	212	95	307	13.6
1923–1927	351	471	822	36.4
1928–1932	183	631	814	36.0

SOURCE: Nakamura (1979: 19), based on a 1934 municipal survey.

the leading village-era landlord families. A batch of photographs owned by the Ide family, as well as those in the collection of the Shinagawa library, include several formal and semiformal group portraits of the volunteer fire brigade, also posing before the local shrine. In these photographs members of the landlord families figure more prominently, particularly in the higher positions, although young men—recent arrivals to the area—made up the rank and file of the brigade. Other important sources of information on the leadership and composition of local groups in the prewar period are the many monuments in the shrine's precincts, each elaborately inscribed with the names of officers active at the time the plaque was erected.

24. See the accompanying table on the establishment of chōkai in various sections of Tokyo.

25. Among the Occupation authorities who considered neighborhood associations, Braibanti was the most favorably disposed toward them. Despite his criticism of their wartime roles, he advocated their preservation as institutions with a potential for fostering principles of democratic local self-government.

26. Local legend maintains that the Doolittle raids of 1942 were aimed at these factories, and that the area was therefore the first in Tokyo to be attacked by American planes.

27. Because of the extensive wartime destruction of local records, the postwar amalgamation of Ebara and Shinagawa, and the fact that Miyamoto-chō almost disappeared as a separate entity in government

records after the early 1960's, it is difficult to get disaggregated population data for Ebara-ku or for Miyamoto-chō for the war years or for much of the postwar period. The following discussion and the data reported in Table 6 therefore rely on material drawn from several different levels, rather than presenting a single consistent unit of analysis.

28. More detailed discussions of the social and political roles chōkai played during the war are provided by Havens (1978). J. Cohen (1949) provides a general picture of the wartime Japanese economy, including information on the role neighborhood institutions played in labor mobilization.

29. Woodard (1972: chap. 12 and appendix B: 7) gives a detailed account of Occupation policy on Japanese religion, including the severing of links between community organizations and Shintō shrines.

30. As ward officials now explain it, the current household registry system arose in the immediate postwar years from the need to maintain accurate rationing records; many of the registry cards kept on file at the branch offices still include notations about rice rationing, although it ended almost 30 years ago.

CHAPTER THREE

1. In 7 of the 8 municipal elections between 1955 and 1983 (the exception being 1975), a resident of Miyamoto-chō was elected to a 4-year term in the ward assembly.

2. See Curtis (1970) for a discussion of the role of kōenkai as a general feature of contemporary Japanese politics. Curtis (1971) examines one candidate's campaign for the Diet; that man's activities did not differ greatly from Tsurumi-sensei's although his campaign was conducted over a much larger area.

3. The monthly payments are collected by the group's treasurer, Mr. Kobayashi, who takes care of all the shared expenses for the trip. The individual members need bring money only to purchase gifts for family and friends back home, to cover gambling losses (which can be very steep), and to pay for personal forays to bars and cabarets at the hot springs resort the group visits. The member who wins most at gambling during the trip is expected to stand the entire group to a meal and evening of drinks on the journey home.

4. Tsurumi-sensei, Mr. Asanuma, and Mr. Izumi are all *mukoyōshi*, adopted sons-in-law, who have taken their wives' family names and succeeded their wives' fathers as heads of their respective households. This pattern of adopted heirs is a customary practice in the Japanese family system, most common in the past in rural, agricultural households. In contemporary times, and particularly in urban areas, the prac-

TABLE TO NOTE 5
Election Results, 1971–1983

Category	1971	1975	1979	1983
Miyamoto-chō's electoral district				
Registered voters	8,735	8,105	7,320	8,351
Votes cast	6,518	4,704	4,561	4,700
Voting rate (pct.)	74.62%	58.04%	62.31%	56.28%
Ward voting rate (pct.)	72.42%	55.20%	55.48%	50.69%
Total number of candidates for				
48 seats	65	66	63	56
Ward vote counts				
Front runner	6,198	3,974	3,567	3,918
Last winner	2,330	1,804	1,836	1,474
Tsurumi	—[a]	1,767	2,026	2,077
Tsurumi's standing	—	49	39	35

SOURCES: Shinagawa-ku Senkyo Kanri Iinkai (1971–79, 1983).
  [a] The 1975 election was Tsurumi's first try for office. In 1971 Miyamoto-chō's candidate, Motofuji, won his 5th and last 4-year term to the ward assembly with 2,487 votes, placing him 44th among the winning candidates.

tice is less common, but among families that own and operate their own businesses—where the household has real property and assets to be maintained intergenerationally, requiring a clear line of succession—adopting a son-in-law to carry on the family name and the family business is still practiced. In Miyamoto-chō I encountered at least 9 cases of households with family businesses who had mukoyōshi among the living generations. Johnson (1964) and Befu (1971: chap. 2) discuss the Japanese stem family (*ie*) system in general and the significance of *mukoyōshi*.

5. Miyamoto-chō's polling district closely corresponds to the half dozen neighborhoods from which the local junior high school draws its students; the election district contains about 8,000 registered voters. In the 1979 and 1983 ward elections, the voter turnout was only a bit over 50%. Tsurumi-sensei received 2,026 votes throughout the ward in 1979 and 2,077 votes in 1983, placing him in 39th and 35th position respectively for the 48 seats in the ward assembly. (Since the ward's election office only keeps vote totals for the ward as a whole, there is no way to determine how many of Tsurumi-sensei's votes come from this or any of the ward's other 39 polling districts.) The results from the four municipal elections between 1971 and 1983 are shown in the accompanying table.

6. Politicians have to be careful about how they and their supporters act and the extent to which political activities become intermingled with the normal ebb and flow of community life. The laws gov-

erning campaign activities are very strict (see Curtis 1971), and in close contests, are strictly enforced as well. During the summer of 1986, when my wife and I paid a short visit to Miyamoto-chō, the women of the folk-dance troupe my wife had joined during our 1979–81 stay decided they should throw a banquet in her honor (and I was invited, too, as one of only 2 males present). As it happened, our visit coincided with a national Diet election and a bitter contest for the district seat. After the banquet—held in the Buddhist temple's rental hall—had been going on for an hour or so, a late arrival rushed in and reported that several plainclothes police were loitering outside, suspecting this was an illegal campaign meeting or an illegal banquet served to influence voters. When my wife and I left some time later, we did indeed encounter a half dozen rather obvious men in plainclothes, who were clearly astonished by our presence. A few days later, as I was eating dinner at a friend's home, we were interrupted by a police detective. He was investigating reports that my friend's wife (who had not been part of the dance troupe's banquet) had helped organize a farewell party (held several months before) for a retiring teacher at the local elementary school, and that this party had actually been a cover for illegal solicitations of support for a candidate before the officially sanctioned start of the campaign. In neither case did the police find evidence to substantiate the rumors of election-law violations, but their investigations had a chilling effect. Normal social life in Miyamoto-chō (particularly among men) ground to a halt out of fears that ordinary sociability would be construed as illegal electioneering.

7. Much of the following discussion is based on Steiner's extensive treatment of Tokyo's administration and the legal standing of its 23 wards in *Local Government in Japan*.

8. The *ondo* is a musical genre that accompanies rhythmic group dancing. In loose translation the lyrics run as follows:

> *First verse*
> Shinagawa, a good place.
> In the past the Tōkaidō's 53rd station.
> Today too a good place to live—
> Constructing a community with a single heart.
>
> *Chorus*
> The "Shinagawa Ondo" is everybody's *ondo*!
> Singing, dancing, smiling brightly like a
> flower blooming!
>
> *Second verse*
> Shinagawa facing tomorrow—
> The wide land reclamation, the industrial zone,

The twin lines of wharves:
Dreams running throughout the world.

Third verse
Shinagawa's pride, what do we have?
We have flowers, and greenery, and the ocean.
In the center is Togoshi park:
Leaves full of youth grow lushly.

To be sure, the lyrics lose a lot in translation. But they are set to a catchy little tune, which I still find myself humming from time to time.

9. Although changes like these would seem to be a matter for municipal decision-making, it is, as Steiner notes (1965: 218n), "symptomatic" of the government's views of local autonomy and local communities that these efforts were directed by the national government.

10. In the system of names used before the 1960's, what is now known as Miyamoto-chō was part of a district called Yanagi-chō, itself divided into 6 chōme; Miyamoto-chō was the 5th chōme. Today the same district is simply Yanagi, and it is divided into 4 chōme. In creating the 4 new chōme, the ward added a fragment of an area not formerly part of Yanagi-chō to the otherwise essentially intact old 1st chōme, still named 1-chōme; the new 2-chōme took the old 2d chōme and combined it with half of the old 3d; the other half of the old 3d chōme was combined with the entire old 4th to create the new 3-chōme; the new 4-chōme combined the old 5th and 6th chōme. As far as local organizations are concerned, however, Yanagi is still made up of 6 neighborhoods, and the chōkai's boundaries correspond to the old chōme boundaries, not the new.

The naming and renaming of neighborhoods and the redrawing of their boundaries illustrate the arbitrary nature of definitions of local community areas imposed by officials at the ward and higher levels, as well as the ways in which official designations bear little if any relation to the units considered significant by local residents and groups. Apparently the area now called Yanagi was not considered any sort of unified district until the ward government designated it as such during the early 1930's. During the 19th century what is now Yanagi extended across two wedge-shaped hamlets, Kumodani and Arigawa. In the early 1930's, in the first wave of reorganization accompanying the amalgamation of Ebara-machi into the City of Tokyo, the ward government designated the river valley that ran along the wide edge of both Kumodani and Arigawa to be Kiyogawa-chō; the plateau bordering the valley in both old hamlets was called Uehara-chō; beyond Uehara-chō the remaining portions of both Kumodani and Arigawa were combined with fragments of other areas to create Hirota-chō. In the reshuffling of neighborhood boundaries on the eve of the war, the government changed the name of Kiyogawa-chō to Yanagi-chō but left the names Hirota-chō and Uehara-chō unchanged, although in all 3 districts the boundaries of chōme themselves were altered by government direction. In the mid-1960's the ward's campaign to reorganize existing chōme left district names unchanged (except for dropping chō from Yanagi) but similarly transformed the official boundaries of chōme in the 3 districts. And in both Uehara-chō and Hirota-chō, as in the new Yanagi, local organizations ignore the new boundaries and maintain the old.

Oddly, despite the ward government's efforts over the past several generations to create new districts, it has never seriously attempted to unify them institutionally. For example, Yanagi and Uehara-chō extend across the boundaries of several contemporary shutchōjo, and during the prewar years, when Shintō was directly under state control (and was frequently manipulated to bolster new systems of local administration), the old shrine parishes of Kumodani and Arigawa remained separate, as they still are. Thus, today Yanagi covers parts of the territory of 2 distinct shrine parishes and 2 volunteer fire brigades, extends across jurisdictional lines of 2 different shutchōjo, and includes parts of 4 different elementary school districts. The only institutional link among all 4 (or 6) of Yanagi's neighborhoods is a federation of 7 shōtenkai along the shopping street that traverses the entire district.

11. The old hall was razed during the summer of 1986 and replaced with a modern two-story building. The new hall, however, does not contain either shops or apartments, and like the old hall, it is used solely for neighborhood events.

12. Kurasawa contrasted the significance of community centers and community baths during his general discussion of informal bases of community life, presented in a seminar at the Japan Foundation, Tokyo, in January 1981.

CHAPTER FOUR

1. Bottles of the leading brand of domestic scotch are colloquially called daruma, because the shape of the short, squat bottle resembles the papier-mâché figures of the Buddhist saint, Daruma, which are popular good luck charms.

2. In Miyamoto-chō, as elsewhere in Japanese urban neighborhoods, some houses bear small plaques that proclaim them to be Bōhan Renrakujo, or Crime Prevention Liaison Posts. The Ebara police sta-

tion is responsible for this loose network of householders who agree to assist the police. The bōhan renrakujo system has no connection with the chōkai, and in Miyamoto-chō, at least, there is no significant overlap between these households and those of the chōkai leaders.

3. There are no separate statistics for Miyamoto-chō, but in the ward as a whole in 1982 there were 7,275 reported crimes of all types (excluding traffic violations). The ward's rate of reported criminal offenses was 20.94 per 1,000 population; for the 23 wards of Tokyo that year the rate was 24.45 (Tōkyō-to Tōkei Kyōkai 1982: 223).

4. Seidensticker (1983) chronicles the destruction of Tokyo's shitamachi districts in the Kantō earthquake; his first chapter, in particular, examines the physical disaster. Havens (1978) gives a general account of Tokyo's wartime years and the devastation of the bombings. Daniels (1975) and Saotome (1971) focus on the great air raid of March 9–10, 1945, which destroyed central Tokyo and killed as many as 150,000 civilians.

5. The statistics compiled by the chōkai's traffic spotters appear in Chap. 1, note 11.

6. The proposal to locate a station near the shopping street—a few blocks up from Miyamoto-chō—took an interesting twist. An opponent of the project—apparently opposed to the new commuter line for the increased noise and vibration it caused—successfully held up construction of the station for several years with a lawsuit charging that it was unconstitutional for one arm of the government (the ward office) to subsidize the activities of another (the Japanese National Railway) by donating land and underwriting some of the construction costs for the new station. Eventually the suit was resolved, and the station opened in the spring of 1986, several years after packed commuter trains began to rumble down the tracks.

7. While watching the NHK program Rensō Geimu ("The Association Game")—similar to the American show "Password," in which contestants try to guess words from the one-word clues their teammates give them—I was pleasantly surprised to find that the teams were trying to guess the word "chōkai." A contestant needed only to be prompted with "kairanban" to get the right answer on the first try.

8. I am indebted to Victoria Lyon-Bestor, who went on several of the fujinbu trips, for appropriately veiled versions of the goings-on.

CHAPTER FIVE

1. Apaato are distinguished from manshon by their smaller size, cheaper rents, and lesser amenities, and by all the connotations of so-

cial class that accompany these differences. The apartment in which my wife and I lived during our research was considered a manshon. Occasionally when talking to my landlady I would slip and refer to it simply as an apaato (using the term as one would its original English, apartment, in a generic sense). She would look very hurt and would gently but firmly correct me.

2. The landlord accepts the responsibility for collecting the dues from each tenant household, whether by taking it out of the rent payment or collecting it directly. Often apartment dwellers' chōkai membership fee is written into the legal rental contract as part of the miscellaneous "management fees" (*kanri-hi*) the tenant must pay for garbage collection, water, and other charges above and beyond the basic monthly rent.

3. The fujinbu is not exclusively for wives. Unmarried adult women and widows are also considered members insofar as their households (of which they may be the head and the only member) belong to the chōkai.

4. Lebra's description of "age-peer grouping" (1984: 269–78) makes much the same point about the informal age segregation that local women's organizations reflect and maintain.

5. During the 1970's the exact number of kumi varied between 53 and 57. In 1981 there were 54, including a cluster that included only the 2 company dormitories near the shrine. Kumi can be created or disbanded as the population in a particular corner of the neighborhood warrants; the recent fluctuations reflect the creation of kumi upon the erection of a new apartment building or the demolition of an old one.

6. Between 1977 and 1981 85% of the paired riji and renrakuin positions for each kumi were filled simultaneously by members from the same household (most frequently by a male household head and his wife).

7. Over a span of 5 years, between 1977 and 1981, 89% of the riji positions passed from one household to another each year. In 41 of the 52 kumi that existed through the whole of that period the position rotated each year. In 8 kumi, though it rotated most years, some households served for 2 or 3 consecutive years; and in 3 kumi the same household served all 5 years. Even with regular rotation a household is likely to fill the riji position frequently, though not necessarily in consecutive years, particularly in smaller clusters or those with a high proportion of nonparticipating households (e.g., apartment-dwellers). But in only 17 clusters (including the 11 mentioned above whose riji were held over for consecutive years) did households repeat as riji within the

5-year span; in two-thirds of the clusters therefore the position rotated every year with no repetition of households.

8. From time to time geographical sections may be subdivided if the number of kumi (and hence the number of households) in a particular area is large enough to make it necessary. During the late 1970's one section was subdivided in this manner, then later reconsolidated, as the population in that corner of the neighborhood fluctuated.

9. In the geographical sections only 24% of the paired positions of chōkai permanent representatives and section leaders for the women's auxiliary were held simultaneously by members of the same household during the period 1977–81, as compared with the 85% at the kumi level.

10. The senior treasurer's position is largely honorific. It is the junior treasurer who handles day-to-day financial affairs and possesses real influence, and normally he belongs to the inner circle of the chōkai's leadership. Though the senior treasurer is an important and influential member of the community, he is not necessarily a central leader.

11. Many of the issues revolved around my violations (only sometimes intentional) of the neighborhood's ladder of seniority and status. In my desire to observe and be part of as many local activities as possible, I successfully (and I delude myself into thinking, sometimes subtly) insinuated myself into roles and events from which most residents were normally excluded. As Mr. Hasegawa once explained it, a typical Japanese newcomer would not be accepted enough to participate in chōkai activities to the extent I did for at least 10 years. He used a military metaphor: as a new resident I should have been a private second class, but I had been given the honorary rank of second lieutenant.

12. Neighborhood groups do not permit a person to hold more than one high-level office at a time in a single organization, but the households of higher-level chōkai and fujinbu leaders take their normal turns in the kumi rotation. It is possible, but rare, for a husband and wife to simultaneously hold high-level (hence individual) positions. For example, Tsurumi-sensei served as sōdanyaku and his wife was a member of the fujinbu cabinet from 1979 through 1981.

CHAPTER SIX

1. The term "2DK" refers to an apaato (apartment) or a manshon (a slightly fancier apartment) with 2 general-purpose rooms and a DK, or "dining-kitchen," a kitchen large enough to contain a small table. Room sizes are calculated in jō (a counter for the number of tatami

mats a room could contain, whether or not the room is actually floored with tatami); in Tokyo tatami customarily measure 1.8m by 0.9m, though today new buildings often use smaller and unstandardized *"danchi saizu"* (apartment-size) tatami. In Miyamoto-chō a modern, spacious 2DK would have 2 6-mat tatami rooms and a 4- or 6-mat kitchen, as well as a bathroom and a separate toilet.

In Miyamoto-chō most apartments built since the early 1970's are 2DK manshon. There are a few larger apartments known as 3DK or 3LDK (for living-dining-kitchen, if the room is large enough to be used as a family parlor). And in the early 1980's tiny studio apartments, known as *"wan rūmu manshon"* (1-room manshon), began to appear.

In 1979–81 an unfurnished modern 2DK with its own bath rented for between 75,000 and 90,000 yen a month, plus utilities and 3,000 or 5,000 yen a month as a *kanri-hi*, or management fee. On the standard 2-year apartment lease, the renter would have normally paid 5 months' rent in key money: 1 month's rent for the real estate broker, 2 as a security deposit (*shikikin*), and 2 as a gift to the landlord (*reikin*). Renewal of a lease for another 2 years meant paying additional reikin.

2. As a local construction labor boss, Mr. Ozawa seems to hold a couple of local monopolies. For almost all construction that takes place in Miyamoto-chō, certainly for all projects done in the neighborhood by local contractors (which is almost all construction), Mr. Ozawa supplies the ordinary laborers, hiring them from his networks throughout the city. The specialized contractors—for carpentry, plumbing, roof tiling, electricity, painting, and plastering—supply their own workmen (or in small remodeling jobs, often just do the work themselves with the aid of an apprentice), but all projects require at least a few semiskilled laborers, and they all come through Mr. Ozawa.

In addition, like tobi throughout Tokyo, Mr. Ozawa holds a localized customary monopoly for the production and sale of New Year's decorations. The last week or so of December each year, he and members of his family erect a tiny booth near the entrance to the public bath across from the temple, from which they sell the braided straw ropes and the swags of branches, paper streamers, and mandarin oranges with which people decorate their gateways (and sometimes the hoods of their cars).

3. Once, as I chatted with Mrs. Horie and Mrs. Ikeda in front of the shrine, shortly after an elaborate funeral of a local notable that had been held outside Miyamoto-chō, they commented on the trend toward commercialized ritual. Both recalled that in their youth, local weddings were simple things, held in the hall of the Tenso Jinja, not today's extravagant events costing millions of yen and held at fancy ho-

tels and the wedding halls of famous shrines. This, they gloomily predicted from their observations of funerals of Miyamoto-chō residents
in recent years, is happening with rituals of death as well, with large,
famous Buddhist temples increasingly favored for the last rites.

4. The sumo world is organized around patron-client ties, expressed
through fictive kin ties centering on the *heya* (usually translated as
"stable"), a group of wrestlers who train together under the tutelage of
a single master, and who throughout their careers (and afterward) are
identified as belonging to that particular "stable."

5. Stereotypically Japanese men go out drinking in all-male groups,
leaving their wives at home. But in Miyamoto-chō, at least, several
couples may occasionally go out together for dinner at, for example, a
sushi bar, followed by a stop at a local bar featuring karaoke singing.
From time to time groups of women may go out for a night on the town,
leaving their husbands and families at home for the evening.

6. The sociological effects of educational competition in Japan
have been widely studied. Examination preparation schools are discussed in depth by Rohlen (1980, 1983) and Riggs (1977). The psychological pressures the examination system exerts on children have been
examined by Vogel (1962) and Kiefer (1970). Yamamura and Hanley
(1975) discuss parental educational aspirations and their interaction
with family dynamics and fertility.

7. Old school ties offer great potential for linking residents of the
area in and around Miyamoto-chō. Of the over 8,600 people who graduated from the elementary school between 1928 and 1978, slightly
over 20% still live within the boundaries of the school district; they
constitute about one-fifth of the district's total population (figures
based on a directory of all the school's alumni, published by the alumni
association to commemorate the school's 50th anniversary).

CHAPTER SEVEN

1. Washoi! Washoi! is a shouted rhythmic chant used only for keeping the cadence of mikoshi carrying.

2. The prefix "*O-*" is an honorific attached to words such as matsuri
or mikoshi to signify the respect in which these events or objects are
held because of their quasi-sacred character.

3. Parking space is at such a premium in Tokyo that to license and
register a car people must present proof to the authorities that they
own or rent an off-street parking space (Bayley 1976: 26). The shrine
earns a considerable income by renting some 20 spaces for 10,000 yen
each a month.

4. These purification rituals are discussed in Sadler (1970b), one of his extensive series of articles on festivals, shrines, and popular Shintō practices in Tokyo.

5. In theory the festival occurs in a 2-year cycle, with alternate years designated the Hon-matsuri (the main festival) and the Kage-matsuri (the shadow festival). In local practice, there is virtually no difference between the two, except that the Hon-matsuri is the occasion for selecting a new pattern for the festival yukata that the women make for themselves and their husbands. When asked about the significance of this distinction between main and shadow festivals, most festival leaders simply shrugged or muttered that though they did not fully understand it, there was some good theological reason behind it.

6. In the understanding of local residents, few of whom are terribly concerned with theological niceties, the deity is divisible, or perhaps is simply omnipresent. Thus the deity resides in the mikoshi of all 7 neighborhoods simultaneously, once the priest has made the rounds to bless the mikoshi. The temporary installation of the deity into each mikoshi is symbolized by a tiny slip of carefully folded white paper that the priest puts behind the wooden doors of the shrine replica that forms the bulk of the mikoshi. Since most neighborhoods have 2 or more mikoshi, the priest blesses them all, and in each the kami resides. At the end of my first festival, I waited and watched to see how the deity returned to the main shrine; when the slip of white paper was roughly removed and discarded by the men who were disassembling and packing the festival paraphernalia for storage, I quietly asked someone about what happens to the deity when the matsuri is over, only to receive a puzzled shrug in reply.

7. The festival as a neighborhood event is so linked to the dynamics of local organizations and the interpersonal politics of community life as to be divorced from religious belief even among adherents of Shintō. For example, Shintō beliefs about ritual purification and pollution call for members of households that have experienced a death during the year to abstain from participating in the matsuri. During the summer of 1981, after neighborhood leaders had designated Mr. Uegahara as the chairman of the festival committee for that year, but before active preparations for the festival got underway, Mr. Uegahara's father (who was also a prominent citizen of Miyamoto-chō) died unexpectedly. Mr. Uegahara went ahead and chaired the festival, taking a part not only in the logistical planning, but also in the various ritual roles expected of the chairman, such as welcoming the priest to the chōkai hall and presiding over the collective prayers of neighborhood leaders and residents

before the altar. His actions caused some discomfort to older residents, but no public opposition.

8. This contrasts with many festivals in Japan (see, e.g., Akaike 1976) and elsewhere (see, e.g., Cancian 1965, on Mexico), in which ritual officeholding and community status are closely linked. Akaike's study describes local status systems in which a man's progress through the ranks of community leadership depends on his having passed through a rigidly defined, nonrepetitive sequence of festival positions, filling a specific series of posts over several festival cycles.

9. The drum group, revitalized during the late 1970's, is loosely affiliated with a tiny shrine near Otani station. A couple of dozen children from the local elementary and junior high schools, including the Tsunodas' daughter, belong to a junior troupe. In July 1986 30 members of the group, including 12 of the children, traveled to Maine to visit Shinagawa-ku's sister city, Portland, and to perform at the Maine State Fair. Though the trip was privately financed by the participants, they went with the blessings of the ward government, to present to Americans the traditions of Shinagawa's culture.

10. My observations of the festival cover 4 years: 1979, 1980, 1983, and 1984. In the first 2 years the neighborhood possessed 2 small mikoshi. From the 1982 festival onward, as is discussed elsewhere, the neighborhood also owned a very large, very heavy, and very expensive new mikoshi. The 2 small mikoshi then came to be considered "children's mikoshi." In those aspects of the festival where the introduction of the new mikoshi has significantly altered the performance of the matsuri, my descriptions are generally of the more recent events.

11. There is clear though informal age segregation (as well as gender segregation) in the mikoshi processions. During the children's circuits only younger elementary school children participate. (Toddlers and preschoolers accompany the drum cart [or *dashi*], helping their mothers and a few fathers pull the cart with a long hawser.) The adult mikoshi processions (which until 1982 used the same mikoshi the children carried earlier) rarely had anyone younger than a college student or an exceptionally husky high school student.

Until 1980 women were explicitly excluded from carrying the mikoshi, in conformity with customary Shintō beliefs about the ritual pollution of women. In that year, the middle-aged women of the fujinbu were allowed to carry the mikoshi for about a block, after they had finished their own folk-dance procession throughout the neighborhood.

Until the neighborhood obtained its new mikoshi in 1982, almost no men in their teens or early twenties participated. One motive for building a flashy new mikoshi was to attract young men, some of whom would (it was hoped) get involved not only in the festival, but in neighborhood affairs more generally. The new mikoshi has been successful at least in the first regard, and has also attracted females in their teens and twenties. But the new heavy mikoshi puts a premium on physical strength and agility, in a sense lowering the upper age limits for mikoshi bearers. Ironically, some of the "young leaders" of Miyamoto-chō who had lobbied so long and hard to purchase it now find themselves a bit too old to help carry it for more than a few minutes, though they still plunge into the fray to steer the mikoshi bearers and to keep the frenzied cadences going.

12. Another link between the mikoshi and the ideology of communal life was revealed in a discussion I had in 1980, some years before Miyamoto-chō acquired its heavy new mikoshi. Mr. Kitano, a widowed craftsman who devotes himself to neighborhood affairs and to the local elementary school from which he graduated in the 1930's, expressed the common opinion that both of the mikoshi the chōkai then owned were too small and really should be used only as children's mikoshi. He explained that even the larger one was light enough that a single bearer could influence its course and behavior. Ideally, he said, a mikoshi should be so heavy that no single person's actions could affect, or even be noticeable in, its movements.

13. A similar procession of children costumed as ancient court nobles took place to commemorate the rebuilding of the shrine in the early 1970's. Several mothers commented to me that it was nice to have this aspect of the festival repeated every decade so that every child could have at least one chance to wear (and be photographed in) the gorgeous costumes.

14. The meaning and origin of this chant are unknown to local residents. It is simply regarded by children and adults alike as a festival custom, though not one with any particularly local significance. Many residents reported similar chants in their hometowns in various regions of Japan. The young heir to Yokokawa-ya speculates that it may be a survival from premodern days when *sake* dealers were among the wealthiest merchants and salt was a valuable commodity. The children's chant is echoed later in the afternoon, when the adults carry the mikoshi on the same circuits of Miyamoto-chō. As the men approach the Araharis' *sake* shop near the shrine, Mr. Seto starts up the cry, "*Sakaya wa kechinbō, sake o dase!*" ("The *sake* dealer is a skinflint, roll out the drinks!"). Obligingly the Araharis' young daughter-in-law un-

locks a vending machine and distributes cans of chilled beer, despite the formal prohibition of drinking during the mikoshi processions. The men take a break.

15. The Miyamoto-chō leaders did not follow the path of their next-door neighbors in organizing a group of young men to build a mikoshi, but opted to have one built by a firm in Gunma prefecture that specialized in them. An introduction to the firm was arranged through the local undertaker (the firm also specialized in funeral equipment). Organizers of the mikoshi campaign made a number of trips to Gunma, several hours away by train, to inspect the firm's products and oversee the job. The decision to purchase a mikoshi instead of building it partly reflected the young leaders' self-imposed deadline, but it was also a recognition that Miyamoto-chō did not have enough residents capable of doing the intricate carpentry and metalwork that building a mikoshi requires.

16. In 1979 and 1980 the adult mikoshi was small enough and light enough that almost any able-bodied adult could help carry it. The new mikoshi imposed its own new standards, not just of strength and endurance but also of height. The greater weight and bulk required greater coordination among the bearers; Mr. Kitayama (who attended college on a basketball scholarship) and I both found that we were just a bit too tall to carry the new mikoshi. If we tried to join, we would throw off the balance and the rhythm of the group (and bring a crushing weight down on our shoulders).

17. The availability of festival hanten is one means of restricting outsiders. The Mikoshi Action Committee prohibits anyone from helping carry the mikoshi without wearing a Miyamoto-chō hanten, 200 of which were ordered when the new mikoshi was commissioned. Almost immediately 150 were sold to residents, and the others were retained by the committee for rentals. Residents can reserve them— for their own use or for the use of family members or friends—several days before the festival for a nominal fee to cover dry-cleaning. Of course, the rule on hanten and their restricted availability limit but do not eliminate the participation of outsiders in the festival. The rule is most effective at discouraging casual bystanders and eager but basically respectful festival buffs; it does not deter serious gate-crashers, nor does it prevent residents from sharing their hanten with family, friends, or even unknown onlookers.

18. George DeVos has discussed Japanese "instant tradition" in several public addresses, and it is from him that I borrow the term; Keith Brown (1976) has shown how traditions are created in a provincial city; Jennifer Robertson (1985) has examined the process in a suburb of To-

kyo. As Donald Keene, in remarks prepared for the Suntory Foundation, observed, "Many traditions persist in Japan but, like the wooden buildings in Nara which are always described as being 1,200 years old, probably every element in the fabric has been subjected to renewal and change, and some traditions were born only yesterday."

CONCLUSION

1. My article, "Craft Life in a Tokyo Neighborhood" (Bestor 1984a), was commissioned for a special issue on Japanese arts and crafts. Unlike most of the articles, which focused on the "specialness" of crafts—on professional potters, on the making of expensive handmade papers, on crafts as fine art—mine examined the ways in which traditional Japanese handicrafts and hand-crafted forms of production were integral to daily life. I focused on such things as how tatami are made and used, on how neighborhoods sometimes build their own mikoshi, on how various kinds of handwork including sewing and flower arrangement are feminine recreations, to try to illustrate how the lines between crafts as fine arts and hand-crafted objects as items of daily life are often artificial. In pursuing this argument, of course, I had presented only one side of neighborhood reality, ignoring microwave ovens, sports cars, video cameras, high-tech furnishings, and other "modern" aspects of local material culture. (I also showed Japanese friends the draft of a brief article that appeared later—Bestor 1984b—which concentrates on events such as the New Year's Eve fire patrol and the autumn festival.)

2. Japanese sociologists follow the lead of Mills (1953: 3–10, 63–76) in distinguishing between the old middle class and the new, between self-employed small-scale entrepreneurs and white-collar bureaucratic organization men (see, e.g., Fukutake 1981: 26–30; Kishimoto 1978; Tominaga 1978). Just as Mills analyzed the historical origins of the American old middle class—situating its rise in the 19th-century transition from an agrarian to an industrial society—so too these scholars place the origins of the Japanese old middle class in the class dynamics and feudal social structure of the premodern era. The presumed identification of the old middle class with the ancien régime is among its most salient defining characteristics, and one Japanese dictionary of sociological terms states, "The basis of life of the old middle class is a survival of feudalism" (*kyū-chūsankaikyū . . . wa sono seikatsu jiban ga hōkenshugi no zanzonbutsu de ari;* Kanba 1966: 114).

3. Wimberley (1973: 423) argues that the merchant lifestyles he found in Kanazawa—a city today noted by Japanese for its traditionalism—originated in "the colorful and culturally rich tradition of the

chōnin (townsman) social class of preindustrial Japan." He contends that "style as a set of cultural prescriptions by which alternate modes of social intercourse and consumption may be differentiated and selected is not necessarily related to economic organization, but is an index of the degree of social interaction obtaining within the group which expresses it, as well as an index of communication between that group and other groups" (p. 428). On this construction, the traditionalistic lifestyle of the old middle class is maintained primarily by the dynamics of relations occurring within that class.

4. The popular phrase *kuroyon* (lit., "nine, six, four"), commonly used in newspaper accounts of tax inequities, describes the differential rate of taxes paid by various classes. Popular belief has it that employees, both white collar and blue collar, whose taxes are deducted directly from their pay checks, pay on 90% of their income; that the self-employed who can take advantage of various loopholes and can both hide income and inflate deductible expenses, pay on only 60%; and that farmers, who have the greatest potential for underreporting their incomes, pay on only 40%.

There is no question that the old middle class of Miyamoto-chō is generally prosperous. One reader of my manuscript reminded me of the possessions Dore found among Shitayama-chō's residents in 1958: bicycles, electric fans, radios. Today the list would have to include such things as gigantic home karaoke audio systems, central air conditioning, home copying machines, electronic facsimile machines attached to multiple incoming telephone lines, large collections of seasonally appropriate kimono, and diamond rings. As another indicator, one might count the number of Miyamoto-chō's shopkeepers and factory owners who have visited Paris, Las Vegas, Tahiti, New York, Rio de Janeiro, San Francisco, New Caledonia, Hong Kong, London, or Honolulu.

Education is still another area of conspicuous consumption. Although in some ways families with businesses to pass on seem to take more casual attitudes toward education than sarariiman households, children from old middle-class families attend some of the best high schools and universities in Tokyo, and the families are willing to spend vast sums of money on educational preparation. Children from Miyamoto-chō regularly go abroad during summer vacations for homestays with foreign families and with relatives of local families who live overseas.

Certainly most local merchants are not wealthy, but almost all are quite comfortable, in part because the economic rewards of self-employment are good and in part because their occupations are flexible enough to allow them the time to enjoy the fruits of their labors. Almost no merchant I spoke with ever indicated jealousy toward sarariiman. Commonly merchants viewed sarariiman as victims of the system, suckers who could not escape from the big corporations that ruled their lives. A few local merchants in fact had been sarariiman for a time before starting a business or returning to take over a family business; none of them expressed regret at the change.

5. Kelly's study (1986) of new middle-class ideals among farm families provides a rural Japanese example of this process.

6. Of course criteria for status and social stratification are complicated and cannot be reduced to a single axis; an important aspect of class stratification in present-day Japanese society is the spread of status inconsistencies arising from "the pluralistic nature of criteria for distributing social resources and rewards" (Tominaga 1978: 10–11). Rank, power, status, and prestige are distributed throughout society according to such criteria as income level, occupational category, and educational attainments, but the correlations between the rankings along these different scales are slight. Tominaga points out, for example, that although Japan is a *"gakureki shakai"* (a society in which position is based on one's educational résumé), higher educational levels do not correspond to higher income levels. He also sees a continuing trend toward the greater and greater domination of society's high-status positions by people in the white-collar, bureaucratic sectors of society. Therefore, criteria such as educational level (necessary to obtain employment in major bureaucratic organizations) or the prestige of the bureaucratic organization one is employed by (based on the organization's size, prominence, and political or economic centrality) become more important determinants of a person's social standing than income, for example.

7. Murakami (1978: 2) notes that studies consistently report that over 90% of the Japanese population considers itself to be "middle class," and takes this, as well as the trend over recent decades toward the homogenization and standardization of Japanese lifestyles, as evidence that distinctions between the new and old middle classes are disappearing: "There are no longer any fundamental differences in ways of talking, dressing or living among office supervisor, office worker, plant foreman, factory worker, store-owner, clerk or farmer." He argues, here and elsewhere (Murakami 1982), that the various components of the old and new middle classes are merging into the "new middle mass." Other scholars disagree, contending that the structural bipolarity of the economy has not lessened: the new middle class made up of salaried white-collar employees and their families continues to

be distinguishable from "the old middle class [that] has always secured its livelihood from personal assets" (Kishimoto 1978: 8) On this argument, even if Japanese lifestyles and consumption patterns are becoming less diverse, underlying class differences remain.

8. I do not emphasize the "he" of sarariiman accidentally here, for one of the effects of the alternative social world created in Miyamoto-chō is to intermingle class and gender identities. In a sense, within the neighborhood there is more equality among women than among men, and local institutions both limit the participation of male white-collar workers and encourage the participation of new and old middle-class wives as equals.

9. This localized status is something Miyamoto-chō's leaders can quite literally demonstrate by identifying themselves on their *meishi*, the business cards that are the sine qua non of male white-collar life, as the chōkai president, or the leader of the merchants' association, or the PTA treasurer, or the leader of a trade association of rice dealers.

APPENDIX A

1. The increase in the number of households between 1975 and 1980 resulted from the reconstruction and expansion of a large company dormitory in the late 1970's. The dormitory now houses about 175 residents, each of whom is counted by the census as a separate single-person household.

2. The household registers identified 98 people (10.2% of all inmigrants) whose previous residence outside the metropolitan region was clearly recorded. An additional 144 residents (15.0%) were ambiguously recorded only as coming from "outside Shinagawa-ku." I have conservatively classified all ambiguous cases as migrants from outside the metropolitan region.

APPENDIX B

1. The special reserve fund had a balance forward from 1978–79 of 287,417 yen. There is also a Bon Odori reserve fund. At the beginning of the budget year it had a balance of 60,679 yen. The current year's contribution of 27,021 yen brought the 1979–80 reserves to 87,700 yen.

2. The parish delegates are representatives to the governing board of the local Shintō shrine, appointed by the chōkai. The chōkai president is 1 of the 2 delegates and serves ex officio.

3. The social welfare representatives are nominated by the chōkai to work with the ward government's social welfare department.

4. The woman is the chief of the women's auxiliary, a position that makes her an ex officio vice-president of the chōkai.

APPENDIX C

1. The status of sewanin is achieved simply by having made a contribution to the previous year's festival. Sewanin is simply a residual category for past contributors who otherwise are assigned no position or responsibility for the actual management of the festival.

2. All 30 people listed in this category are current riji for their household clusters who did not contribute to the previous year's festival and are not assigned any festival duties for the current year.

3. Chiefs and assistant chiefs of the various committees (*kakari*) are known as *kakarichō* and *fukukakarichō*, respectively.

4. During the festival the chōkai hall is called the O-mikisho (lit., "the place of sanctified *sake*"). It serves both as the local headquarters for the neighborhood's festival and as the site of prayers and rituals performed by the shrine's priest on the first day of the festival.

5. Under this heading, 18 women are named (though without explicit titles or offices), followed by a blanket inclusion of all officers of the fujinbu.

BIBLIOGRAPHY

Bibliography

The place of publication on all Japanese-language works in the list below is Tokyo. The following abbreviations are used in the citations:

MITI Japanese Ministry of International Trade and Industry
SCAP Supreme Commander for the Allied Powers
SKKI Shinagawa-ku Kyōiku Iinkai [Board of Education of Shinagawa Ward]
SKNT *Shinagawa-ku no Tōkei* [Statistics of Shinagawa Ward]. Annual publication of the Shinagawa Ward Office.
SKS *Shinagawa-ku Shi, Tsūshihen* [The history of Shinagawa Ward, narrative volumes]. 2 vols. Tokyo, 1973–74.
TMG Tokyo Metropolitan Government (for English-language publications)

Akaike, Noriaki. 1976. "Festival and Neighborhood Association," *Japanese Journal of Religious Studies*, 3(2–3): 127–74.
Allinson, Gary D. 1978. "Japanese Cities in the Industrial Era," *Journal of Urban History*, 4(4): 443–76.
———. 1979. *Suburban Tokyo: A Comparative Study in Politics and Social Change.* Berkeley: University of California Press.
———. 1980. "Opposition in the Suburbs," in K. Steiner, E. S. Krauss, and S. C. Flanagan, eds., *Political Opposition and Local Politics in Japan.* Princeton, N.J.: Princeton University Press, pp. 95–130.
Ames, Walter L. 1981. *Police and Community in Japan.* Berkeley: University of California Press.

Aoyagi, Kiyotaka. 1983. "Viable Traditions in Urban Japan: *Matsuri* and *Chōnaikai*," in G. Ansari and P. Nas, eds., *Town-Talk*. Leiden: E. J. Brill, pp. 96–111.

Atsumi, Reiko. 1979. "Tsukiai—Obligatory Personal Relationships of Japanese White-Collar Company Employees," *Human Organization*, 38(1): 63–70.

Bayley, David H. 1976. *Forces of Order: Police Behavior in Japan and the United States*. Berkeley: University of California Press.

Befu, Harumi. 1963. "Network and Corporate Structure," *Studies on Asia*, 4: 27–41.

———. 1968. "Gift-Giving in a Modernizing Japan," *Monumenta Nipponica*, 23(3–4): 445–56.

———. 1971. *Japan: An Anthropological Introduction*. San Francisco: Chandler.

———. 1980. "The Group Model of Japanese Society and an Alternative," *Rice University Studies*, 66(1): 169–87.

Bellah, Robert N. 1957. *Tokugawa Religion: The Values of Pre-Industrial Japan*. Glencoe, Ill.: Free Press.

Benedict, Ruth. 1946. *The Chrysanthemum and the Sword*. Boston: Houghton Mifflin.

Bennett, John W., and Iwao Ishino. 1963. *Paternalism in the Japanese Economy*. Minneapolis: University of Minnesota Press.

Berger, Bennett M. 1960. *Working-Class Suburb: A Study of Auto Workers in Suburbia*. Berkeley: University of California Press.

Bestor, Theodore C. 1984a. "Craft Life in a Tokyo Neighborhood," in J. Mock, ed., *The Sociology of Craft: Japan 1984*, special issue of *Craft International*, Jan./March 1984, pp. 10–12.

———. 1984b. "Life in a Tokyo Neighborhood: An Anthropologist's Journal," *Japan Society Newsletter*, December 1984, pp. 3–6.

———. 1984c. "Land, Households, and Mobility in Tokyo," paper presented at the annual meeting of the American Anthropological Association, Denver, Nov. 18.

———. 1985. "Tradition and Japanese Social Organization: Institutional Development in a Tokyo Neighborhood," *Ethnology*, 24(2): 121–35.

———. 1991. "The *Shitamachi* Revival," *Transactions of the Asiatic Society of Japan*, fourth series, 5: 71–86.

Braibanti, Ralph J. D. 1948. "Neighborhood Associations in Japan and Their Democratic Potentialities," *Far Eastern Quarterly*, 7(2): 136–64.

Broadbridge, Seymour. 1966. *Industrial Dualism in Japan: A Problem of Economic Growth and Structural Change.* Chicago: Aldine.

Brown, L. Keith. 1976. "Community and the Territorial Principle: Neighborhood Relations in a Japanese Town," paper presented at the Workshop on the Japanese City, Mt. Kisco, N.Y., April 23–27.

Caldarola, Carlo. 1965. "Socio-economic Dualism in Japan," *Monumenta Nipponica,* 20(3–4): 359–73.

Cancian, Frank. 1965. *Economics and Prestige in a Maya Community.* Stanford, Calif.: Stanford University Press.

Cohen, Abner. 1969. *Custom and Politics in Urban Africa: A Study of Hausa Migrants in Yoruba Towns.* Berkeley: University of California Press.

Cohen, Jerome B. 1949. *Japan's Economy in War and Reconstruction.* Minneapolis: University of Minnesota Press.

Curtis, Gerald L. 1970. "The *Kōenkai* and the Liberal Democratic Party," *The Japan Interpreter,* 6(2): 206–19.

———. 1971. *Election Campaigning Japanese Style.* New York: Columbia University Press.

Daniels, Gordon. 1975. "The Great Tokyo Air Raid, 9–10 March 1945," in W. G. Beasley, ed., *Modern Japan: Aspects of History, Literature, and Society.* Berkeley: University of California Press, pp. 113–31.

Davis, Winston. 1980. *Dojo: Magic and Exorcism in Modern Japan.* Stanford, Calif.: Stanford University Press.

De Mente, Boye, and Fred Thomas Perry. 1967. *The Japanese as Consumers: Asia's First Great Mass Market.* New York: Walker/Weatherhill.

DeVos, George A. 1979. "Industrialization and the Growth of Tokyo," *The Journal of the Oriental Society of Australia,* 14: 34–42.

DeVos, George A., and Hiroshi Wagatsuma. 1973. "The Entrepreneurial Mentality of Lower-Class Urban Japanese in Manufacturing Industries," in G. A. DeVos, *Socialization for Achievement: Essays on the Cultural Psychology of the Japanese.* Berkeley: University of California Press, pp. 201–19.

Dore, R. P. 1958. *City Life in Japan: A Study of a Tokyo Ward.* Berkeley: University of California Press.

———. 1968. Introduction to H. Nakamura's "Urban Ward Associations in Japan," in R. E. Pahl, ed., *Readings in Urban Sociology.* Oxford: Pergamon, pp. 186–90.

Ebara-ku [Ebara Ward]. 1943. *Ebara-ku Shi* [History of Ebara Ward]. Ebara-kuyakusho.

Embree, John F. 1939. *Suye Mura: A Japanese Village.* Chicago: University of Chicago Press.

———. 1945. *The Japanese Nation: A Social Survey*. New York: Farrar and Rinehart.

Falconeri, G. Ralph. 1976. "The Impact of Rapid Urban Change on Neighborhood Solidarity," in J. W. White and F. Munger, eds., *Social Change and Community Politics in Urban Japan*. Chapel Hill: Institute for Research in Social Science, University of North Carolina, pp. 31–59.

Fridell, Wilbur M. 1973. *Japanese Shrine Mergers, 1906–12: State Shintō Moves to the Grass Roots*. Tokyo: Sophia University Press.

Fujii, Masao. 1983. "Maintenance and Change in Japanese Traditional Funerals and Death-Related Behavior," *Japanese Journal of Religious Studies*, 10(1): 39–64.

Fukawa, S. T. 1963. "Neighbourhood Associations in Japanese Cities and Their Political Implications." Unpublished M.A. thesis, University of London.

Fukutake, Tadashi. 1962. *Man and Society in Japan*. Tokyo: University of Tokyo Press.

———. 1981. *Japanese Society Today*, 2d ed. Tokyo: University of Tokyo Press.

Geertz, Clifford. 1973. *The Interpretation of Cultures*. New York: Basic Books.

Hastings, Sally Ann. 1980. "The Government, the Citizen, and the Creation of a New Sense of Community: Social Welfare, Local Organizations, and Dissent in Tokyo, 1905–1931." Unpublished Ph.D. dissertation, University of Chicago.

———. 1984. "District Welfare Committees in Prewar Tokyo," paper presented to the Triangle East Asian Colloquium, Raleigh, N.C., April 7.

Havens, Thomas R. H. 1978. *Valley of Darkness: The Japanese People and World War Two*. New York: Norton.

Hobsbawm, Eric, and Terence Ranger, eds. 1983. *The Invention of Tradition*. Cambridge: Cambridge University Press.

Hozumi, Shigetoh. 1943. "The Tonari-gumi of Japan," *Contemporary Japan*, 12(8): 984–90.

Hunter, Albert. 1974. *Symbolic Communities: The Persistence and Change of Chicago's Local Communities*. Chicago: University of Chicago Press.

Inoue, Kenji. 1932. *Ebara-chō Shi* [Chronicle of Ebara Town]. Ebara-chō Shi Henshūiinkai.

Ishida, Takeshi. 1971. *Japanese Society*. New York: Random House.

Ishikawa, Atsushi, and Michihiro Okuda. 1959. "Toshi no chiiki shūdan ni kansuru kenkyū: Toshika no katei ni okeru chiiki shūdan no chii [Research on urban regional groups: the status of regional groups in the process of urbanization]," *Tōyō Daigaku Kiyō*, 13: 91–115.

Ishizuka, Hiromichi. 1977. *Tōkyō no Shakai Keizai Shi: Shihonshūgi to Toshi Mondai* [The socio-economic history of Tokyo: capitalism and the urban problem]. Kinokuniya Shoten.

Isomura, Eiichi, and Michihiro Okuda. 1966. "Recent Trends of Urban Sociology in Japan," in P. Halmos, ed., *Japanese Sociological Studies, The Sociological Review*: Monograph No. 10, pp. 127–50.

Johnson, Erwin H. 1964. "The Stem Family and Its Extension in Present-Day Japan," *American Anthropologist*, 66(4): 839–51.

Kagami, Zenkō. 1935. *Dai Ebara Sōran* [A general view of Ebara]. Asahi Shuppansha.

Kamishima, Jirō. 1961. *Kindai Nihon to Seishin Kōzō* [The mental structure of modern Japan]. Iwanami Shoten.

Kanba, Toshio. 1966. *Shakaigaku Yōgo Kaisetsu* [Dictionary of sociological terminology]. Tōyō Keizai Shinposha.

Kelly, William W. 1986. "Rationalization and Nostalgia: Cultural Dynamics of New Middle-Class Japan," *American Ethnologist*, 13(4): 603–18.

Kiefer, Christie W. 1970. "The Psychological Interdependence of Family, School, and Bureaucracy in Japan," *American Anthropologist*, 72(1): 66–75.

Kishimoto, Shigenobu. 1978. "Can the 'New Middle Class' Theory Be Sustained?," *The Japan Interpreter*, 12(1): 5–8.

Kokumin Seikatsu Sentaa, comp. 1974. *Gendai Nihon no Komyuniti* [Contemporary Japanese communities]. Kawashima Shoten.

Kornhauser, David H. 1976. *Urban Japan: Its Foundations and Growth*. London: Longman.

Kurabayashi, Yoshimasa. 1983. "Kantō daishinsai no SSDS [A system of social and demographic statistics of the great Kantō earthquake]," *Keizai Kenkyū*, 34(2): 97–111.

Kurasawa, Susumu. 1968. *Nihon no Toshi Shakai* [Japanese urban society]. Fukumura Shuppan.

Kuroda, Toshio. 1979. "The Impact of Internal Migration on the Tokyo Metropolitan Population," in J. W. White, ed., *The Urban Impact of Internal Migration*. Chapel Hill: Institute for Research in Social Science, University of North Carolina, pp. 33–52.

Lebra, Takie S. 1984. *Japanese Women: Constraint and Fulfillment*. Honolulu: University of Hawaii Press.

Lee, Changsoo, and George DeVos. 1981. *Koreans in Japan: Ethnic Conflict and Accommodation*. Berkeley: University of California Press.

Lewis, Jack G. 1983. "Where Security Begets Security: Concurrent Careers of Local Politicians," in D. W. Plath, ed., *Work and Lifecourse in Japan.* Albany: State University of New York Press, pp. 116–34.

Littleton, C. Scott. 1985. "Tokyo Rock and Role," *Natural History*, August, pp. 48–57.

———. 1986. "The Organization and Management of a Tokyo Shintō Shrine Festival," *Ethnology*, 25(3): 195–202.

Loftus, Ronald P. 1977. "*Bōsōzoku*," *The Japan Interpreter*, 11(3): 384–94.

McKean, Margaret A. 1981. *Environmental Protest and Citizen Politics in Japan.* Berkeley: University of California Press.

Masai, Yasuo. 1975. *Edo no Toshiteki Tochi Riyō-zu, 1860-nen Goro* [Urban land-use map of Edo, ca. 1860]. Privately published.

Masland, John W. 1946. "Neighborhood Associations in Japan," *Far Eastern Survey*, 15(23): 355–58.

Mills, C. Wright. 1953. *White Collar.* New York: Oxford University Press.

MITI (Ministry of International Trade and Industry). Small and Medium Enterprise Agency. 1977. *Small Business in Japan: 1977 White Paper on Small and Medium Enterprises in Japan.*

———. 1980. *Chūshōkigyō Hakusho* [White paper on small and medium enterprises].

Mock, John A. 1980. "Social Change in an Urban Neighborhood: A Case Study in Sapporo, Japan." Unpublished Ph.D. dissertation, Michigan State University.

Morioka, Kiyomi. 1966. "Changing Neighborhood Associations in a Fringe Area," in Social Science Research Institute, ed., *Transformation Process of a Suburban City in Japan.* International Christian University Publication II.A, Social Science Studies 11. Mitaka, Japan: International Christian University, pp. 4–6.

Murakami, Yasusuke. 1978. "The Reality of the New Middle Class," *The Japan Interpreter*, 12(1): 1–5.

———. 1982. "The Age of New Middle Mass Politics," *Journal of Japanese Studies*, 8(1): 29–72.

Nakagawa, Gō. 1980. *Chōnaikai* [Neighborhood associations]. Chūōkōronsha.

Nakamura, Hachirō. 1963. "Some Types of Chōnaikai in the Process of Urban Development," in Social Science Research Institute, ed., *Local Community and Urbanization.* International Christian University Publication II.A, Social Science Studies 9. Mitaka, Japan: International Christian University, pp. 1–14.

———. 1968. "Urban Ward Associations in Japan," in R. E. Pahl, ed., *Readings in Urban Sociology.* Oxford: Pergamon, pp. 190–208.

———. 1979. *Senzen no Tōkyō ni okeru Chōnaikai* [Neighborhood as-

sociations in prewar Tokyo]. Ningen to shakai no kaihatsu puroguramu kenkyū hōkoku HSDRJE-3J/UNUP-23. Kokuren Daigaku.

———. 1980a. "The Concept of Community Transplanted in Japan," in
S. Koyano, J. Watanuki, and H. Komai, eds., *Asian Perspectives on
Social Development*. Tokyo: Japan Sociological Society, pp. 79–89.

———. 1980b. *Chōnaikai no Soshiki to Un'ei-jō no Mondaiten* [Prob-
lems in the management and structure of neighborhood associa-
tions]. Ningen to shakai no kaihatsu puroguramu kenkyū hōkoku
HSDRJE-3J/UNUP-204. Kokuren Daigaku.

Nakane, Chie. 1970. *Japanese Society*. Berkeley: University of California Press.

Norbeck, Edward. 1962. "Common-Interest Associations in Rural Japan," in R. J. Smith and R. K. Beardsley, eds., *Japanese Culture: Its
Development and Characteristics*. Chicago: Aldine, pp. 73–85.

———. 1972. "Japanese Common-Interest Associations in Cross-Cul-
tural Perspective," *Journal of Voluntary Action Research*, 1(1):
38–41.

———. 1977. "Changing Associations in a Recently Industrialized Japanese Community," *Urban Anthropology*, 6(1): 45–64.

Ohsato, Katsuma, ed. 1966. *Hundred-Year Statistics of the Japanese
Economy*. Tokyo: Bank of Japan.

Ohshio, Shunsuke. 1964. "The Urban Phenomenon in Japan," *Journal
of Asian Studies*, 24(1): 122–29.

Okuda, Michihiro. 1964. Kyūchūkansō o shūtai to suru toshi chōnaikai [Urban neighborhood associations centered on the old middle
class], *Shakaigaku Hyōron*, 14(3): 9–14.

Park, Robert E. 1976. Introduction to H. W. Zorbaugh, *The Gold Coast
and the Slum*. Chicago: University of Chicago Press. Originally
published in 1929.

Patrick, Hugh, and Thomas P. Rohlen. 1987. "Small-Scale Family Enterprises," in K. Yamamura and Y. Yasuba, eds., *The Political Economy of Japan*, Vol. 1: *The Domestic Transformation*. Stanford,
Calif.: Stanford University Press, pp. 331–84.

Price, John A. 1967. "The Japanese Market System: Retailing in a Dual
Economy." Unpublished Ph.D. dissertation, University of Michigan.

———. 1968. "Retail Market Associations in Japan," *Kroeber Anthropological Society Papers*, No. 39, pp. 20–29.

Ratcliffe, C. Tait. 1975. "Approaches to Distribution in Japan," in I.
Frank, ed., *The Japanese Economy in International Perspective*. Bal-
timore: Johns Hopkins University Press, pp. 101–33.

Reischauer, Edwin O. 1981. *Japan: The Story of a Nation*, 3d ed. New
York: Knopf.

Riggs, Lynne E. 1977. "*Ranjuku jidai,*" *The Japan Interpreter,* 11(4): 541–49.

Rikuchi Sokuryōbu. 1886. *Tōkyō Kinbō Nanbu* [Environs of Tokyo: southern portion]. 1:20,000 map from an 1880 survey reprinted (date unknown) as one of five maps in a set entitled *Tōkyō Kinbō-zu* [Maps of the environs of Tokyo]. Kochizu Shiryō Shuppan.

Robertson, Jennifer. 1985. "The Making of Kodaira: Being an Ethnography of a Japanese City's Progress." Unpublished Ph.D. dissertation, Cornell University.

Rohlen, Thomas P. 1974. *For Harmony and Strength: Japanese White-Collar Organization in Anthropological Perspective.* Berkeley: University of California Press.

———. 1980. "The *Juku* Phenomenon: An Exploratory Essay," *Journal of Japanese Studies,* 6(2): 207–42.

———. 1983. *Japan's High Schools.* Berkeley: University of California Press.

Sadler, A. W. 1969. "The Form and Meaning of the Festival," *Asian Folklore Studies,* 28(1): 1–16.

———. 1970a. "O-kagura: Field Notes on the Festival Drama in Modern Tokyo," *Asian Folklore Studies,* 29(1): 275–300.

———. 1970b. "Of Talismans and Shadow Bodies: Annual Purification Rites at a Tokyo Shrine," *Contemporary Religions in Japan,* 11(3–4): 181–222.

———. 1972. "Carrying the Mikoshi: Further Field Notes on the Shrine Festival in Modern Tokyo," *Asian Folklore Studies,* 31(1): 89–114.

———. 1974. "At the Sanctuary: Further Field Notes on the Shrine Festival in Modern Tokyo," *Asian Folklore Studies,* 33(1): 17–34.

———. 1975a. "Folkdance and Fairgrounds: More Notes on Neighborhood Festivals in Tokyo," *Asian Folklore Studies,* 34(1): 1–20.

———. 1975b. "The Shrine: Notes Towards a Study of Neighborhood Festivals in Modern Tokyo," *Asian Folklore Studies,* 34(2): 1–38.

———. 1976. "The Grammar of a Rite in Shintō," *Asian Folklore Studies,* 35(2): 17–27.

Salamon, Sonya. 1975. "The Varied Groups of Japanese and German Housewives," *The Japan Interpreter,* 10(2): 151–70.

Sanseidō, comp. 1974. *Tōkyō Chimei Kojiten* [Pocket dictionary of Tokyo place names].

Saotome, Katsumoto. 1971. *Tōkyō Daikūshū* [The great Tokyo air raid]. Iwanami Shoten.

SCAP (Supreme Commander for the Allied Powers). 1947. *Two Years of Occupation: Economic.* Tokyo: SCAP, GHQ, Public Information Office. August.

————. 1948. *A Preliminary Study of the Neighborhood Associations of Japan*. Tokyo: SCAP, Civil Information and Education Section, Public Opinion and Sociological Research. Jan. 23.

————. 1949. "The Abolition of the Tonari Gumi System," in Supreme Commander for the Allied Powers, Government Section, *Political Reorientation of Japan, September 1945 to September 1948*, Vol. 1. Washington, D.C.: U.S. Government Printing Office, pp. 284–87.

Seidensticker, Edward. 1983. *Low City, High City: Tokyo from Edo to the Earthquake*. New York: Knopf.

Shinagawa-ku [Shinagawa Ward]. 1971. *Shinagawa-ku Shi, Shiryōhen* [The history of Shinagawa Ward: documents]. All Shinagawa Ward volumes are published by Shinagawa-kuyakusho.

————. 1972. *Shinagawa-ku Shi, Shiryōhen, Chizu Tōkei Shū* [The history of Shinagawa Ward: documents: collected maps and statistics].

————. 1976. *Dai-Jūnikai Kokusei Chōsa Kekka no Gaiyō (Sokuhō)* [Overview of the results of the 12th national census (preliminary report)].

————. 1978. *Shinagawa-ku Chōki Kihon Keikaku* [The fundamental long-term plan for Shinagawa Ward].

————. 1979. *Shutchōjo no Kinō oyobi Chii-zuke narabi ni Kumin Shūkaijo no Kanri Un'ei ni tsuite* [Concerning the function of Branch Offices and the administration of ward residents' meeting halls].

————. 1980. *Shinagawa-ku no Aramashi* [About Shinagawa Ward].

————. 1981. *Dai-Jūsankai Kokusei Chōsa Kekka no Gaiyō (Sokuhō)* [Overview of the results of the 13th national census (preliminary report)].

————. n.d. *Jūsho o Wakariyasuku Suru Hōhō* [The way to make addresses easy to understand].

Shinagawa-ku Senkyo Kanri Iinkai [Election Management Commission of Shinagawa Ward]. 1971–79. *Chihō Senkyo no Kiroku* [Records of the regional elections].

————. 1983. *Chihō Sangiin Senkyo no Kiroku* [Records of the regional and House of Councillors elections].

Silverman, Sydel. 1979. "On the Uses of History in Anthropology: The Palio of Siena, *American Ethnologist*, 6(3): 413–36.

SKKI (Shinagawa-ku Kyōiku Iinkai [Board of Education of Shinagawa Ward]). 1973. *Shinagawa no Rekishi Shiriizu: Chimeihen* [The Shinagawa history series: volume of place names].

————. 1979. *Shinagawa no Rekishi* [The history of Shinagawa].

SKNT. 1961–84. *Shinagawa-ku no Tōkei* [Statistics of Shinagawa Ward]. Published annually. Shinagawa-kuyakusho.

SKS. 1973–74. *Shinagawa-ku Shi, Tsūshihen* [The history of Shinagawa Ward: narrative volumes]. 2 vols. Shinagawa-kuyakusho.

Smith, Henry D., II. 1978. "Tokyo as an Idea: An Exploration of Japanese Urban Thought Until 1945," *Journal of Japanese Studies*,
4(1): 45–80.

———. 1979. "Tokyo and London: Comparative Conceptions of the
City," in A. M. Craig, ed., *Japan: A Comparative View*. Princeton,
N.J.: Princeton University Press, pp. 49–99.

———. 1986. "The Edo-Tokyo Transition: In Search of Common
Ground," in M. B. Jansen and G. Rozman, eds., *Japan in Transition:
From Tokugawa to Meiji*. Princeton, N.J.: Princeton University
Press, pp. 347–74.

Smith, Robert J. 1960. "Pre-industrial Urbanism in Japan: A Consideration of Multiple Traditions in a Feudal Society," *Economic Development and Cultural Change*, 9(1.II): 241–57.

———. 1961. "The Japanese Rural Community: Norms, Sanctions,
and Ostracism," *American Anthropologist*, 63(3): 522–33.

———. 1963. "Aspects of Mobility in Pre-industrial Japanese Cities,"
Comparative Studies in Society and History, 5(4): 416–23.

———. 1973. "Town and City in Pre-modern Japan: Small Families,
Small Households, and Residential Instability," in A. Southall, ed.,
Urban Anthropology. New York: Oxford University Press, pp. 163–
210.

———. 1977. "Diversity and Variability in Japanese Society," *Papers in
Anthropology*, 18(2): 1–9.

———. 1983. *Japanese Society: Tradition, Self and the Social Order*.
Cambridge: Cambridge University Press.

Soeda, Hiroshi. 1973. "Festivity and the City: Mobile Stages of the
Gion Festival," *Concerned Theatre Japan*, 2(3–4): 190–207.

Sōrifu Tōkei-kyoku [Statistics Bureau, Prime Minister's Office]. 1960.
1960 Population Census of Japan, Vol. 4, Part 13: *Tokyo-to*.

———. 1975. *1975 Population Census of Japan*, Vol. 3, Part 13: *Tokyo-
to*.

———. 1980. *1980 Population Census of Japan*, Vol. 2: *Results of the
First Basic Complete Tabulation*, Part 2, 13: *Tokyo-to*.

Steiner, Kurt. 1965. *Local Government in Japan*. Stanford, Calif.: Stanford University Press.

Steiner, Kurt, Ellis S. Krauss, and Scott C. Flanagan, eds. 1980. *Political
Opposition and Local Politics in Japan*. Princeton, N.J.: Princeton
University Press.

Suttles, Gerald D. 1972. *The Social Construction of Communities*.
Chicago: University of Chicago Press.

Teikoku Dōshinkai. 1908. *Tōkyō-fu Ka Hachi Gun Shūgiin Giin Senkyosha Hikkei*. [Directory of parliamentary electorate in the 8 counties of Tokyo Prefecture]. Teikoku Dōshinkai Shuppanbu.

TMG (Tokyo Metropolitan Government). 1978a. *An Administrative Perspective of Tokyo*.

———. 1978b. *City Planning of Tokyo*.

———. 1981a. *Organization of the Tokyo Metropolitan Government*.

———. 1981b. *Plain Talk About Tokyo: The Administration of the Tokyo Metropolitan Government*.

———. 1981c. *Tokyo at a Glance*.

Tōkyō-fu [Tokyo Prefecture; pre-1943 entity]. 1900–1940. *Tōkyō-fu Tōkeisho* [Statistical handbook of Tokyo Prefecture]. Published annually.

Tōkyō-shi [City of Tokyo; pre-1943 entity]. 1928. *Tōkyō-shi Kōgai ni okeru Kōtsū Kikai no Hattatsu to Jinkō no Zōka* [The development of transportation systems and rapid population increases in the outskirts of the City of Tokyo]. All City of Tokyo volumes published by Tōkyō-shiyakusho.

———. 1931. *Shiiki Kakuchō Chōsa Shiryō: Ebara-gun Kaku Chōson Genjō Chōsa, (no.6) Ebara-machi* [Documents for surveying the expansion of city boundaries: surveys of present conditions in the towns and villages of Ebara County (No. 6), the Town of Ebara].

———. 1935. *Tōkyō-shi no Kugyōsei Seido ni Kansuru Chōsa* [Survey of the ward administrative system of the City of Tokyo].

———. 1937. *Shōwa Jū-nen Kokusei Chōsa Futai Chōsa: Ku-hen, Ebara-ku* [Supplementary survey to the 1935 national census: ward volumes: Ebara Ward].

Tōkyō Shōbōchō [Tokyo Fire Department]. 1978. *Chōkai Jichikai oyobi Bōsai Shimin Soshiki nado Ichiranhyō (Tokubetsu Ku Hen)* [Directory of neighborhood associations, self-governing associations, and citizens' disaster-relief organizations (volume for special wards)]. Tōkyō Shōbōchō-kannai Seikatsu Anzen Bu.

Tōkyō-to [Tokyo Metropolitan Prefecture]. 1979. *Tōkyō Hyakunen-shi* [The hundred-year history of Tokyo]. 7 vols. Gyōsei.

Tōkyō-to Tōkei Kyōkai [Tokyo Statistical Association]. 1982. *Tōkyō-to Tōkei Nenkan* [Tokyo statistical yearbook].

Tominaga, Ken'ichi. 1978. "An Empirical View of Social Stratification," *The Japan Interpreter*, 12(1): 8–12.

Turkle, Sherry R. 1975. "Symbol and Festival in the French Student Uprising," in S. F. Moore and B. G. Myerhoff, eds., *Symbol and Politics in Communal Ideology*. Ithaca, N.Y.: Cornell University Press, pp. 68–100.

Vogel, Ezra F. 1961. "The Go-Between in a Developing Society: The Case of the Japanese Marriage Arranger," *Human Organization*, 20(3): 112–20.

———. 1962. "Entrance Examinations and Emotional Disturbances in Japan's Middle Class," in R. J. Smith and R. K. Beardsley, eds., *Japanese Culture: Its Development and Characteristics*. Chicago: Aldine, pp. 140–52.

———. 1971. *Japan's New Middle Class*, 2d ed. Berkeley: University of California Press.

Vogel, Suzanne H. 1978. "Professional Housewife: The Career of Urban Middle Class Japanese Women," *The Japan Interpreter*, 12(1): 16–43.

Wagatsuma, Hiroshi, and George A. DeVos. 1980. "Arakawa Ward: Urban Growth and Modernization," *Rice University Studies*, 66(1): 201–24.

———. 1984. *Heritage of Endurance*. Berkeley: University of California Press.

Watanuki, Joji. 1964. "The Political Consciousness and Behavior of the Old Middle Class," *Journal of Social and Political Ideas in Japan*, 2(3): 127–32.

———. 1977. *Politics in Postwar Japanese Society*. Tokyo: University of Tokyo Press.

White, James W. 1970. *The Sōkagakkai and Mass Society*. Stanford, Calif.: Stanford University Press.

———. 1973. *Political Implications of Cityward Migration: Japan as an Exploratory Test Case*. Sage Professional Paper in Comparative Politics 01-038. Beverly Hills, Calif.: Sage Publications.

———. 1976. "Social Change and Community Involvement in Metropolitan Japan," in J. W. White and F. Munger, eds., *Social Change and Community Politics in Urban Japan*. Chapel Hill: Institute for Research in Social Science, University of North Carolina, pp. 101–29.

———. 1978. "Internal Migration in Prewar Japan," *Journal of Japanese Studies*, 4(1): 81–123.

———. 1982. *Migration in Metropolitan Japan*. Berkeley: Institute of East Asian Studies, University of California.

Wimberley, Howard. 1973. "On Living with Your Past: Style and Structure Among Contemporary Japanese Merchant Families," *Economic Development and Cultural Change*, 21(3): 423–28.

Woodard, William P. 1972. *The Allied Occupation of Japan 1945–52 and Japanese Religions*. Leiden: E. J. Brill.

Yamamura, Kozo, and Susan B. Hanley. 1975. "*Ichi hime, ni Tarō*: Educational Aspirations and the Decline of Fertility in Postwar Japan," *Journal of Japanese Studies*, 2(1): 83–125.

Yanagisako, Sylvia J. 1985. *Transforming the Past: Tradition and Kinship Among Japanese Americans*. Stanford, Calif.: Stanford University Press.

Yazaki, Takeo. 1968. *Social Change and the City in Japan: From Earliest Times Through the Industrial Revolution*. Tokyo: Japan Publications.

———. 1973. "The History of Japanese Urbanization," in A. Southall, ed., *Urban Anthropology*. New York: Oxford University Press, pp. 139–61.

INDEX

Index

An "f" after a number indicates a separate reference on the next page, and an "ff" indicates separate references on the next two pages; "passim" is used for clusters of references in close but not consecutive sequence.

Library of Congress Cataloging-in-Publication Data

Bestor, Theodore C.
  Neighborhood Tokyo / Theodore C. Bestor.
    p.   cm.
  Bibliography: p.
  Includes index.
  ISBN 0-8047-1439-8 (alk. paper)
  ISBN 0-8047-1797-4 (pbk)
  1. Neighborhood—Japan—Tokyo.   2. Tokyo (Japan)—Social
conditions—1945—   I. Title.
HT147.J3B45   1988
307.3'362'095213—dc19   88-12383
                                                          CIP